Working in Teams

To my wonderful daughters Caitlyn, Chelsea, Emma, and Tessa.
Brian A. Griffith, PhD

To my family, the most important people in my life.
Ethan Dunham, EdM, MBA

Working in Teams

Moving From High Potential to High Performance

Brian A. Griffith
Peabody College, Vanderbilt University

Ethan B. Dunham
Human Capital Performance Partners

Los Angeles | London | New Delhi
Singapore | Washington DC

Los Angeles | London | New Delhi
Singapore | Washington DC

For information:

SAGE Publications, Inc.

2455 Teller Road

Thousand Oaks, California 91320

E-mail: order@sagepub.com

SAGE Publications Ltd.

1 Oliver's Yard

55 City Road

London EC1Y 1SP

United Kingdom

SAGE Publications India Pvt. Ltd.

B 1/I 1 Mohan Cooperative Industrial Area

Mathura Road, New Delhi 110 044

India

SAGE Publications Asia-Pacific Pte. Ltd.

3 Church Street

#10–04 Samsung Hub

Singapore 049483

Printed in the United States of America

Acquisitions Editor: Patricia Quinlin

Associate Editor: Maggie Stanley

Editorial Assistant: Katie Guarino

Production Editor: Libby Larson

Copy Editor: Talia Greenberg

Typesetter: C&M Digitals (P) Ltd.

Proofreader: Rae-Ann Goodwin

Indexer: Sheila Bodell

Cover Designer: Candice Harman

Marketing Manager: Liz Thornton

Copyright © 2015 by SAGE Publications, Inc.

Library of Congress Cataloging-in-Publication Data

Griffith, Brian A. Working in teams : moving from high potential to high performance / Brian A. Griffith, Peabody College, Vanderbilt University, Ethan B. Dunham, Human Capital Performance Partners

pages cm
Includes bibliographical references and index.

ISBN 978-1-4522-8630-3 (pbk.)
ISBN 978-1-4833-1328-3 (web pdf)
1. Teams in the workplace. I. Dunham, Ethan B. II. Title.

HD66.G743 2014
658.4'022--dc23   2013040658

This book is printed on acid-free paper.

SFI label applies to text stock

14 15 16 17 18 10 9 8 7 6 5 4 3 2 1

Brief Contents

Detailed Contents

3. Interpersonal Dynamics and Conflict

4. Leadership

5. Communication

6. Decision Making

7. Creativity and Innovation   133

8. Diversity   149

9. Project Management 167

10. Performance Evaluation 189

Preface

Individuals who affiliate with groups and learn to cooperate with others increase their chances of personal success and collective survival. Families, communities, workgroups, and organizations are but a few of the many social contexts in which individuals work together to achieve shared goals, solve common problems, and meet personal needs. Given the shift in our economy to a more team-based and collaborative workforce, it is not surprising that a recent study by the Association of American Colleges and Universities (AACU) found that 71% of employers want colleges to place a greater emphasis on teamwork. It is more important than ever for college graduates to be prepared to work in a team-based environment.

While it is not uncommon to encounter group projects and team-based assignments throughout college, the robust working knowledge and subtle interpersonal skills required for team success may not be effectively developed within the college experience. Success in most organizations after graduation requires individuals to work effectively in high-pressure team environments that may be ambiguously defined and poorly run. Whether in business, government, not-for-profit organizations, or a vast array of other professional pursuits, being able to contribute to and lead teams is of central importance to personal success and organizational sustainability.

The primary focus of this text is to prepare students for task-oriented groups in which individuals have joined together to accomplish specific goals. Having smart and competent people on a team roster is not enough; members must learn to work together effectively to harness the power that each individual brings to the team. The evidence-based concepts and skills that are presented in this text can help both leaders and members alike as they work together to achieve success. The best teams not only foster the development of individual members; they also achieve their collective goals in a convincing, efficient, and satisfying way. When that happens, a team has moved from "high potential" to "high performance."

Audience

Working in Teams: Moving from High Potential to High Performance is a college textbook that prepares students to work in collaborative, interdependent environments. This book is ideal for business courses but could be used in a variety of disciplines, including education, communication, psychology, industrial psychology, sociology, organizational studies, and leadership. It could also be used as a supplemental text for any class in which students are working in teams. For example, students in an engineering class in which projects are done collaboratively would greatly benefit from some training on how to maximize team performance.

Key Features

Working in Teams is written in an engaging style, with illustrations and examples that are of interest to students. It has a well-balanced approach between theory and practice that does not sacrifice depth or substance. It is grounded in solid research, with a strong theoretical foundation, yet at the same time is practical and applicable in nature. Interesting case studies at the beginning of each chapter draw readers in, provide accessible context for the material, and create a desire to know *more*. The content is intentionally written in a very readable style and draws upon illustrations and examples that are of interest and applicable to college students.

Each chapter includes a "Leadership in Action" section that helps the reader translate the conceptual material from the chapter into a practical leadership framework. Thus, students should be able to take something from each chapter and immediately apply it to their living communities, student organizations, or employment settings. Our hope is that they will put these leadership strategies into practice and then observe the effects they have on team performance.

At the end of each chapter are discussion questions, group activities, and cases that help reinforce and apply the concepts that were presented in the chapter. This added step of engagement increases learning and prepares students to transfer the concepts from the classroom to their work and life experiences outside the classroom. New skills are rarely perfect the first time they are attempted, so we suggest that students practice them, evaluate their effectiveness, and continue to develop and improve their leadership and interpersonal skills.

Overview of the Book

The first chapter presents an *introduction to teams* by discussing the concepts, practices, and importance of teams. It describes the common problems people encounter when working on teams and provides the conditions that lead to success. The chapter ends with a discussion about team development that presents multiple theories to explain the stages and changes groups go through as they reach maturity.

Chapter 2 presents a broad overview of *team design*. Structure is comprised of the norms, roles, and culture of a team and is a strong predictor of performance. In addition, team design and launch are discussed in order to provide practical information that maximizes the potential of new teams from their inception.

Interpersonal dynamics and conflict are a normal part of teams. Chapter 3 describes the major components of those interpersonal undercurrents and how they affect team performance. A model of interpersonal behavior is presented that can be a helpful guide for identifying our own interpersonal strengths and weaknesses. Later in the chapter, the most common interpersonal problems that generate conflict are discussed with the hope that we can identify potential problems before they start, and make the necessary corrections before team performance suffers.

The importance of team *leadership* cannot be overstated. While members must be motivated to do their part, strong leadership is often the difference between the success and failure of a team. Chapter 4 presents a brief history of traditional management models in organizations before discussing the emergence of self-managed work teams. Various theories of leadership are discussed, including a model that has identified five important practices of exemplary leaders that everyone can learn and apply. The chapter concludes with a detailed framework leaders can use to persuade and motivate others.

Chapter 5 focuses on the lifeblood of groups: *communication*. Communication is a complex set of verbal, nonverbal, and information-processing skills that can lead to stellar team performance or decay into murky misunderstandings and frustration. Thus, we discuss the process of communication in detail and highlight the two components of effective communication: inquiry and advocacy. After discussing centralized versus decentralized models of communication, the chapter concludes with a discussion about the benefits and challenges of virtual communication.

Decision making is the subject of Chapter 6. Teams make decisions on a regular basis; some are well thought out, while others are poorly conceived. After describing the typical mistakes teams are prone to making, this chapter presents a functional model of decision making that increases the ability of teams to make good decisions. The chapter concludes with a discussion about the major influences on group decision making.

Chapter 7 involves the important components of *creativity and innovation*. First, we begin with an overview of the importance of innovation with respect to today's teams. Then we explore the concept of creativity in detail, including a discussion of the characteristics of creative people. Brainstorming is one of the most important, though relatively underdeveloped and underutilized, team activities related to creativity, so we present practical guidelines to improve team performance in this area.

Creativity and innovation are often improved through *diversity,* which is the subject of Chapter 8. Unfortunately, team diversity can prove to be more of a hindrance than an advantage. Thus, in this chapter we describe the challenges and benefits of diversity with an emphasis on practical suggestions for using it to improve team performance. Technology has made diversity much easier to obtain, so we discuss in detail the prevalence, characteristics, and performance of virtual teams as a contemporary strategy to increase diversity.

Chapter 9 delves into the world of *project management.* This chapter explores the importance of goal-setting and performance benchmarks that motivate team members and generate commitment. Two models of project management are presented to give the reader an idea of the various ways to identify, analyze, solve, and implement solutions to the types of problems teams are often enlisted to address. The chapter closes with suggestions to make meetings more efficient and productive by reducing the amount of time and resources that are wasted.

Finally, Chapter 10 focuses on *performance evaluation.* In order to assess the relative strengths and weaknesses of a team, we have to understand the various frameworks that can be used to evaluate teams. Many teams get bogged down in common dysfunctions that hinder performance and compromise member satisfaction. Thus, we discuss how teams can evaluate their performance, learn from their mistakes, and apply the lessons and principles explored in depth throughout this text to improve their outcomes.

Supplementary Materials

This textbook helps students become more proficient in participating in and leading teams. In order to support that learning objective, we have prepared detailed supplemental materials including a sample syllabus, a facilitator's guide with weekly exercises and teaching notes, PowerPoint lectures for each of the chapters, exam questions, and suggested *Harvard Business Review* cases to accompany the text. Students rate the Vanderbilt University course that uses this material highly, both at the time they take the class and five years later, on alumni surveys.

Visit www.sagepub.com/griffith1e to access the instructor teaching resources and student study resources that accompany this book.

Team-based classes often include an experiential component in which students work together in project teams to gain an applied understanding of the theoretical material. A major part of the learning in this experience is the feedback students give to and receive from one another. Yet it can be difficult to facilitate open, honest dialogue that is productive and leads to personal growth. As a result, we have developed an online, multirater instrument that gives each student feedback about his or her performance on team projects. The G360 Personal Development Survey provides confidential feedback from classmates about each team member's personal character, interpersonal skills, problem-solving skills, and leadership skills. Project teams will also receive a G360 Team Survey Report that identifies the strengths and weaknesses of the project team as a whole. More information about both surveys can be found at www.g360surveys.com.

Acknowledgments

First and foremost, we are grateful to our families and the many people who have mentored, modeled, and taught us the meaning of teamwork. And we feel especially grateful for the opportunity to work together on this important text. Our efforts were born out of deep appreciation and respect for one another. We would also like to thank our students. As a result of teaching team courses over the past 15 years at Vanderbilt University, our students have not only made us better teachers, they have made us better writers. Their feedback and openness to the learning process have been inspiring. This book is the fruit of our collective collaboration in discovering the best ways to understand, experience, and drive team performance. In addition to the many students of HOD 1100 Small Group Behavior who have given excellent critical feedback on early versions of this text, we especially want to thank Lisa Koenig and Ariel Clemons. Their dedication and editing expertise helped research, organize, and improve early drafts of this manuscript. While the current errors, omissions, and shortcomings rest solely on our shoulders, we are in their debt for the good work they have done.

For their insightful comments and helpful suggestions, we would like to thank the following reviewers:

Ashour Badal, California State University, Stanislaus

Wendy Jo Bartkus, Albright College

Robert E. Beaudoin, University of New Haven

Elizabeth J. Brown-Jordan, Pace University

Alvin D. Lewis, Pima Community College

Marilyn L. Lutz, Barry University

Beth Patrick-Trippel, Olivet Nazarene University

Gianna H. Phillips, Golden Gate University

Bob Sindoni, Montclair State University

Alvin Snadowsky, Brooklyn College

Dorscine Spigner-Littles, University of Oklahoma

Doug Steele, Lewis-Clark State College

Finally, we are indebted to all the fine people at Sage Publications. Writing a textbook is a collaborative effort; the suggestions, guidance, and feedback from the Sage team were invaluable. We would like to give a special word of thanks to Pat Quinlin, who encouraged us and believed in us from the very beginning. Thank you, Pat.

Brian A. Griffith, PhD, and Ethan Dunham, MEd, MBA

Introduction to Teams

Working in teams to solve problems and achieve collective goals is a common experience for many. While teams can achieve extraordinary results, they can also deteriorate into an ineffective and immobilized group of frustrated individuals. This chapter introduces the concept of teams and describes common team problems as well as the conditions that are associated with team success. As individuals join together and build trust, groups develop a shared identity and a common purpose as they progress through predictable stages of development. Team leaders that understand those stages are able to facilitate growth. The chapter concludes with a look at the current trends in team research.

CASE 1.1: ALTERNATIVE SPRING BREAK

Alternative Spring Break (ASB) began at Vanderbilt University in 1986, when four students decided to form a team and spend their spring vacation together serving others. Although they had the best of intentions, being with a group of friends under stressful conditions for a week can be quite a challenge. Under duress, the very best of human nature comes out and the very worst of human nature comes out. The sheer logistics of organizing and planning a week-long service trip can be daunting. Once teams are on site, interpersonal problems often emerge as people start working together. As soon as a leader or a coalition of members decides to do one thing, other people will question those decisions and advocate a different direction. Even though ASB participants are well meaning and eager to contribute to the common good, problems almost inevitably emerge.

Whitney was a typical student and would be quick to attest to the life-changing power of her ASB experience. She spent every spring break during her college career volunteering at different ASB sites. She remembers her first spring break as setting the stage for involvement in a student group that would forever change her life. During that year, her team conducted conflict resolution workshops in some of the most troubled public schools in Detroit, Michigan. While the work was overwhelming at times, it was also extremely meaningful. Team members called the Detroit experience that year the "all-star site" because of the incredible friendships they forged and the important work they accomplished together.

The "all-star site" was not without its problems, though. One of the memorable experiences for Whitney was an argument that took place between two of the male members of the team. It was a heated debate about whether or not sports should be presented to urban kids as a viable career option. One member viewed sports as an opportunity for disadvantaged youth, while the other saw it as an unrealistic dream and barrier to educational success. Interestingly, Whitney found herself pleased that group members had become comfortable enough with one another that they were able to disagree so openly after only spending a short amount of time together. Because of the amount of time ASB participants spend with one another and because of the issues they face, they tend to go through the stages of group development quickly. While some teams get bogged down in communication misunderstandings and interpersonal squabbles, most become cohesive units that not only make a difference in the communities in which they serve but also in the lives of the members themselves.

Case Study Discussion Questions

1. If you were screening applications of students who wanted to go on an ASB trip, what are the qualities for which you would seek?

2. What are some of the tasks that need to be done ahead of time to prepare for a spring break trip?

3. Describe the general climate of ASB. What are the collective values and beliefs of students who are involved with this organization?

4. What would you do if you were on a team in which two of the members were hostile toward each other? How do you respond to interpersonal conflict?

5. From an administrative level, what do ASB leaders need to do to ensure a safe and successful experience for students?

In their article "The Discipline of Teams," Katzenbach and Smith (2005) suggest that "The essence of a team is shared commitment. Without it, groups perform as individuals; with it, they become a powerful unit of collective performance. This kind of commitment requires a purpose in which team members can believe" (p. 3). ASB students who are willing to forgo a fun and relaxing spring break in order to provide meaningful service to others are certainly committed to the mission of their teams. But their level of commitment does not ensure a smooth and successful experience. There are a multitude of things that can go wrong because of site leaders who are inexperienced or activities that are poorly planned or team members who do not get along with one another. Any one of these, which come from a much longer list of potential team obstacles, can serve to create disappointment and frustration. As the title of this text suggests, a collection of high-potential individuals does not always develop into a high-performance team. In fact, it is quite the exception (Wheelan, 2005). But with a little bit of knowledge and planning, teams can be rewarding and extremely successful enterprises (Hertel, 2011).

WHAT IS A TEAM?

Perhaps we should begin by defining what a team is. Kozlowski and Bell (2003) define teams as groups of people "who exist to perform organizationally relevant tasks, share one

or more common goals, interact socially, exhibit task interdependencies, maintain and manage boundaries, and are embedded in an organizational context that sets boundaries, constrains the team, and influences exchanges with other units in the broader entity" (p. 334). First and foremost, according to this definition, teams exist to accomplish specific tasks that are related to common goals. In order to do this, people must interact with one another in some form or fashion to accomplish those tasks.

Summarizing the existing definitions, Wageman, Gardner, and Mortensen (2012) define a team as a "bounded and stable set of individuals interdependent for a common purpose" (p. 305). Team boundaries are created so that members know who is on the team and who is not. And finally, we must acknowledge that teams exist within a larger organizational context that influences them to varying degrees. While some organizations give tremendous autonomy to their teams, others require strict adherence to a set of rules, roles, structures, and operating procedures.

Businesses and corporations are well aware of the potential of teams and frequently use them to carry out the missions of their organizations. Take Ford Motor Company, for example. When Henry Ford, the founder and chief engineer of Ford, envisioned his company, he wanted to find a way to efficiently create cars that were both affordable and reliable for the consumer. He developed several teams—each consisting of two to three members—that worked together on a specific part of the assembly process instead of separately building a car from start to finish. This innovative approach pioneered the assembly line method. With several teams working toward a common goal, Ford Motor Company went on to make millions of reliable automobiles and is now the world's fifth-largest automaker in the world. The 21st century business world is marked by the need for quick responses to rapidly changing market conditions. Keeping up with the complexities of a global economy requires businesses to draw upon multiple perspectives and multiple sources of input in order to be able to compete. For this reason, task-oriented teams can be found almost anywhere, from factory assembly lines to corporate executive suites (Polzer, 2003).

WHY DO WE NEED TO LEARN ABOUT TEAMS?

Individuals who affiliate with groups and learn to cooperate with others increase their chances of solving shared problems and meeting personal needs (Qin, Johnson, & Johnson, 1995). Families, neighborhoods, communities, work teams, organizations, and cultures are all attempts to increase collective stability in ways that meet individual needs for survival, personal development, and social interaction. Given the shift in our economy to a more team-based, collaborative, and interdependent approach to work, it is not surprising that an Association of American Colleges and Universities (AACU) survey showed that 71 % of employers want colleges to place a greater emphasis on teamwork (AACU, 2010). It is more important than ever for college graduates to be prepared to work in a team-based environment.

While it is not uncommon to encounter group projects and team-based assignments throughout the college experience, the robust working knowledge and subtle interpersonal skills required for team success may not be effectively developed within the undergraduate curriculum. Another AACU report, "College Learning for the New Global Economy: A Report from the National Leadership Council for Liberal Education and America's Promise" (AACU, 2007) identifies teamwork as 1 of 15 "Essential Learning Outcomes" in college. Success in most work environments after graduation requires individuals to work well with others in collaborative team efforts. Whether in business, government, not-for-profit organizations, or a vast array of other professional pursuits, being able to work within and to lead teams is of central importance to individual success and organizational sustainability.

The primary focus of this text is to prepare students for task-oriented groups in which individuals have joined together to accomplish specific goals. The evidence-based concepts and skills that are presented can help both leaders and members alike as they work together to achieve collective success. After reading the text, students will be able to create meaningful social contexts that foster the development of individual members, changing "high-potential" teams into "high-performance" teams.

TEAMS VERSUS WORKGROUPS

Groups of people who join together to accomplish a specific task do not always exemplify the characteristics of a true "team." Hackman (2009) has identified five basic conditions that must be met if a group is to be considered a team versus a workgroup:

1. "Teams must be real." While many organizations assign people to teams, some of those structures are teams in name only. Real teams are groups of identifiable people who actually work together to achieve a common set of objectives.

2. "Teams need a compelling direction." In order for everyone to be pulling in the same direction, they need to understand and embrace a shared purpose.

3. "Teams need enabling structures." This means involving the right number of the right kind of people on the right tasks in the right ways, and governing them by the right norms and shared values.

4. "Teams need a supportive organization." Everything must facilitate success, from the behaviors and output that are most prized or rewarded, to the structure of the teams' people, systems, and processes.

5. "Teams need expert coaching." An expert third party must lend insight and guidance at key points in any groups' evolution. Too much coaching focuses on the individual, when it should be focused on teamwork and team process.

Clearly, teams and teamwork are nuanced, dynamic, and highly variable. In addition, they are increasingly valued across industries as instrumental in organizational success.

COMMON PROBLEMS

While teams have tremendous potential to accomplish tasks well beyond the reach of any single individual, they are not without problems. As a matter of fact, working in teams can be quite frustrating. Research about teams, personal observations, and personal experience point to five common problems that people experience when working in teams:

- Lack of commitment
- Productivity losses
- Poor communication
- Interpersonal conflict
- Poor leadership

One of the perennial problems in working with others is a lack of commitment among members. It is not uncommon for a majority of the work to be done by only a few members. While this may be extremely frustrating for those who are doing the work, those same team members are often reluctant to give up control in order to allow others to rise to the challenge. As a result, those who are doing little or nothing are content to ride the coattails of higher performing members. This free riding, or social loafing, is a regular irritant for countless team leaders.

Losses in productivity that come from poor structure and a lack of planning and organization are called "process losses." They occur because of the additional layers of complexity that come from working in teams. For example, it may take longer to come to a decision, time may be wasted in trying to schedule meetings, and individual contributions must be integrated into the larger project. Furthermore, conflicts about goals, task assignments, and operating procedures all threaten to slow down the work of a team. Unless a team has specifically defined roles and responsibilities, and has established a sound system of coordinating its efforts, there will likely be losses in productivity.

Poor communication is often at the heart of poorly performing groups. Team members can emerge from the same meeting with completely different perspectives of what was said or what was or was not accomplished. In general, as the number of people working on a task increases, so does the chance for communication problems. Most of what team members perceive comes from highly subjective interpretations of nonverbal behavior including tone, facial expression, and body posture. In addition, members often do a poor job supporting or providing evidence for their positions. Thus, there is a great propensity to miscommunicate or misunderstand what is being said.

Communication problems easily give way to interpersonal conflict. On any given team, there are likely to be people with whom we get along better than others—and there may even be some whom we strongly dislike. Strong dislike for a person is frequently quite evident to them even despite our best efforts to hide it. Furthermore, some members are prone to taking questions or challenges far too personally, and do not realize that banter and spirited debate actually sharpen the ability of the group to make good decisions. When members are emotionally fragile, they are likely to feel threatened by those who play the important role of the deviant or devil's advocate.

Finally, poor leadership can compromise the ability of teams to perform effectively (Sivasubramaniam, Murry, Avolio, & Jung, 2002). Leadership is a delicate dance that both guides and empowers. There is no shortage of cases in which team members were so discontent with their leaders that they disengaged, resisted, or even sabotaged their own teams. Team leaders who do not balance members' need for structure with their need for autonomy will hinder performance.

CONDITIONS FOR TEAM SUCCESS

Druskat and Wolff (2001) have identified three essential conditions for team success: trust among members, a sense of group identity, and a sense of group efficacy. Team leaders and organizers can impact their teams by nurturing the development of each of these components. As teams begin their journey together, trust, identity, and efficacy must be established for optimal performance.

Trust

According to Doney, Cannon, and Mullen (1998), trust can be defined simply as the willingness to rely upon others. Organizational researchers have become increasingly interested in its causes, nature, and effects (Costa, Roe, & Taillieu, 2001; Kramer, 1999; Mayer, Davis, & Schoorman, 1995). Lencioni (2002) suggests that trust is necessary for effective team functioning. Without it, a host of dysfunctions may emerge, including a fear of conflict, lack of commitment, avoidance of accountability, and inattention to results.

Levels of trust are related to the personal characteristics of both those who trust and those who are trusted. Some people, by nature, are more trusting than others. This quality stems from positive past experiences and relationships that have proven others to be generally trustworthy. Thus, core beliefs in the goodness of people are established, which enables attraction and attachment to others. On the other hand, for those who have had negative experiences with people in the past, relying upon others will not be an easy thing to do. Group members with painful past experiences and negative beliefs will likely be less trusting of others and seek to be independent.

Trust in groups is also related to the trustworthiness of the group members. Members are trusted when they are perceived to have characteristics that engender trust. These include competence, benevolence, and integrity (Mayer, Davis, & Schoorman, 1995). First, members will rely upon those who are competent and have ability in an area of concern to the group. In other words, members must be relatively sure that the person has the capacity to perform the task at hand. Second, members will trust colleagues who exhibit benevolence. Benevolent members are kind and generous, and are opposed to intentionally harming or manipulating other people. The third quality that begets trust is integrity. Members who have integrity are true to their word and do what they say they will do before the deadline. If enough members consistently demonstrate these qualities of competence, benevolence, and integrity, the group will establish a foundation of trust that will lead to success and satisfaction.

While trust takes time to establish, it can be compromised after just a single negative interaction. Distrust can become a group norm if members have a lack of confidence in one another or suspect that others are harmful or malicious (Kramer, 1999). Imagine a scenario in a local coffee shop in which a cashier takes an order from a customer and communicates that order to the barista. The line is long, the customers are in a hurry, and the barista inadvertently makes a mistake. When the customer comes back to complain, the cashier makes a condescending remark to the barista. The barista is upset and quickly tries to correct the mistake, only to find that she is still out of the vanilla syrup that the backroom person promised to bring 20 minutes earlier. At this point, the barista thinks the cashier is being overly critical (questioning his benevolence) and that the backroom person is not reliable (questioning her integrity). Meanwhile, the cashier is annoyed at the barista's error (questioning her competence) and no longer wants to work the same shifts because she makes him look bad. One can see how quickly trust can be violated. In a matter of a few short minutes, trust was lost—and it can be difficult to regain.

Team Identity

Team identity is Druskat and Wolff's (2001) second element necessary for team success. Teams that spend enough time together eventually develop a unique identity. When individuals derive their own identity in part from their team affiliation, they become invested in, loyal, and committed to it. Teams develop norms, values, and characteristics that separate them from other teams, and these characteristics can be the difference between an average team performance and a stellar performance.

Alternative Spring Break (ASB) teams are a good example of how team identity can produce superior results. Service organizations such as ASB, Teach for America, or Boys & Girls Clubs are known for their commitment to the common good and enlist members who are aligned with those goals. Their training programs seek to build a sense of camaraderie and unity among their team members that can stand up to the adverse circumstances they will likely encounter together. In the opening case study, the ASB team that went to Detroit dubbed itself the "all-star site." This demonstrated the members' belief that they were both special and unique. This clear sense of identity was one of the reasons the team was so successful.

Collective Efficacy

Collective efficacy concludes the shortlist of the most vital elements leading to team success. We know that optimism and self-confidence can go a long way in enhancing personal achievement. Teams are no different. In order for teams to be most successful, they need to believe they can accomplish their goals (Porter, Gogus, & Yu, 2011). Visit the locker room of any high school football team and you will be inundated with messages of "We Can,"

"Believe," "No Limits," and the like. When members are confident that they can accomplish ambitious goals, their chances of success are much greater (Katz-Navon & Erez, 2005). There exists no shortage of examples of small groups of people accomplishing amazing feats simply because they believed they could.

IDEAL TEAM CLIMATE

Teams are often created and assembled to solve important problems within communities and organizations. For example, a marketing team might be asked to improve annual sales by 10%, a school improvement task force might be asked to identify strategies to reduce student absenteeism by 5%, or a product design group might be tasked with the responsibility of creating a new potato chip bag that will keep chips fresher longer. In each of these cases, team members must "think outside the box" to solve the problem presented to them. Anderson and West (1998) have found four team characteristics that lead to innovation and effective performance. The ideal team climate includes a shared vision, participative safety, task orientation, and support for innovation.

Shared vision describes the importance of developing clear, objective goals that are visionary in nature but also attainable. A shared vision can be dictated by the de facto leader of the group, or it can emerge organically through a collaborative process. Whatever the case, the group ultimately needs to agree upon the purpose of members' collective efforts. Members need to know the answers to questions such as "Where are we headed?," "What are we doing?," and "What are our goals?" Often, the leader can jump-start this process by asking those very questions. Some of the most successful groups begin their work with the question "What do we want to accomplish with this team?" The ensuing conversation invariably covers topics such as goals, benchmarks, balance of responsibility, commitment level, and other similar logistical concerns. A clear vision within the team is essential in order to produce and sustain long-term results.

Participative safety exists when levels of trust and support are such that members feel safe participating freely in group discussions and decisions (Kessel, Dratzer, & Schultz, 2012). This can be established with as little effort as setting ground rules and holding members accountable to those rules. As with shared vision, participative safety is something that the group can facilitate by establishing explicit rules of engagement and expectations for participation during meetings. For example, is everyone expected to "participate fully"? If so, what does that mean? If it's something that everyone understands, this will allow all group members to refer to that "ground rule" to encourage contributions *and* to discourage negative dynamics like condescending or judgmental behavior that hinder the willingness of other team members to offer ideas, voice dissent, or contribute to the shared process.

A task orientation is achieved when teams uphold their commitment to high performance standards by monitoring performance, holding one another accountable, giving one another honest feedback, and engaging in constructive conflict in order to reach their goals. As with other dimensions of successful teams, it is helpful to have an open discussion about this and lay out expectations. Structure is the product of intentional and earnest conversation about the things that matter most to members with regard to the *task* at hand. Leaders should be willing to discuss it in concrete and specific terms. They can begin by saying something like, "I think it will be important for us to have some shared expectations about our group and the work we do. I know we all have our own ways of doing work, so can we take a few minutes to talk about how we work best in teams, giving special attention to how we can stay on task and accomplish our goals." It may be particularly helpful to have an agenda for each meeting and to have someone take minutes in order to record major decisions, action items, and assigned responsibilities.

Groups that have strong support for innovation are open to examining existing ways of doing things and are willing to take risks and experiment with new ideas. Innovation often means change, and change can create anxiety. Teams that support innovation are willing to endure the discomfort of thinking "outside the box" in order to explore new ways of understanding problems and creating solutions. These types of teams also give great latitude to creative members who at first might seem totally off base, but who often see things in very different ways.

Research and development (R&D) teams are often called upon to create new and innovative products and services. The amount of time it takes to design a new product or concept can be the difference between success and failure in a fast-paced, market-driven economy. In a study of 33 R&D teams over a nine-month period, Pirola-Merlo (2010) found that three of the four team climate scales (participative safety, support for innovation, and task orientation) were significantly related to project performance as rated by managers and customers. In addition, two of the scales (support for innovation and vision) were associated with higher levels of project innovation. Those teams with a stronger climate were also able to complete their projects more quickly.

Not only does team climate affect innovation and efficiency, it also influences levels of member satisfaction and general team performance. In a study of 654 general practitioners and staff and 7,505 chronically ill patients from 93 primary health care practices in Australia, researchers found that a strong team climate is related to higher levels of job satisfaction as well as higher levels of patient satisfaction (Proudfoot, Jayasinghe, Holton, Grimm, Bubner, Amoroso, Beilby, & Harris, 2007). An optimal team climate creates both the structure and interpersonal dynamics that can lead to success. But it often takes time and intentional effort to develop that type of atmosphere. It doesn't happen by accident, and it doesn't happen overnight. But an understanding of the typical stages of group development can help team leaders shape the direction and destiny of their teams.

STAGES OF GROUP DEVELOPMENT

Groups are dynamic social systems that change over time; the first few meetings of a newly formed group are substantially different from the twentieth meeting (Arrow, Poole, Henry, Wheelan, & Moreland, 2004). Group development models attempt to explain these differences and identify typical stages through which groups evolve. Knowledge of these stages can help leaders and members alike to understand the changes and manage expectations. Bruce Tuckman (1965) was the first to suggest the stages of development known as forming, storming, norming, performing, and adjourning. Sometime later, Susan Wheelan (1999) constructed a similar linear model that includes many of the same concepts.

During the first few meetings, while the group is in the **forming** stage of its development, members are sizing one another up while self-consciously assessing their own competence. At this stage, members are typically concerned with acceptance and belonging. They have an over-reliance on the leader and are generally cautious and tentative due to both a lack of role clarity and an understanding of the rules of operation (norms). Coincidentally, when existing groups add new members or change the composition of the group, they will often return to the forming stage as the existing members and the new members size one another up. New members can provide a fresh perspective that encourages an examination of the existing team structure that propels the group into the next stage of development.

Storming is the stage of group life characterized by members becoming increasingly impatient with the existing structure and directly or indirectly challenging the leaders of the group. Because there is rarely one right way to solve problems or achieve goals, it is nearly impossible for everyone in the group to be completely happy with decisions and plans.

Disagreement over procedures, role assignments, and any number of details related to group life are inevitable, and as the newness of the group wears off, members become bolder in questioning and challenging one another. "Individual" roles emerge at this time as members take a passive, passive-aggressive, or aggressive stance against the group (avoider, resister, and dominator roles, respectively). Groups will often become polarized as members form coalitions and alliances with one another as they jockey for status and power (Carton & Cummings, 2012). Although uncomfortable for some, this stage is necessary for optimal cohesion and group functioning.

The **norming** stage is an attempt by the group to restore stability and cohesion after the storm and to develop a more effective structure toward achieving goals. Having gone through conflict, the group has tested its boundaries and (hopefully) developed trust. At this stage, groups not only become more unified, but also better organized. Relationships deepen at the same time that task efficiency increases. During this stage, the storming period has officially given way to a renewed commitment to the goals and purpose of the group, resulting in an examination and redefinition of norms, roles, and relationships.

In the **performing** stage the group's focus is on getting work done. Relationships and cohesion have been built, optimal strategies have been constructed, and the underlying group structure has solidified. The group is now positioned for maximum productivity. During this stage, effective groups spend 80% to 85% of their time on task completion (Wheelan, 1999; Wheelan, Davidson, & Tilin, 2003). In terms of time frame, Wheelan (2004) suggests it takes approximately six months for a group to get to this level of functioning. Unfortunately, not all groups make it to this productive stage. Many groups remain stuck in one of the earlier stages.

In the **adjourning** stage of group development, groups are preparing to disband. The group is coming to an end and members need to prepare for its demise. For some this is a joyful event, but for others there may be disappointment or even sadness. Some group experiences are so positive and so powerful that members do not want them to come to an end. In either case, it is important for members to discuss what they have learned from the experience and to say their goodbyes to one another.

OTHER MODELS OF GROUP DEVELOPMENT

Not all experts agree with the stage model of group development. In Connie Gersick's (1988, 1989) research on team development, she found that by the end of the first meeting, groups had formed an initial structure that remained fairly stable until the middle of the project or life of the group. At that midpoint, Gersick observed a burst of energy and transition whereby members critically examined their progress and reorganized themselves for more effective functioning. Interestingly, whether the groups she studied met four times or twenty-five times over seven days or six months, they all had a major transition at the chronological midpoint of the project. As a result of her studies, Gersick postulated that groups do not progress through stages of development, but phases.

According to her phase theory, the first phase is defined by the stable structure that is established by the end of the first meeting. Thus, the first meeting is extremely important in setting the climate, culture, and direction of the group. Then, at the midpoint, the group goes through a period of instability and transition before entering phase two, with the newly defined structure that will guide the project through to the end. Gersick also noted a flurry of activity and effort toward the end of the project as the deadline approached.

Research partially supports both the Tuckman and Wheelan models and the Gersick model (Chang, Bordia, & Duck, 2003). One way to reconcile them is to use the Tuckman and Wheelan models to describe the relationship dimension of group work while the Gersick model is more aligned with the task dimension. These dimensions of group dynamics (task and relationship) are the two primary components of group dynamics that require the attention of group members and leaders alike. The forming and storming stages often set the relational tone for the later, more task-oriented stages of norming and performing. Both dimensions are important for long-term group success.

Table 1.1 Comparing Models of Group Development		
Tuckman (1965)	**Wheelan (1999)**	**Gersick (1988)**
Forming	Dependency and inclusion	Phase 1 (stability)
Storming	Counterdependency and fight	Transition (instability)
Norming	Trust and structure	
Performing	Work and productivity	Phase 2 (stability)

THREATS TO EFFECTIVE COLLABORATION

Collaboration is the ability of team members to work together effectively, efficiently, and meaningfully. Thompson (2004) asserts, "When groups perform highly uncertain tasks, they need to integrate large amounts of information, form multiple perspectives, and collaborate closely. In such situations, collaboration is necessary" (p. 238). Yet only about a quarter of all teams progress through the normal stages of group development and reach their full potential (Wheelan, 1999). There are numerous threats to effective collaboration, including the size of the team, the degree of virtual participation, the amount of diversity, and the education level of the members (Gratton & Erickson, 2007). Each of these threats will be discussed in detail.

Size of the Team

In the last few decades, teams in organizations have become significantly larger in size (Gratton & Erickson, 2007). Technology has made it easier to include geographically remote members with presumably greater levels of expertise. Yet as teams grow in size, it becomes harder and harder for members to coordinate their efforts (Walsh & Maloney, 2007). Due to process losses and logistical challenges, large teams can be inefficient and, therefore, less effective. Furthermore, interaction among members is often more superficial, and thus less meaningful. Working closely with others to achieve mutual goals is often one of the most rewarding dimensions of team participation, but one that teams that are large and dispersed often lose.

Degree of Virtual Participation

As teams become more "virtual," the quality of collaboration decreases (Gratton & Erickson, 2007). Because the communication process relies heavily on nonverbal cues to interpret verbal statements, electronic messages can be ambiguous at best and grossly misunderstood at worst. Virtual teams have been studied at length, and while there are many benefits, there are drawbacks as well. In order to minimize potential misunderstanding and miscommunication, team leaders have to implement specific strategies that support collaboration in a technology-rich environment.

Amount of Diversity

Similar to technology, diversity can be both a benefit and a threat to collaboration. Differences of opinion and perspective can create innovative and fresh ways to understand and solve problems, but they can also generate distrust and frustration. For example, a university task force that is charged with addressing the role of the Greek system on campus would probably include members from the administration, faculty, and student body. However, such a task force would likely begin with some tension as each group sought to understand the motives and positions of the other stakeholders. Though diverse perspectives are important to the overall discussion, groups might regard one another with suspicion. Theoretically, a diverse team composition creates a more comprehensive approach to problem-solving, yet, in practice, diversity can put a strain on interpersonal dynamics and the ability to collaborate. Diversity can be found in any number of member differences, including personality, gender, age, race/ethnicity, functionality, education level, or length of tenure within the organization or industry.

Education Level

Interestingly, level of education is negatively correlated with group collaboration. According to Gratton and Erickson (2007), "the greater the proportion of highly educated specialists on a team, the more likely the team is to disintegrate into unproductive conflicts" (p. 5). Members who are very knowledgeable and highly trained tend to be resistant to perspectives and ways of doing things other than their own. Simply put, they have a hard time compromising. It is no wonder that academic departments that aspire to the highest ideals of virtue and learning can become mired in endless squabbles over relatively insignificant decisions. True collaboration requires an openness and willingness to understand and agree with other perspectives. The following section will describe specific strategies to increase team collaboration.

IMPROVING COLLABORATION

Team researchers have identified a number of things that can be done to overcome the inherent challenges in teamwork and increase the chances for effective collaboration. Specifically, team composition, meeting space, and leadership practices can all contribute to the conditions conducive for success (Gratton & Erickson, 2007).

Team Composition

New teams that are comprised of members who have successfully worked together in the past are at a distinct advantage as they have a history of trust and interpersonal strengths from which to draw, whereas team members without any history must go through the typical posturing and interpersonal jockeying that take place at the start of a new team. Thus, when possible, designing teams in which 20% or more of the members have successfully worked together in the past can help establish a strong foundation of collaboration (Gratton, 2007). The opposite is also true. People who have had negative experiences working together in the past may not be a good fit for a new team. While a small amount of interpersonal tension can be helpful, too much can engender negative emotional contagion that can sabotage trust and good will.

Meeting Space

The physical or virtual setting where meetings take place can also have a significant impact on collaboration. The setting should reflect the values of the organization and the goals of the team, and it should be conducive to effective and balanced communication. Rooms that are inviting and conducive to allow members to see and hear one another are obviously the most effective. Thus, consideration should be given to seating arrangements and the layout of the room. A study group that meets in a classroom would feel very different from a group meeting in a dorm room. Each setting has its relative strengths and weaknesses. Furthermore, eating a meal together, or simply sharing snacks or soft drinks, may increase the sense of community and cohesion.

Leadership Practices

Team leaders impact team collaboration through the behaviors and attitudes they model, by publicly acknowledging collaborative behavior, by coaching individual members, and by focusing on both task and relationship dimensions of the team. Modeling is a powerful communicator of team norms and values. Thus, what a team leader does is often more important than what he or she says. Leaders that model collaborative behavior are setting the standard for the rest of the group (Ibarra & Hansen, 2011). For example, a leader who is transparent about personal goals and willing to admit mistakes opens the door for others to do the same. In a similar way, when a leader responds nondefensively to a direct challenge or personal attack, he or she increases the team's capacity for collaboration.

In addition to modeling collaborative behavior, team leaders can reward it publicly and coach members on it personally. Acknowledging a member who went above and beyond the call of duty for the sake of the team reinforces collaborative behavior. When leaders "encourage the heart," both the recipient of the comment as well as the rest of the team are reminded of the importance of ideal team behavior. Members who are not aware of their own behavior may need personal feedback and coaching. Effective leaders regularly pull individual members aside to facilitate conversations on how they view their own level of collaboration and team behavior.

TRENDS IN TEAM RESEARCH

Technological advances and trends in globalization are radically changing the ways individuals participate in teams (Wageman, Gardner, & Mortensen, 2012). Technology and globalization have increased both the scope and practice of our work with others. While it is unfathomable to think of a world without e-mail, social networking, and the Internet, these technologies have only been used by a majority of the workforce since the mid-1990s. For example, the popular social networking platform Facebook was only launched in early 2004. In just a few short years, it has revolutionized the ways in which individuals connect with one another. So are Facebook groups that are created to address social problems or discuss political issues actual teams? When some computer programmers voluntarily work together to develop the next release of an open source operating system, are they part of a team? When people join a virtual support group to help one another find medical solutions to diseases from which they all suffer, are they operating as a team? While these groups may not fit the standard definition of a team, they certainly have many characteristics of a team, including shared commitment to a common goal.

Teams in the 21st century are not as stable or bounded as they have been in the past. In contemporary social settings, people float in and out of teams, move quickly among teams, and are part of multiple teams (O'Leary, Mortensen, & Woolley, 2011). Technology has made it easy to be involved in multiple projects at the same time. Since formal team membership is a more loosely understood construct in today's world, researchers are just beginning to explore how to capture the complexities of multiple team membership and its effect on interpersonal dynamics and team performance.

Another trend in team research has been to reexamine the way we understand the concept of interdependence. Once again, technology has allowed us to contribute to collective tasks in novel and creative ways. The person who takes our order at the drive-thru menu of a fast food restaurant may actually be located many miles from the pickup window and may be taking orders from multiple stores at once (Friedman, 2006). This certainly challenges the way we have traditionally understood collaborative work teams. Contemporary team structures are more elusive, dynamic, and difficult to measure. Teams themselves have greater levels of autonomy than in the past to define their own goals and operating procedures. Thus, researchers are concluding that not only is team membership dynamic, so is the way people work together to define and accomplish shared tasks (Wageman, Gardner, & Mortensen, 2012).

LEADERSHIP IN ACTION

Effective team leaders pay attention to both the task and relational dimensions of teams. Clear roles, responsibilities, deadlines, and accountability can go a long way in accomplishing tasks and achieving goals. But on the relational dimension, members must learn to trust one another and create a sense of community in order to work together effectively. The best leaders are able to address both dimensions directly.

First of all, teams must have a clear vision of what they are trying to accomplish. A team mission, charter, or project statement can give a clear vision of the purpose of the group. Then, leaders must coordinate the work of the team to accomplish those goals. For example, a team leader might begin a meeting by asking members to give a status update on their individual tasks. At the end of the meeting, he or she might ask whether or not everyone knows exactly what they need to accomplish before the next meeting. Action plans, deadlines, and meeting agendas help keep teams focused and on task.

On the relational dimension, team members want to feel like they are appreciated and valued. They want to feel connected to the team on some level. This is where team-building activities come into play. It can be hard to trust others when you do not know them. So at the beginning of a new group, it makes sense to do an icebreaker or two to allow members to get to know one another. In addition, leaders can create a positive atmosphere by being enthusiastic about the team and by supporting team members both publicly and privately. When this happens, the group is well on its way to becoming a high-performing team.

KEY TERMS

Lack of commitment   5
Losses in productivity   5
Poor communication   5
Interpersonal conflict   5
Poor leadership   6
Shared vision   8
Participative safety   8

Task orientation   8
Support for innovation   9
Forming stage of development   10
Storming stage of development   10
Norming stage of group development   10
Performing stage of development   10
Adjourning stage of development   10

DISCUSSION QUESTIONS

1. Hackman identifies five basic conditions that distinguish a team from a workgroup. Name and describe each condition.

2. Although teams have great potential to accomplish tasks effectively, there is an array of common problems that can hinder performance. Describe three of those common problems.

3. Druskat and Wolff (2001) state that there are three conditions that are essential to a team's success. Name and explain the importance of each condition.

4. Levels of trust are strongly related to team success. Identify individual qualities that are related to trustworthiness.

5. Explain why each the following characteristics of team climate can impact team success: shared vision, task orientation, open communication, support for innovation, and interaction frequency.

6. Describe Tuckman's five stages of group development. Provide an example of each.

7. Name and describe the four threats to collaboration. What can be done in order to increase collaboration? Give at least two examples.

GROUP ACTIVITIES

EXERCISE 1.1 PAST TEAM EXPERIENCES

Get into groups of four to five and describe the positive experiences you have had in groups and/or teams in the past:

- What made the team exceptional?

- What was the shared goal of the group or team?

- Were members committed to the team? How do you know?

- Describe your past experiences with unsuccessful teams. What made them frustrating? Why did they fail? What was lacking in the leadership of the team?

Create a list of the top three reasons teams succeed and a list of the top three reasons teams fail. Be prepared to share your list with the rest of the class.

EXERCISE 1.2 BUILDING TRUST

Trust is an important component of relationships. Form groups of three or four and discuss the following questions:

1. What is trust?
2. Can you describe a trusting relationship in your life?
3. What does it take to form trust/a trusting relationship?
4. How do trusting relationships differ from relationships that may lack trust?
5. What ground rules and team guidelines will help build trust?

Be prepared to present your ground rules to the rest of the class. After all the groups have shared, you will have a final opportunity to add additional items to your list of ground rules.

CASE 1.2 WORKING WITH THE LONE WOLF

You have just finished a summer-long stint with your family's business, an office products supplier. The company generates about $3 million of revenue per year and employs 27 people. Employees are organized in three primary teams: sales and marketing, warehouse operations and distribution, and the executive team. Your mother, the CEO, has brought you on for the summer so you can rotate through each team to get a first-hand look at how the company operates.

You spent the first month with the warehouse team, sweating in the June heat with warehouse workers and delivery people. In spite of the backbreaking work, this crew proved to be a tight, strong community that ate lunch together, spent breaks playing basketball on the temporary hoop behind in the back parking lot, and often grabbed a beer together after work. Though they didn't immediately trust you as "the owner's kid," you worked hard to prove your worth through hard work and a minimal amount of complaining.

The second month, you went out with the sales team. Rick, your mentor for the month, referred to himself as "the lone wolf." He has been the top salesperson for the last two years and is vocal about his financial success and the value he brings to the company. Rick confides in you that he thinks other salespeople are jealous of his success and are actively trying to steal his customers. At the weekly sales team meetings, you notice a lot of competitive jabbing among sales representatives. There are also a lot of complaints about the commission structure and criticism of the "lazy warehouse workers" who drag their feet and take too long to process orders.

By August, you moved inside the main office with the executive team. The executive team is made up of middle-aged, highly educated professionals who are the highest-paid people in the company. You often hear them complain about the "lack of effort" they see from the salespeople and the hourly employees. Lately, company executives have appeared frazzled and stressed out due to what they describe as "shrinking profits." At executive meetings nobody seems to know what to do to turn the company around. There appears to be a growing sense of pessimism about whether or not the company is going to make it.

By the end of the summer, you have experienced three different teams with three distinct cultures operating within the organization.

Describe and assess each of the teams according to the following:

- The problems each team is experiencing

- The conditions for team success they may or may not be experiencing

- Whether or not they have the characteristics associated with the ideal team climate.

Team Design

Team design affects how a group of individuals interact as a unit and serves as a key determinant of success. This chapter will describe the major components that make up team design, including member roles and responsibilities and team culture. In order to build a successful team, leaders need to be well versed in the specific goals and tasks that need to be completed, as well as the levels of interdependence needed among members. Once team members have been selected, work can begin. The first few meetings in the life of a team strongly influence its ongoing structure, so planning *how* to launch a project and *how* to conduct those first few meetings is an important consideration in developing an effective and efficient team structure. Thoughtful planning and active participation increase the chances for outstanding team performance.

CASE 2.1: JOINING THE STARBUCKS TEAM

Jennifer is like many college students. She enjoys her classes and the whole college experience—but she's broke. It's only November, and the money she saved from her summer job as a retail clerk is almost depleted. As she withdraws the last of her final paycheck, she can't help but recount how the hours in the clothing store seemed to drag on and on while the workers continuously engaged in petty bickering and complaining. Jennifer stayed to herself that summer in an attempt to avoid the store drama. She hated going to work and often felt irritated by her demeaning customers or demanding bosses. Now that the hard-earned money she made during those months was gone, she knew she would have to find another part-time job, but she couldn't bear the thought of having another experience like the one she had over the summer.

One of Jennifer's favorite places to study had always been the local Starbucks. She loved to drink her coffee and enjoy the atmosphere of the shop—particularly the friendly and helpful staff who worked there. The obvious enjoyment the employees seemed to get from their jobs soon convinced Jennifer to apply for a position. After an interview that went pretty well, she got the job. When Jennifer arrived for her first of several days of training, she was encouraged by the store manager's kind words of introduction to the rest of the team. He named several of the achievements that he remembered from her résumé and assured them that she would be a great asset to the team.

Her training program allowed Jennifer to acquire new knowledge and to learn new skills. She was taught a host of information about the coffee industry and the Starbucks philosophy, while simultaneously gaining experience in every area from drink mixing to cashiering and inventory logging. Her coworkers were patient, helpful, and kind to her during her training process, and she soon began to build meaningful relationships with them. She even went out to dinner a few times with them and genuinely enjoyed their company.

Jennifer was both surprised and pleased with the positive environment at Starbucks and soon became loyal to the company's mission. Instead of simply putting in her time and counting down the hours, Jennifer saw herself as part of a group of people working toward a common goal. This job proved to be nothing like the experience she had over the summer. Working at Starbucks began as a simple solution to her financial woes, but it quickly became something much more.

Case Study Discussion Questions

1. What was Jennifer's primary reason for working at Starbucks? What kind of environment was she looking for?

2. What are some of the typical problems in working with others in a team environment?

3. List some characteristics of successful team experiences.

4. What is the primary mission of each Starbucks location? How does each store maintain high levels of commitment to that mission?

5. Field experiment: Next time you find yourself inside a Starbucks, observe the employees. What do you see? Ask them if they enjoy working there, and why. Ask them how their performance is measured as individual employees and as a team.

Jennifer's experiences as a team member at the clothing store and then at Starbucks were very different. When people join new teams, they eagerly observe the way team members communicate with one another and the way they work in order to figure out how they are supposed to act and what they are supposed to do. These observed "operating procedures" can be understood as the group's structure. As expectations, roles, and relationships become clear, team members find their place on the team and attempt to fit in. A well-conceived team design provides (a) **predictability**, by reducing ambiguity and, thereby, lowering anxiety; (b) **efficiency**, by maximizing resources and reducing coordination losses; and (c) **member satisfaction**, through improved relationships and task achievement. Unfortunately, work environments like the one Jennifer experienced at the clothing store are not uncommon. Much of the frustration and inefficiencies can be linked back to a faulty or ill-defined structure.

Team design can be imposed from an external source, or it can emerge organically from within the team itself. In a democratically oriented group, structure is mutually decided upon by members and emerges from the bottom up. Team members might volunteer for specific jobs and have the freedom to vote on when and where they will meet. For example, a group of community volunteers who have come together to address rising property taxes in their town will likely decide for themselves what they want to accomplish and how they will do it. This kind of empowerment and shared decision making can be an adjustment for many (Thoms, Pinto, Parente, & Druskat, 2002). Members who are conscientious, open to new ideas, and emotionally stable will be most successful and satisfied with self-structured groups (Molleman, Nuata, & Jehn, 2004).

Conversely, teams that operate in strict, hierarchical social systems, organizations, or cultures will have their structure defined from the top down. Some institutions have stringent regulations about the behavior and expectations of their members in terms of dress code, rules about communication, and policies regarding attendance, to name just a few. Employee handbooks and office protocol can take a lot of the guesswork out of knowing what is expected of members. Though individuals tend to experience higher levels of satisfaction when teams function more democratically in nature (Foels, Driskell, Mullen, & Salas, 2000), teams that are defined by the larger organizations within which they operate may be more efficient. In some cases, it may be more effective to be told exactly what to do and how to do it instead of spending a lot of time creating the right set of rules, roles, and interpersonal dynamics that satisfy the particular tastes of any given team. Furthermore, teams that need to respond quickly in crisis situations require strong autocratic leadership in order to maximize efficiency and minimize coordination losses. For example, the military requires a highly structured, top-down hierarchy of authority in order to accomplish tasks in potentially confusing and life-threatening situations. Surgical teams and cockpit crews are other groups in high-intensity situations where rules and roles are dictated by strict institutional policies and predetermined task assignments.

Figure 2.1   The Search for Stability

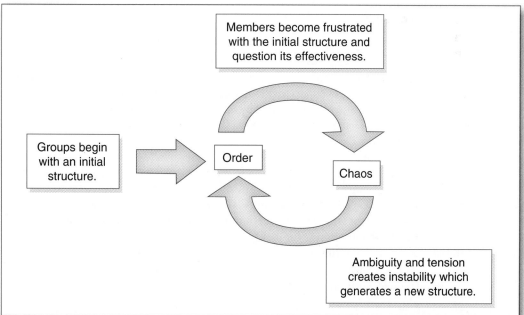

While initial structure provides security and stability for teams, it is important to note that social systems don't remain stable for very long. They frequently oscillate from stability (order) to instability (chaos) and back again (order). This fluid dynamic makes groups unpredictable, yet it also provides the potential for learning and development. Because of the diversity of opinion and experience within teams, members bring multiple perspectives regarding how they should operate; as a result, they often challenge the existing structure. The "storming" and "norming" stages of group development are necessary to move the team into "performing." In this way, ongoing reorganization and restructuring can be seen as a creative force that has the potential to maximize group effectiveness.

For example, imagine a fraternity that has just elected a new set of officers. Not surprisingly, the brothers were elected on the basis of popularity and not necessarily on their administrative experience or skills. After the "chaos" of elections, the new executive board is in the forming stage and the members settle into their roles and responsibilities according to their positions. Unfortunately, the new treasurer is not a detail person, and bills from outside venders start to fall through the cracks. Things get so bad that the president gets a letter from the local electric company threatening to turn off the house's electricity if it is not paid immediately. The president confronts the treasurer, but he gets defensive and blames the secretary for not delivering the bills to his mailbox. The rest of the officers are briefed on the situation and there is full-blown "storming" between those loyal to the treasurer and those critical of him. How can this team pull out of the downward spiral? The executive committee needs to have a "norming" session to get all the issues on the table and redefine procedures or reassign responsibilities to ensure the board is able to "perform" its function properly. These types of meetings can be messy, but they are necessary. After this, things will settle down as the leadership team stabilizes and members learn to work together more effectively.

ROLES AND RESPONSIBILITIES

As teams work on common goals, members fill various roles and responsibilities to contribute to the group effort. Roles are a "set of prescriptions that define the behaviors required of an individual member who occupies a certain position" (Bray & Brawley, 2002, p. 234). These roles can be assigned by the leader, decided by the team, or volunteered for by specific members. For example, the leader of a team working to raise money for a worthy cause might ask a certain member to contact various agencies with whom they might partner. Presumably, the leader perceives that the member to whom he or she gives the assignment either has the skills, commitment, or appropriate attitude to carry out the task. Other, less formal roles evolve through the group's process. After a few meetings, the service team mentioned above might realize that it would be advantageous to partner with other organizations and suggest that a particular member who has strong community ties explore that possibility.

Finally, members will often volunteer for those tasks that they feel most comfortable, confident, and competent doing (Bray & Brawley, 2002). For example, a member who has a lot of experience working for nonprofit organizations might be quick to volunteer to make initial contact with other groups.

As individuals consistently take on similar tasks and functions, other members will come to expect to see them in those roles. This is one way groups become predictable and

stable. When roles are ambiguous and unclear, members experience frustration and group performance suffers. But when everyone understands their role within the group, misunderstandings and process losses can be minimized. Consistent patterns of behavior from individual members can be associated with one or more of the three major categories of group roles: task roles, relationship roles, and individual roles (Forsyth, 2006).

Task roles are roles that contribute to the ultimate goal of the group. Members who primarily fill these roles provide critical thinking and strong organizational skills. They are able to analyze problems and overcome obstacles to success. These roles include the ability to make plans and create accountability structures. Sometimes perceived as driven, those immersed in task roles are goal-oriented and keep the group focused and on track. Productivity, efficiency, and achievement are important values to those who are in task roles, causing them to become frustrated if the group wastes time or becomes inefficient.

Relationship roles, on the other hand, are roles that build cohesion in the group. They fulfill the important functions of creating trust and increasing member satisfaction (Ilgen, Hollenbeck, Johnson, & Jundt, 2005). Members who fulfill relationship roles are aware of the interpersonal dynamics of the group and strive to encourage and validate others. While some may perceive these roles as overly concerned with non-task-related issues, both task and relationship roles are needed to balance the group experience and increase the chance for success.

The third type of role describes behavior patterns that are not often beneficial to the group. Individual roles work against the group's goals and distract the group from its mission. People who are playing individual roles are often frustrating to other members, as they passively or actively resist the work of the group. While they may serve a function by challenging and thereby establishing boundaries, individual roles are generally seen as more of a hindrance than a help to performance. The following list of team roles is adapted from a larger list of functional group roles originally developed by Benne and Sheats (1948).

At times, roles can become overly rigid to the point where members either get stuck in less than optimal roles or they become stagnant. This not only hurts their own development but can also prevent others from having the opportunity to experience that role. Family systems theory suggests that the healthiest families allow members to try different roles at different times. For example, the "rebel" of the family does not always have to be the rebel. Likewise, the family "hero" does not always have to be perfect. Applied to groups, the person who has played the role of "recorder" does not always have to be the one who takes notes. He or she may like a break, and someone else may want to take on that task for a while. Members who previously served as negative forces in the group should also be

Table 2.1

Task Roles	Function
Information seeker	Asks for facts, opinions, and ideas from the group, and for clarification and elaboration about existing concepts
Information giver	Contributes facts, opinions, and novel ideas to the group
Discussion facilitator	Facilitates the discussion by engaging the group
Task manager	Keeps the group on task and focuses on practical details
Skeptic	Challenges ideas and evaluates potential solutions
Recorder	Takes notes and records the decisions of the group

Table 2.2

Relationship Roles	Function
Encourager	Validates, affirms, and supports others
Harmonizer	Mediates conflict among group members
Process observer	Observes and periodically comments on the groups progress
Advocate	Helps quieter members to speak up and be heard in the group

Table 2.3

Individual Roles	Function
Resister	Opposes the group by being negative and passive-aggressive
Dominator	Dominates discussions and intimidates others
Avoider	Tries to do as little work as possible
Attention seeker	Calls attention to self to meet personal needs

given the opportunity to participate in more productive roles. However, groups often make it challenging, even for members playing negative roles, to change roles. Once initial impressions have been formed, it can be difficult to change them.

Interestingly, a given role can change the typical behavior of the role carrier. Commonly held beliefs about how a particular role should be carried out can determine an individual's behavior regardless of whether or not that behavior had previously been characteristic of that individual. The classic Stanford Prison Experiment is an example of the strength and influence of role expectations. In 1971 social psychologists at Stanford University enlisted 24 male students to participate in an experiment conducted in the psychology building on campus. Each was assigned, by the flip of a coin, to act as either a prisoner or a guard in a convincing mock prison that was constructed in the basement.

On the first day of the experiment, prisoners were "arrested" by local law enforcement officers, taken to the Palo Alto police station, and charged with armed robbery. They were booked, fingerprinted, had their mug shots taken, and then placed in a holding cell. When they were transported to the mock prison, their individual identity was largely taken from them; they were given ill-fitting muslin smocks to wear and were no longer referred to by name, but by number. The guards were dressed in military-style uniforms and wore mirrored sunglasses to prevent eye contact. They wore whistles around their necks and carried billy clubs borrowed from the local police department. Although the guards were forbidden to use physical force, they were otherwise encouraged to use any means possible to control the prisoners and maintain order in the prison.

By the second day of the experiment, the prisoners had already become weary of the humiliating environment and attempted to stage a rebellion. They ripped off their numbers, barricaded themselves in their cells, and began taunting the guards. The guards responded with anger and hostility, using a fire extinguisher to force prisoners back as they entered their cells. The guards then stripped the prisoners naked, put the leaders into solitary confinement, and began to harass and intimidate them. As they strongly identified with their arbitrarily assigned roles, the guards became abusive and the prisoners became passive and depressed. The entire experiment had to be stopped prematurely after only six days into the projected two-week timetable. The power of roles in conjunction with the power of peer influence ensured that everyone knew their place and were expected to behave accordingly. After a short time, the roles were no longer roles—they became identities.

In the case of the Stanford Prison Experiment, roles were exaggerated and, ultimately, dysfunctional. But well-defined roles can also be used in a very positive way. Members with clear roles know what they are expected to do and can execute their responsibilities with efficiency. Little time is wasted in confusion about which responsibilities belong to whom. In contrast, without clearly defined roles and agreed-upon division of responsibilities, teams sacrifice productivity and potentially even induce chaos. This would certainly be the case during the morning rush at Starbucks if the employees didn't have clearly defined roles for cashiers, baristas, backroom staff, and supervisors. Over time, standard operating procedures and interpersonal patterns are established and become part of the culture. These patterns of interaction create stability, predictability, and efficiency.

TEAM CULTURE

Culture is the learned set of shared beliefs, values, customs, and history that unifies a group of people, helps them make sense of their world, and influences their behavior. Southwest Airlines has been proactive and deliberate about creating a corporate culture that fosters mutual respect and a commitment to customer service. It devotes significant time and resources transmitting these particular values to new and existing employees. The culture of a group or organization can be communicated in many ways and through many symbolic mediums (Bolman & Deal, 2003). Organizational developers and team leaders often pay close attention to how these messages are communicated.

Myths, folklore, and stories represent and perpetuate the values and shared beliefs that tie a group of people together. For example, the hallways of Southwest Airlines' corporate headquarters are lined with pictures of the early days; these images of heroes, heroines, and milestones reinforce the company's shared set of beliefs and values. They are reminders of what is important to the organization. Group and organizational histories are rich with clues about the development of their cultures.

Company logos, team names, performance measures, and job titles all communicate distinct messages. The way people dress, the physical layout of offices and meeting rooms, and the way people talk to one another impact the overall environment. These symbolic messages are always present to influence what people are to believe and how they are to behave. Some team leaders are very deliberate about the kind of culture they want to create, while others let the group culture emerge organically. In either case, a team culture takes shape.

Rituals and ceremonies celebrate important moments in the life of the team (Martin, 2002). For example, initiation rituals indoctrinate new members, enhancement rituals recognize exemplary conduct, and degradation rituals publicly reprimand or remove poorly performing members from the group. Ending rituals signal the time when a member

transitions out of a group. Whether they operate within a prison gang or on a corporate executive board, rituals reinforce the identity and structure of groups. This is because rituals are explicit ways that groups communicate and reinforce group culture. Walmart's founder, Sam Walton, conducted the following ritual with over 100,000 employees over TV satellite in the mid-1980s: "Now, I want you to raise your right hand—and remember what we say at Walmart, that a promise we make is a promise we keep—and I want you to repeat after me: From this day forward, I solemnly promise and declare that every time a customer comes within ten feet of me, I will smile, look him in the eye, and greet him. So help me, Sam" (Walton and Huey, 1992, p. 223.) This ritual helped create a culture that is reinforced every time a customer walks past a Walmart greeter. When customers walk into a Walmart store, they are welcomed with a warm, friendly greeting that is distinctly personal and engaging.

As individuals work together and form relationships, they develop a shared identity that distinguishes their group from others. According to social identity theory, this happens when individuals "identify themselves in the same way and have the same definition of who they are, what attributes they have, and how they relate to and differ from specific out-groups or from people who are simply not in-group members" (Hogg, 2005, p. 136). As people experience various groups, either as members or outsiders, they create categories with which to associate individuals of that group. Thus, if a person has created an internal definition, or schema, that describes "chess players," then all new people who describe themselves as chess players are ascribed those attributes (Hogg & Reid, 2006).

Characteristics and attitudes that define a group's identity can have a strong influence on its members (Hogg & Reid, 2006). Social identity theory suggests that members adopt a common set of beliefs and behaviors when they associate with a certain group. Those that

are strongly associated with a particular group will readily adopt the beliefs and goals that define that group (Christensen, Rothgerber, Wood, & Matz, 2004). Social norms that are integrated into personal identity then become standards against which to evaluate one's own beliefs and behavior. For example, in the highly polarized world of national politics, those who identify as either Democrats, Republicans, or independents are prone to having an overly optimistic assessment of their own party's views while discounting any ideas or proposals coming from a different group. When this happens, meaningful dialogue is compromised, as groups engage primarily in offensive and defensive posturing to gain or maintain power.

In the same way that individuals construct internal working models that include beliefs, goals, and strategies for daily functioning, groups create a shared working model or mental model to define the life and structure of the group (Ilgen, Hollenbeck, Johnson, & Jundt, 2005). Internal working models are cognitive roadmaps that provide a framework for understanding experiences (what is) and for defining ideals (what should be). They are established from previous group experiences and influenced by the larger sociocultural context within which they exist. Because groups establish unique and distinct mental models, two groups might perceive the same event in very different ways. For example, a group of homebuilders might be very enthusiastic about a large, highly desirable piece of land that was rezoned for residential building and put up for sale. But a neighboring homeowners' association might be upset due to potential problems with overcrowded schools or additional traffic. The local school administration could interpret this event in an altogether different way, seeing it as a way to increase funding and visibility in the district. But then, a group of conservation enthusiasts might be concerned about the potential impact on the environment. Each group has a unique set of shared beliefs, goals, and strategies that influence the way it interprets and evaluates new information.

Shared mental models include a common set of beliefs, attitudes, and values that guide group thinking and decisions. They define beliefs about the team in terms of group description, collective self-esteem, and group efficacy. As a result, an assessment of one's team can create a sense of pride and confidence. Individual members experience increased personal self-esteem when they are affiliated with a highly desirable and successful group (Aberson, Healy, & Romero, 2000). Because of these benefits, groups have a tendency to view their own group in overly inflated ways while viewing other groups, especially competing groups, in an overly negative way. This tendency is called the ingroup/outgroup bias, whereby individuals consider their group as better than other groups.

Members are not only influenced by the culture, but they also impact the culture in a reciprocal fashion. The personality of individual members contributes to the personality and identity of the larger group. The personalities of leaders, especially, can have a ripple effect upon a social context. Because of their stature and influence, they have the ability to establish and enforce policies that reflect their own values. For better or worse, charismatic leaders such as Herb Kelleher, CEO of Southwest Airlines, have tremendous influence over their organizational cultures. But it is not only top leaders that have influence; leaders and influential members (i.e., culture carriers) at all levels contribute to the collective atmosphere and often set the tone for group meetings. For example, skilled facilitators can create warm, inviting environments, where discussion is vibrant and engaging in contrast to ineffective facilitators, who can shut down conversations and discourage members from speaking up.

Have you ever wondered while you're placing an order for a vanilla latte or caramel macchiato at Starbucks, why the baristas are so friendly and helpful? They seem to enjoy their jobs and seem to be enjoying the camaraderie of their fellow teammates. In his autobiography, Howard Schultz, chair and CEO of Starbucks (Schultz & Yang, 1997), describes the passion and devotion of his employees as their "number one competitive advantage. Lose it, and we've lost the game" (p. 138).

By harnessing the power of teams, Starbucks grew from a single Seattle location in 1971 to 20,000 stores in 59 countries by 2012—and its success is not just numerical. Starbucks has won a multitude of awards including the "Ten Most Admired Companies in America" by *Fortune* magazine in 2003, 2004, and 2005, a trend that continues to date. In fact, Starbucks is one of the most admired companies in the world. It is frequently listed by the press and business literature in categories such as "most admired," "most influential," "top performers," and "best companies to work for." This last distinction deserves further discussion. What makes Starbucks so effective, and why is it such a great place to work?

One reason may be the shared culture that the company works to inspire among its employees. New Starbucks baristas receive a full 24 hours of in-store training that informs them not only about how to mix drinks and operate a cash register, but also about the coffee industry and the Starbucks franchise itself. And note that the term is always *barista* or *partner,* and not merely *worker* or *counter help,* thus further individuating Starbucks employees from other standard coffee shop workers. And finally, the company accepts and responds to an average of 200 mission review queries per month from employees with concerns or suggestions regarding the company mission. The care that Starbucks takes to institute both a unique training and team environment, coupled with the empowering feedback-oriented relationship established around the company's mission, help to make employees feel as though they are a valued part of a greater shared vision. It comes as little surprise to learn that the first of Starbucks' six-point mission statement is to "provide a great work environment and treat each other with respect and dignity."

With the shift away from hierarchal authority structures in recent decades, organizations have relied upon self-managed groups to establish their own unique ground rules and operating procedures that produce results (Pfeffer, 1992). This popular management strategy of empowerment utilizes the dynamics of group conformity to hold members accountable to high standards. High-performance standards and "cult-like cultures" often exist in the most successful organizations (Collins & Porras, 2002). A concrete ideology reinforced by strong methods of indoctrination can create cohesive group environments that socialize members into proven strategies for success.

However, it is important to note that a strong team culture can have negative consequences as well. Groupthink is a condition that occurs when teams are overly cohesive or when one or more members have too much power and influence over the group as a whole. For example, the Senate Intelligence Committee (2004), which assessed the U.S. intelligence systems' conclusion in falsely identifying Iraq's possession of weapons of mass destruction, identified groupthink as one of the contributing factors to the error. Apparently, the general presumption that Iraq had such weapons was so strongly felt by top members of the administration that individuals were reluctant to question what they perceived as the majority position. When a single dominant member or small group of members have enough influence to make judgments that others in the group are reluctant to question, the checks and balances of group decision making are compromised. The process and potential pitfalls of team decision making is discussed in length in Chapter 7.

BUILDING A TEAM

Team design begins with a clear understanding of the task that the team is being asked to accomplish. After that has been established, it is time to begin identifying and enlisting the members that will give the team the best opportunity to fulfill its purpose. Some important and highly interrelated aspects to consider are the complexity of the task; the amount and type of interaction that will be required of members; and, finally, the number and type of members to enlist. Not all teams have a discreet beginning. In fact, most group memberships evolve over time. In those cases, existing teams can regularly evaluate their performance to determine if they have the right mix of people along with an enabling structure and positive culture that lead to results. If not, the following concepts can help improve performance.

Task Complexity

Groups that engage in complex tasks require greater levels of coordination, participation, and decentralized communication (Brown & Miller, 2000; Lafond, Jobidon, Aubé, & Tremblay, 2011). There are simply more details and interdependencies to monitor and manage. Task complexity increases with the following:

- Task unfamiliarity (lack of previous experience)

- Task ambiguity (absence of clear mission or goals)

- The volume of information required to understand the task
- The number of alternatives available in reaching the desired outcome
- The number of subordinate tasks to be defined and coordinated

For example, restructuring a student organization would be a more complex task than collaboratively writing a research paper. Imagine yourself as an executive council member of a fraternity that has had repeated alcohol violations and must either restructure the house or face possible expulsion from campus. The leadership team is likely to have had little or no previous experience with the task before it. In addition, the students will be challenged by the relative ambiguity of the goal of "restructuring." In contrast, writing a group research paper for a history class does not have this same level of complexity. The desired outcome is fairly straightforward, as students will have had plenty of experience writing papers by the time they have reached college.

Group members performing highly complex tasks need to work together closely to determine their best options for success. These higher levels of interdependence and cooperation mean that, depending on the type of interdependence required (see next section), extra attention may need to be paid to selecting team members with superior communication skills. When task complexity stems from a lack of familiarity or background information, teams will benefit from the advice of experts in the field. If a team doesn't have the expertise within its ranks, it must find it outside the team. Finally, regardless of the source of complexity, teams performing complex tasks must clearly define their vision, create detailed action plans, and have regular status updates to ensure that members are informed of the team's progress.

Types of Interdependence

As stated in the previous section, the amount of cooperation needed for success is strongly related to the type and complexity of the tasks being undertaken. When high levels of interdependence are required, clearly defined roles must be in place in order for teams to be successful (Allen, Sargent, & Bradley, 2003). The nature of these roles will largely be determined by the type of interdependence needed to accomplish the task. Thompson (2004) identifies three distinct types of interdependence within groups: pooled, sequential, and reciprocal interdependence.

Pooled interdependence refers to group work that may simply be divided among members in order to be compiled into a finished product at a later time. For example, a group of workers cleaning up after a big football game might each take a section of the stadium from which to pick up trash and sweep. Though they work independently of one another, the workers collectively clean the entire stadium. These types of tasks require the least amount of cooperation and communication.

Pooled interdependence is more effective when teams have the following structural procedures in place: (a) a reporting structure in which a supervisor or leader can hold members accountable for their part of the project, (b) regular team meetings where members can discuss potential problems and improve policies and procedures, and

| Figure 2.2 | Pooled Interdependence |

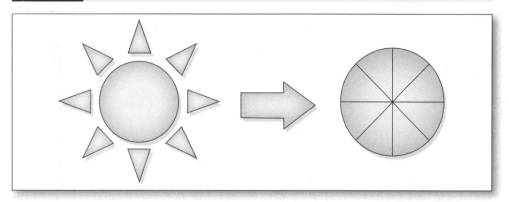

(c) a way to keep members committed to the overall task by reinforcing and updating each member's understanding of how their part will be integrated into the finished product.

Other tasks require more coordination among members. **Sequential interdependence** occurs when group members are dependent on the completed work of other members prior to being able to complete their own part. As one person finishes a portion of the task, he or she hands it off to the next person. The "hand off" can be a bottleneck in the process, so it requires thoughtful attention. In the case of a relay team, track and field athletes will rehearse the simple act of handing the baton to the next runner countless times before competing in an actual race. Efficiency in the handing of the baton could be the difference between victory and defeat, especially in a sport that is decided by milliseconds.

In another example, before a Starbucks barista can make a coffee drink, he or she is dependent upon someone else to order and then to stock the ingredients that are needed to brew the coffee. Thus, each member's work is dependent on other members fulfilling their portion of the task. Therefore, sequentially interdependent groups must pay close attention to the transition points between each member's portion of the task. Groups may want to establish a routine for notifying the next member in sequence when a task has been completed. It may also be beneficial to create a procedure for informing the next member of delays or changes that will affect their segment of the work. High-performance teams identify mistakes or problems early on and learn from them as opposed to hiding them or covering them up.

Reciprocal interdependence requires the greatest level of interaction among members as they work together simultaneously. Members influence one another as tasks are accomplished simultaneously with input from others. For example, sailing teams in the America's Cup races have a highly defined structure that dictates who does what and when. Every member is needed to successfully complete the task, and there is little room for role negotiation.

Figure 2.3 Sequential Interdependence

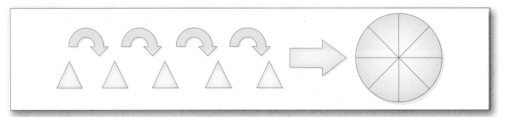

Figure 2.4 Reciprocal Interdependence

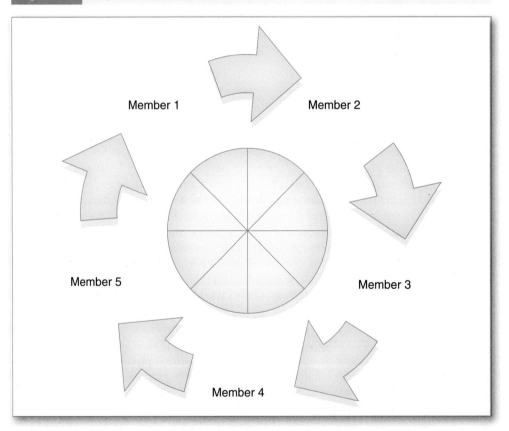

Examples of this type of interdependence include zone defenses in football, marching bands, and Broadway plays. Each member is required to do his or her part according to well-defined protocols in order for the whole group to be successful.

Team Composition

The success or failure of a team is strongly related to the quality of its membership. Collins's (2001) popular book, *Good to Great: Why Some Companies Make the Leap . . . and Others Don't,* stresses the importance of finding the best people possible. Metaphorically speaking, he suggests that "getting the right people on the bus" is even more important than deciding where the bus is going, because high-caliber individuals will be able to figure out where the bus needs to go and determine the best route for getting there. Research on sports teams suggests that "the best individuals make the best team" (Gill, 1984, p. 325). This correlation between individual talent and team performance is strongest in sports such as baseball (.94) and football (.91). However, it is entirely possible for a group of highly skilled players to be a poorly performing team. For example, though a soccer team of eleven all-star goalies may boast an extraordinary amount of individual talent, their performance as a team may suffer because their one-dimensional level of expertise does not encompass all of the skills required to play a well-rounded game of soccer. Thus, not only do teams need to have talented members, those members need to have skills that complement one another.

Ideally, each member will possess task-related knowledge and skills along with interpersonal skills that enable them to work with others. The relative amount of each type of skill that a given member should possess will depend on the complexity of the task and the level of interdependence required to achieve the desired outcome. More specifically, task-related knowledge and skills are especially important on tasks that are complex and that require highly specialized knowledge and skills to achieve results. On the other hand, members of reciprocally interdependent teams will need stronger interpersonal skills than do members of groups that use sequential or pooled methods. Regardless, group work will always call upon some mixture of both sets of skills; thus, it is important to be aware of each when building a team.

While task-related competence is important to consider in choosing potential members, ideal members also possess strong interpersonal skills. Members who are considered "team players" are enthusiastic, optimistic, collegial, cooperative, and flexible (Rousseau, Aubé, & Savoie, 2006). Furthermore, they are self-motivated and conscientious, and have strong communication skills. Communication skills such as active listening and assertiveness are used both to support and to challenge other team members. Yet individuals who have strong interpersonal skills are self-aware enough to know that they are not being overly assertive, derogatory, or offensive. In addition, they are able to accept negative feedback from others and respond in a nondefensive manner. Of course, those with strong interpersonal skills also know how to give critical feedback in a way that is motivated by a desire to help others, not tear them down. Spirited banter through which members challenge one another's assumptions is often the hallmark of high-performing teams; it is described in detail in Chapter 6, on communication.

Stevens and Campion (1999) have developed the Teamwork-KSA Test to measure team knowledge, skills, and abilities (KSAs). After reviewing the research, they determined five specific areas associated with effective participation in groups:

Interpersonal Knowledge, Skills, and Abilities

Conflict resolution: Recognizing types and sources of conflict; encouraging desirable conflict but discouraging undesirable conflict; and employing integrative (win-win) negotiation strategies rather than distributive (win-lose) strategies.

Collaborative problem-solving: Identifying situations requiring participative group problem-solving and using the proper degree of participation; recognizing obstacles to collaborative group problem-solving and implementing appropriate corrective actions.

Communication: Understanding effective communication networks using decentralized networks where possible; recognizing open and supportive communication methods; maximizing the consistency between nonverbal and verbal messages; recognizing and interpreting the nonverbal messages of others; and engaging in and understanding the importance of small talk and ritual greetings.

Self-Management Knowledge, Skills, and Abilities

Goal-setting and performance management: Establishing specific, challenging, and accepted team goals, and monitoring, evaluating, and providing feedback on both overall team performance and individual team member performance.

Planning and task coordination: Coordinating and synchronizing activities, information, and tasks among team members, as well as aiding the team in establishing individual task and role assignments that ensure the proper balance of workload among members.

Sources: Miller (2001, p. 748); Stevens and Campion (1994, p. 505).

The Teamwork-KSA Test is just one of many assessment tools available commercially for assessing current and potential members, and its results are often used for member selection or staff development.

Team Size

After team designers clarify the team's task, predict the level of interdependence that will be required for success, and identify potential members, they must decide how many members to enlist. In smaller groups of three or four, members may have to take on multiple roles and responsibilities. But in groups of more than eight or ten members, coordination can become cumbersome. The complexity and breadth of the task to be completed will help to inform the minimum number of members required to complete the task. In other words, the number of specializations or fields that the task will call upon, added to the human capital that will be required in order to carry out the job, will yield an estimate as to the number of individuals that should be called to the team. Noted team expert J. Richard Hackman (2002) emphasizes the importance of team size and specifically warns against the common error of placing too many members on a team.

What are the risks associated with oversized teams? Coordination losses increase as the number of people involved on any given task increases and relational bonds weaken (Mueller, 2012). As group size grows, individual members may also become passive due to a diffusion of responsibility, a lack of accountability, and ultimately a reduction in commitment

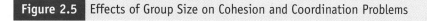

Figure 2.5 Effects of Group Size on Cohesion and Coordination Problems

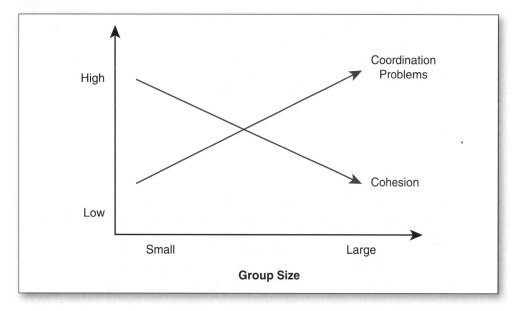

(Wagner, 1995). In a study of group performance on a decision-making task, three-person groups consistently outperformed seven-person groups (Seijts & Latham, 2000). This means that not only did having an extra four people fail to contribute positively to the outcome of the group, the additional members actually hindered performance. One reason for this is that smaller groups tend to have higher levels of commitment among their membership. Similarly, they have fewer members who engage in **social loafing**, which is the desire to do as little work as possible. Smaller groups simply cannot afford to have members slacking off. It's also harder for members to fly under the radar in smaller groups. Laughlin, Hatch, Silver, and Boh (2006) found that three-, four-, or five-member groups outperformed individuals and dyads on a problem-solving task but did not differ from one another.

As groups increase in size, it is also more difficult to maintain a sense of connection with fellow group members. Individuals have a limited capacity for the number of people with whom they may feel reasonably close. As groups get larger, it is increasingly difficult to establish and maintain high levels of cohesion (Gammage, Carron, & Estabrooks, 2001). Hackman (2002) suggests that the optimal size for a group is the fewest number of members who can feasibly accomplish the tasks assigned to them. The **ideal size** for most groups is typically between four and eight members, once again depending upon the complexity and breadth of the task.

LAUNCHING A TEAM

Once team membership is determined, team builders must give thought to how they will introduce team members to their task, and to one another. The first face-to-face meeting is a critical event in the life of a team. Patterns of relating and general operating procedures can become established in the opening minutes of the first meeting. Various components such as the physical setting, seating arrangements, task description, and introductions forge a lasting impression on the members of the team. In addition, interpersonal dynamics such as communication patterns and status hierarchies will influence the emerging structure of the group. Thus, it is important to conduct a well-structured and thoughtfully planned launch meeting, since it is generally much easier to establish effective team processes at the beginning of a team's development than to correct faulty ones later (Polzer, 2003). This first meeting sets the foundation upon which the group and its work will be built, so consistency, foresight, transparency, and candor must be used throughout the following four preliminary steps.

Introductions

One of the first tasks of running a successful launch is taking the time to make thorough and thoughtful introductions. Introductions help begin the process of forging bonds and developing trust. Tasks that are highly interdependent require significant amounts of mutual trust, and it is difficult for members to trust those they do not know. Members often come into new teams with some measure of anxiety and uncertainty because they don't know how they will compare to other members. For teams with individuals who have never worked together before, it can be very helpful to share brief biographies of each member to familiarize the team with one another. This allows members to become aware of the unique value and expertise each member will bring to the team, including their own potential contribution. Take, for example, the introduction that Jennifer's manager at Starbucks made on her first day of work. Not only did his kind words infuse a feeling of initial respect from her new coworkers, they helped contribute to her own self-confidence in that new and unfamiliar work setting.

Since introductions can be stressful, leaders might want to consider ways to minimize the need for members to try to prove themselves or promote their own superiority. Thus, leaders can use a prepared description of each member so that the members themselves do not feel put on the spot. In this way, the team designer or leader can highlight the strengths that each team member brings to the team in order to establish the norm that all members have been carefully selected and are important for the team's success. Another strategy is for members to pair up, interview one another, and then introduce their partner to the rest of the team. In general, this is a time for members to learn about one another. They should have more confidence in their teammates after going through this exercise.

Ground Rules

The launch meeting is also a prime opportunity to establish initial rules and expectations for members. Setting concrete ground rules is an effective way to reduce uncertainty and establish what will be expected of each member. Ground rules differ from implicit norms. Implicit norms, which we will cover in more depth in a later chapter, are the unstated yet generally accepted rules that are established based on the team members' experiences together. Ground rules, on the other hand, are the specifically stated regulations and standards to which every member is expected to adhere. The launch meeting provides the team leader with an important opportunity to establish these rules because everyone is likely to be present, attentive, and eager to comply with what is asked of them. Here are some typical ground rules established at the first meeting: (a) meetings will start and end on time, (b) members should let others know if they cannot attend or will be late, (c) texting and cell phones are not appropriate during team meetings, (d) everyone is expected to contribute to discussions, and so on. Publicly stating these guidelines, even those that seem obvious, will eliminate ambiguity and serve as a foundation for other rules and norms that will be added throughout the team members' time together.

Some rules will be established by the leader while others will be left up to team members themselves. In fact, it can be helpful to ask members to describe how they best work in teams or about the types of team dynamics that have worked best for them in the past. This will help them to establish ownership in the functioning of the group and create a collaborative team environment.

Shared Vision

High-performance teams go much further beyond mere compliance or perfunctory obedience to group expectations. The most effective teams are committed to a shared vision. An engaging vision defines the purpose for which the group exists. From that purpose, specific goals emerge that have the potential to motivate members and guide collective efforts (Van Mierlo & Kleingeld, 2010). A compelling direction that captures the hearts and minds of team members separates true teams from mere workgroups (Hackman, 2002). Launching the team in a way that lays out the task in a compelling way can help motivate and jump-start the process.

In the movie *Braveheart*, William Wallace (played by actor Mel Gibson) rode to the battlefield at Stirling, Scotland, to confront a group of Scottish peasants fleeing before a superior British army. In the film, Wallace was faced with the daunting task of inspiring a shared vision of such proportions that the peasants would be willing to give up their own lives to fight the British in order to become a free nation. Much to Wallace's credit, the peasants, who had been nothing more than pawns with which the Scottish nobles bargained for their own personal gain, began to embrace Wallace's vision as they considered the possibilities for their children and grandchildren. Because of their shared vision, the peasants were willing to make great personal sacrifice and commit themselves to battle. According to the Hollywood version of this thirteenth-century historical event, Wallace challenged the enemy to a battle, and with the help of the peasants, nobles, and some clever strategy, managed to defeat the British in a surprising victory.

Motivational speeches alone rarely generate the long-term commitment required for group success. Eventually, motivation must come from within the group itself, not imposed from an outside source (Liu, Zhang, Wang, & Lee, 2011). A shared vision often begins with one or two members and then spreads to the rest of the group. In the case of William Wallace, fighting for a free Scotland was his passion, and he was willing to pay the ultimate price for it. In his petition to the Scottish peasants he offered few extrinsic rewards, yet the vision he inspired regarding the possibility of a better life for future generations was enough to motivate the ragtag army.

A shared vision stimulates the interest, enthusiasm, and creativity of group members (Cohen & Bailey, 1997). More important, it generates commitment. Personal goals are put aside as members work for the common good of the group and the ultimate mission of the organization. For instance, if a Starbucks employee is only serving coffee and cleaning tables, he or she may feel disengaged or lack motivation. However, if the employee sees his or her job as providing a meaningful service to others and contributing to the success of the team, then pouring coffee and emptying trash cans take on a whole new meaning. This transformation of thinking can be a wonderful benefit of working in teams or groups. Collaborating with a group of friendly, outgoing people on a meaningful task can make an otherwise wearisome 5:00 a.m. shift significantly more enjoyable.

Levels of Commitment

Thompson (2004) suggests that the most common leadership challenge identified by more than half (56%) of the leaders in her study is developing and sustaining high levels of team motivation. Consequently, team leaders should use the launch meeting to set the stage for true commitment from the membership. People are drawn to groups for collective benefits. However, they will also want to preserve personal interests. The result is a tension between conforming to the will of the group and preserving individuality and autonomy. Not all members will be committed to the group's goals; some will resist. This resistance can come in many forms, including a passive response (do nothing to help the group), an aggressive response (actively resist the leader or other members of the group), or a passive-aggressive response (resist indirectly while appearing to be supportive of the group's goals). Leaders can overcome member resistance by creating a shared vision around which members can rally.

Group members can experience various degrees of commitment at different times. The following levels describe the possible ways members might relate to the goals of the team (Senge, 1990):

- *Commitment:* These members are committed to the goal and motivated to achieve it. They are also committed to the group and have interest in and concern for the other group members.

- *Compliance:* Members who are compliant will do what they are asked in spite of not having embraced the importance of the group's mission. While they rarely volunteer or go above and beyond what is expected, they consistently fulfill their responsibilities.

- *Resistance:* Group members who are resistant are working against the group. They are actively trying to sabotage particular members or even the group as a whole for their own personal reasons. If the leadership of the group is fairly authoritarian, these resistant members tend to be passive-aggressive, as they secretly try to enlist other members to join in working against the group.

- *Disengagement:* These members are physically present but are apathetic toward the work of the group. Their clear disinterest and lack of engagement likely render them undependable in the eyes of their colleagues.

One undergraduate student offered the following example of how member commitment affects the team:

My junior year of high school, I played bass and guitar for a band with some friends from church. After performing three songs for a local battle of the bands, we got a call from a guy at the Dallas House of Blues to play in a battle of the bands downtown. The winning band got a recording contract and $3,000. We had one month to get ready. Immediately, I started writing original songs for the battle of the bands. In the meantime, we asked the other band members to begin learning some cover songs that we would perform as well. When it came time to practice five days later, I asked everyone if they were ready to practice the covers. The female vocalist said she "never got around to it." The drummer and other guitarist nodded in agreement. "What do you mean 'you never got around to it?'" the band's male vocalist asked. "Learning those cover songs was the only thing we told you guys to do. How can we have a productive practice if no one knows their parts?" "Okay, I'm sorry," the female vocalist said. "Let's just go to dinner, and practice next weekend." Reluctantly, TJ and I agreed. "But for next time we need everyone to know those cover songs, because we will really need to practice our original songs as well." A week passed and I practiced and spent some more time writing with TJ and our other guitarist, Matt. When next week came, once again, no one knew the cover songs. TJ and I cancelled practice and sent everyone home to learn the covers for a practice in the next few days. However, when TJ asked everyone when they could practice, no one could practice until the next weekend. Two weeks from the House of Blues battle of the bands, the band had no songs prepared. By the weekend before the battle of the bands, my band only knew one cover and had half of a song written and rehearsed. After briefly discussing practicing during the weekdays, everyone decided it would be best if we just did not perform at the battle of the bands, and focused on other things. After that the band never played together again.

Each member's commitment level contributes to the collective strength of the group. Compliant members are loosely connected to the group, while resistant or disengaged members are negative forces that serve to weaken the group. Effective leaders pay attention to group interactions from day one to assess the commitment level of each member and appropriately address those members whose commitment is lacking.

LEADERSHIP IN ACTION

Throughout this chapter, we have provided theories, suggestions, and examples outlining the foundational steps of building a healthy team. However, think back to the last time you were a part of forming a team. Was it a structured, logical, and effective process? More likely, you found yourself and your team down a road you hadn't planned to take, fumbling along toward a general outcome or product without a formalized system of values, expectations, or shared agreement about how often you would meet, the quality of the ultimate deliverable, and the distribution of responsibilities. At that point, the enthusiasm and optimism of a new team most likely deteriorated into frustration and even dread.

In order to start a new team in the right direction, there are a few key agreements to strike early. Much of this can be achieved by calling the foundational components by name and requiring the group to engage the issues directly and explicitly. For example, in the first meeting of a group of students working together on a class project, members should introduce themselves to one another. Introductions should include each member's name, where they are from, what they are studying, what they like to do in their free time, and what they think their academic strengths are. Leaders should take notes during this round-robin introduction session so they can identify common interests, complementary strengths, and levels of motivation. A discussion about ground rules can easily emerge with the following prompt: "Okay, now that we see how much potential we have, I think we should take a few minutes to set up a few ground rules for how we want to work together."

Ground rules include "rules of engagement" that regulate participation, interaction, conduct, and productivity. One of the ground rules that most teams should adopt is "everyone must offer their full and earnest participation." This bars individuals from holding back, biting their tongue, or "checking out." From those rules and from the shared personal details that emerged from the introductions, trust begins to form. Trust builds upon the safety and consistency provided by the ground rules (and their necessary enforcement). Next, the leader can describe the task and, thus, begin building a vision for success. And from the vision, common ground, shared rules, and trust, the group can achieve an identity. This may seem or feel like a forced or overly intentional approach to building a team, but the best results don't occur by accident. They are the result of an earnest, consistent, and dedicated architecture. Real-world examples include the 1980 U.S, men's Olympic hockey team portrayed in the movie *Miracle*; the 2008 U.S. men's Olympic basketball team; and Earnest Shackleton's Antarctic expeditionary crew that survived against all odds in the face of isolation, starvation, and hopelessness from 1914 to 1917. They are all the products of an effectively and intentionally built team.

The complex challenge of assembling, coordinating, and motivating high-performance teams requires dedication and know-how. By applying the key concepts described in this chapter and building a solid structural foundation, teams are positioned for success.

KEY TERMS

Predictability   20

Efficiency   20

Member satisfaction   20

Task roles   23

Relationship roles   23

Individual roles   23

Ingroup/outgroup bias   28

Groupthinkm29

Pooled interdependence   30

Sequential interdependence   31

DISCUSSION QUESTIONS

1. Explain the difference between task roles, relationship roles, and individual roles.

2. Discuss the importance of rituals in respect to corporations such as Walmart, Southwest Airlines, and Starbucks.

3. Describe the three types of interdependence in groups: pooled interdependence, sequential interdependence, and reciprocal interdependence. Give examples of each.

4. Describe Stevens and Campion's five types of skills associated with ideal team members.

5. Describe the strengths and weaknesses of a large versus a small team. How do you know how many members to place on a new team?

6. Explain the importance of introductions and facilitating a successful launch. How do these contribute to a shared vision?

7. Group members can have any of the following attitudes toward the group's main goal: commitment, compliance, resistance, and disengagement. Describe each of these attitudes and provide examples.

GROUP ACTIVITIES

EXERCISE 2.1 GROUP ANALYSIS

Get into groups of four and complete this task: Compare and contrast two different student groups on campus. Before you begin, assign roles for the discussion. Each person should either be a task leader, recorder, time keeper, or skeptic.

What is the primary objective or goal of the groups? How are members selected to be a part of the groups? Describe the culture of each of the groups. What are the strengths and weaknesses of each of the groups?

You are to submit a written analysis at the end of the prescribed time and present your analysis to the rest of the class.

EXERCISE 2.2 PRESENTATIONS ABOUT GROUP STRUCTURE

Form groups of five to seven people and prepare a three-minute presentation on the three most important concepts in this chapter. Describe the concepts, illustrate the concepts with examples, and apply the concepts to an actual group or team that could benefit from this information. Assign one of your team members to observe how you accomplish this task. That person will watch and take notes but will not participate in the actual task. After each group presents, the observer will describe how his or her group approached this task.

CASE 2.2 PLANNING A COMMUNITY OUTREACH

It's the first week of your summer internship at Futura Industries, and you've been asked by Jasmine, the company's internship coordinator, to meet with her in the conference room. She lets you know that she is putting together a group of interns to form a team charged with the responsibility of planning a community outreach event for the company to raise money for a local animal shelter. Because you have had a class on teams, she is asking you to be the team leader and to identify potential members. She has given you a deadline and some goals in terms of how many summer associates at the company she would like to have participate and how much money Futura Industries wants to raise.

- What kind of team members would you pick from the other interns? Describe their characteristics.

- How many people would you ideally like to have on your team, and why?

- Create a detailed agenda for your first meeting with the internship coordinator.

CHAPTER 3

Interpersonal Dynamics and Conflict

Working with other people can be one of the most rewarding aspects of being on a team, but it can be one of the most challenging as well. This chapter begins with a discussion about social norms and how they develop. Then we explore how individual social styles differ and contribute to the interpersonal dynamics of a team. Often, differences in the way people interact can create misunderstandings and frustration. Fortunately, there are a number of common interpersonal problems that, once understood, can be minimized. But even in the best of circumstances, conflict tends to affect both team members and the team atmosphere. Conflict is not always bad. As a matter of fact, the right kind of conflict is characteristic of high-performing teams and can lead to strong cohesion and team success.

CASE 3.1: *SURVIVOR*

The participants are dirty, malnourished, and tired. Their clothes are in tatters. They scowl and are so exhausted that they don't even bother to wave the flies from their faces. They have resorted to tribalism and clandestine alliances to make it to the next day, seeking strength in numbers against the faceless, ethereal, insidious specter that threatens to snuff out their flame of life. They lie, they cheat, they steal, they fight . . . yet hardly anyone tries to escape. This is not some deranged parallel universe, or sci-fi show, or post-apocalyptic vision of the world. This is Survivor, *the reality television series in which people compete for prizes, money, and the title of "sole survivor."*

Anyone who has watched the series knows the structure. Sixteen strangers are dropped off on a remote island and divided into two teams or "tribes" to fight for survival. With the limited resources of a machete, cooking pot, and canteens, they have to quickly build a shelter and find food and water. At regular intervals, the two tribes compete with one another for prizes and supplies. After each competition, the losing team convenes at a "tribal council" to choose a team member to eliminate from the game.

Under such duress, strained and contentious interpersonal dynamics quickly develop within the two teams. During every episode, contestants lie to one another to gain an advantage and instill loyalty from others. There are threats that strain the group, outbursts that alienate allies, and displays of dominance that intimidate, inspire, and divide tribal sentiment. One fascinating aspect of the show is when a person is "voted off," the host snuffs out the player's flame/torch and dramatically states, "The tribe has spoken. It's time for you to go." Whether they are seen as a weak link or a threat to win the $1 million prize, the person is singled out from the group, judged, and sent away.

One of the interesting paradoxes that team members have to confront is their degree of loyalty to the team versus personal survival. For example, it is in the best interest of the team for every member to forage for food and water; but it is in the best interest of each individual to conserve his or her energy and allow others to do the majority of the work. Indeed, a difference in work ethic is often one of the first issues of contention that emerges on the remote islands. Members who are working hard to help the team survive become extremely frustrated with those who aren't doing their fair share of the work.

Another interpersonal issue that comes up early in the Survivor season is the question of alliances. Tribal members quickly realize that they need to form coalitions with other teammates who will watch their backs and protect them. Subgroups strategize and work together to get to the final stages of the game when they will ultimately compete against one another. Issues of trust, honesty, manipulation, and betrayal create the tumultuous drama that has made this show a success.

When participants become hungry, tired, and stressed out, they get grumpy and irritable. Tempers flare. People storm off in disgust. Teammates think the worst about one another and become suspicious of every word or action. The remote islands of Survivor are a crucible of human interaction. Everything is intensified. While most group experiences are not as volatile, the same dynamics that are dramatically highlighted on the show are present in some form or fashion.

Case Study Discussion Questions

1. What fundamentals of interpersonal dynamics are evident in *Survivor*? What do we learn about human nature?

2. What lessons can we learn from *Survivor* about the balance of team alliances and personal survival?

3. Describe the type of people who end up winning *Survivor*.

4. What, if any, parallels exist between *Survivor* and our experience of everyday life?

The producers of the TV show *Survivor* know exactly how to create a social setting that leads to high drama. The structure of reality shows such as *The Real World* and *The Bachelor/Bachelorette* create interpersonal dynamics that are extreme and evocative. Yet viewing statistics prove that these shows are clearly popular and entertaining to many despite their exaggerated storylines. Viewers are captivated by the interpersonal dynamics among contestants who are trying to capitalize on the basic need of human beings both to fit in and stand out. We all want to fit in and be part of the group. Getting along with others and forging alliances is the key to survival, if not success, in many of these shows. But contestants also want to be special and have a unique place within the group. They want to be the sole survivor. They want to stay in the *Real World* house and parlay their fame into future success. They want to get a rose and possibly find the love of their lives.

Interpersonal dynamics describes the interaction among members in a specific social context. It describes the way members relate to one another within a certain setting. Each setting is different depending on the purpose of the group, the unique constellation of members, and the physical or virtual setting. In order to assess the socio-emotional environment of a group, observers might ask themselves the following questions:

- Do members seem to enjoy working together?

- What do members do when they enter and exit meetings?

- Is there an atmosphere of lightheartedness and laughter in the meetings?

- Is everyone participating equally?

- What nonverbal messages do people seem to be communicating?

- Do members express frustration directly or indirectly?

- Are members assertive, passive, passive-aggressive, or aggressive?

NORMS

Norms are the interpersonal rules that members are expected to follow. They are established and at times enforced in order to get members to conform to certain expectations and standards of behavior (Hogg & Reid, 2006). These rules or expectations create order and stability by acknowledging what is expected of members—though this acknowledgement does not necessarily require any explicit declaration or statement. Instead, through the group members' interactions and time spent together, norms are often established through unspoken behavior protocols that simply come to be. Norms shape many aspects of group life, including seating arrangements, communication patterns, language, attire, humor, and respect for the leader; and the list goes on.

Similar to the function of traditions, norms define roles and behavior in such a way that makes social settings predictable through repetition over time. For example, many of us expect to be served turkey on Thanksgiving Day. Over the years, through much repetition, and with the support of family elders, this has become an accepted ritual in many cultures. Of course, much like traditions, norms can either become outdated or outgrow their original purpose and therefore need to be periodically examined and updated when necessary.

Norms not only describe "what is" (descriptive norms) but also "what should be" (injunctive norms). For example, imagine a group of students meeting to discuss a class project. Suppose a member jokingly makes an inappropriate racial comment; because this is a new group, a norm about racial comments has not yet been established. If everyone laughs, a descriptive norm that endorses these kinds of comments is established. On the other hand, if a member says, "That's not cool. I'm uncomfortable with those kinds of comments," and others nod their heads or give their assent in some way, then an injunctive norm is established, and the member who made the comment is now in jeopardy of losing status and being ostracized by the group. This all takes place in a matter of seconds, but the ramifications can last a long time.

Some norms are explicitly communicated by one or more members of the group while implicit norms operate through more indirect means. Often, implicit norms are not clearly defined, or made explicit, until a member has been found in violation of one of them. Adherence to team norms is more likely to occur when (a) members perceive a behavior to be universally performed by other group members, (b) there is a risk of social sanctions being imposed in light of not upholding any particular attitude or behavior, or (c) there is a reward associated with complying with the perceived norm. One of this book's authors has established a cell phone policy (i.e., norm) by answering students' phones that ring during class. He puts the unsuspecting caller on speaker phone and lets the class listen while he asks the caller to share an interesting story about the phone's owner. It only takes one or two experiences like this for students to remember to turn their cell phones off during class. Even though this norm was explicitly stated at the beginning of the semester, it often takes a mild "social sanction" like this to change behavior.

Team norms can develop in one of four ways (Feldman, 1984). First, a team's initial meeting often establishes a pattern of norms that determines future interpersonal behavior and expectations. Gersick (1988, 1989) has observed that the structure set in the first meeting of a team's existence becomes the default pattern for the group, remaining unchallenged until the midpoint of the group, when it is reexamined in order to find more effective ways to achieve objectives. This being the case, it should be reiterated just how important it is for group leaders to be deliberate about the kind of norms they directly or indirectly establish in that first meeting. For example, will the group be focused on relationships or only tasks? How will members relate to one another? How will group meetings be conducted? And so on. The leader models behavior that will translate into default norms for the group.

Second, norms are often established when the leader or influential member makes an explicit statement or deliberate action regarding a particular norm. In the previous example, the class instructor stated the norm about his cell phone policy at the beginning of the semester and then called attention to it when it was violated. Not everyone in a classroom has the credibility to create such norms. For example, if an upset student were to suggest that midterm exam grades should not count toward the final grade, nobody would take him or her seriously. Group members must have enough status and authority either to challenge an existing norm or create a new one.

Another way norms are established is through the experience of a critical event. At times, teams experience significant events that force the examination or establishment of various norms. For example, a college football team that violates NCAA recruiting regulations might have to voluntarily alter the norms, values, and practices of its coaches in order to avoid serious sanctions and penalties. This major policy violation and the subsequent probationary period would be a critical event that would force the athletic program to examine old norms and create new ones that honor the spirit and letter of NCAA guidelines. Again, organizations and institutions are wise to periodically evaluate their policies and practices before a negative critical event catches them unprepared.

Finally, team norms are inevitably carried over from prior group experiences. Individuals do not enter new groups as blank slates. Past group experiences are the springboards from which each new group is entered. Team members apply the norms from past team experiences that are similar in kind to their current team. For example, college students beginning a new class at the beginning of the semester will have 12-plus years of prior educational experiences from which to draw in order to know both what to expect in class and what is expected of them. These prior experiences will serve as the basis for understanding the new class environment until new norms are identified.

Source of Group Norms

- Initial group patterns

- Explicit behavior or statements

- Critical events

- Past group experiences

Hackman (2002) argues that two specific group norms are necessary for maximum group functioning: ongoing self-evaluation and ethical standards of behavior. Effective groups are, first, proactive and self-critical as they develop project management and problem-solving strategies (Postmes, Spears, & Cihangir, 2001). They continually scan the environment to determine the best course of action for any given situation. These groups are also willing to discard outdated or poorly conceived strategies that are no longer effective. This norm is important in combating the general human tendency to respond to problems and demands with automatic and habitual responses (Cannon & Witherspoon, 2005). Groups and organizations have a tendency to take a strategy or solution that worked in the past and apply it to new situations until it becomes an unquestioned operating procedure that may be less than optimal. This practice, clearly, is not productive.

The second norm that Hackman sees as crucial for effective group performance is the commitment to ethical guidelines and operational responsibility. Groups exist within organizational contexts that have rules about proper behavior. When challenges and pressures confront a group, the group must act ethically and responsibly according to organizational guidelines and general ethical principles such as honesty and integrity. Without this explicitly stated norm, it can be easily compromised when clients, bosses, or influential peers are demanding results or when there is great incentive for personal gain. Hackman acknowledges that secondary norms involving issues such as punctuality and conflict can help groups function more efficiently but must be determined by the members of each individual group. The next section presents a model of interpersonal styles that describes how people relate to one another and why there might be potential difficulties.

SOCIAL STYLES

Group members express themselves in a multitude of ways ranging from productive to destructive. As social creatures living in social contexts, people naturally develop interpersonal strategies that become established patterns of social behavior. The characteristics of these interpersonal strategies can then be categorized into various "styles" of verbal and nonverbal interaction. The social style of individuals can be determined by identifying interpersonal characteristics along two continuums: degree of assertiveness and degree of emotional expression (Baney, 2004; Bolton & Bolton, 1996; Merrill & Reid, 1981). Based upon these two variables, group members can be classified as one of four social styles: analytic, driver, expressive, or amiable. While theoretical models like this one may risk artificially reducing complex interpersonal behavior into oversimplified categories, awareness of individual social styles can help reduce the risk of misunderstandings and inaccurate assessments. For example, team leaders who understand the various social styles of their members can tailor their communication in ways that are most appropriate for each style (Wicks & Parish, 1990). In addition, awareness of one's own style may aid in avoiding potential communication problems and can lead to an increase in effective communication.

As seen in Figure 3.1, assertiveness is plotted on the horizontal axis and ranges from "asking" to "telling." While individuals demonstrate different levels of assertiveness depending on their immediate social context, their predominant style tends to prevail in most cases. In general, those with an "asking" orientation are less interested in influencing others than are those with a "telling" orientation. The following descriptions of "asking" and "telling" behaviors help identify an individual's primary orientation:

- *Asking:* States opinions more carefully without a call for action from others. Speaks in a softer voice while using less animated nonverbal gestures.

- *Telling:* States opinions more authoritatively, including a strong call for action from others. Speaks in a louder voice while using more forceful gestures.

Figure 3.1   Social Styles

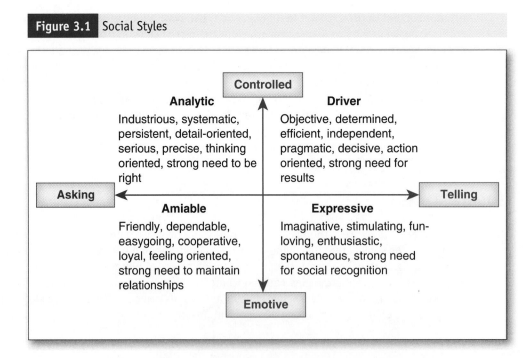

Next, the expression of emotion is plotted on the vertical axis and ranges from "controlled" to "emotive." Someone with a controlled posture expresses very little emotion, whereas an emotive person expresses a significant amount of emotion and energy:

- *Controlled:* Prefers facts and details to feelings. Limits small talk and typically speaks with a limited range of vocal inflection and facial expression.
- *Emotive:* Enjoys stories, jokes, small talk, and the expression of feelings. Speaks with more animated vocal inflection and facial expression.

Based upon these two variables, individuals can be classified as a driver, expressive, amiable, or analytic. While people are complex and do not necessarily fit into discrete categories, this framework is still helpful. It can give us a better understanding of how people relate to one another in general and how they prefer to communicate.

Group members who have identical social styles have the easiest time communicating with one another. Those with adjacent styles (quadrants that are touching each other) have a number of characteristics in common and will also have a relatively easy time working

together. For example, an expressive will have an easier time communicating with another expressive than with a driver. However, those with diagonally opposite styles (amiable-driver and analytic-expressive) tend to have the most difficulty communicating with each other due to the incongruence in their styles.

Different socials styles have preferred ways of communicating with others, and those differences can create interpersonal problems. A developmental goal of this model is to develop interpersonal versatility. Leaders who understand the social styles of their members can adapt their own style in order to communicate in the predominant style of the individual with whom he or she is interacting. For example, an expressive leader may take on a more task-oriented focus in order to engage those with an analytic style. Learning about one's own style and being able to identify the styles of others is one factor contributing to the flexibility necessary for communicating most effectively with others.

In addition to being aware of our own style and accurately assessing the social styles of others, we must adapt our style to match the style of the person to whom we are trying to relate. As a general rule, the driver and expressive styles need to improve their listening skills and use more probing questions and paraphrasing to draw out the opinions of others. Analytic and amiable styles would do well to increase their assertiveness. Tangibly, this means that they must practice expressing themselves more directly and learn to communicate their observations, thoughts, feelings, and desires with confidence.

INTERPERSONAL CIRCUMPLEX

As previously stated, differences in social styles can contribute to interpersonal problems on teams. The interpersonal circumplex model (Birtchnell, 1993) is similar to the social styles model in that it suggests that individuals relate to one another on two important dimensions: dominance versus submission and distant (cold) versus close (warm). The dominance versus submission dimension describes the degree of assertiveness an individual exerts in interpersonal communication and posturing, making it similar to the horizontal "assertiveness" dimension of the social styles model. The distant versus close axis, similar to the emotionality component of the social styles model, is a measure of sociability and friendliness.

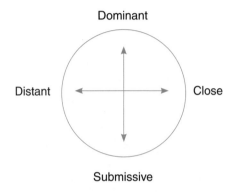

According to the interpersonal circumplex model, interpersonal problems emerge when team members exhibit behavior at the extreme of either dimension. The Inventory of Interpersonal Problems (Gude, Moum, Kaldestad, & Friis, 2000) identifies potential problems at the extremes of these two continuums and suggests a third area of concern: interpersonal sensitivity. Some people tend to be oversensitive to challenges or questions, while others are insensitive and unaware of how they are coming across to others.

Problematic Behavior Within Three Interpersonal Domains

- *Assertiveness dimension:* Being too domineering or too passive

- *Sociability dimension:* Being overly friendly or cold and aloof

- *Interpersonal sensitivity:* Being oversensitive or insensitive

---

The key to interpersonal success is to have the right balance of assertiveness, sociability, and sensitivity within an individual's social settings. Unfortunately, those ideals are not consistent across social contexts. For example, a business meeting might require more assertiveness than a church potluck dinner, which might require a lot more sociability. Individuals have to accurately read the different social cultures within which they interact, and adjust their interpersonal behavior accordingly. In addition, teams have different tolerance levels for each of the dimensions, which makes interpersonal sensitivity an important skill for members to use in order to understand the norms and expectations operational in the team.

Leaders and members alike can check their own behaviors and reactions to others against these dimensions in order better to understand what might be causing interpersonal difficulties. Of course, this requires self-awareness, interpersonal sensitivity, and tenacious honesty. We tend to place blame on others without considering how we might be contributing to the problem. Interpersonal tensions are often unavoidable, but the way members deal with them will determine whether or not they hinder team performance.

Conflicts and personality clashes can make group experiences quite uncomfortable. Negative emotions can have a ripple effect on groups, a concept researchers call emotional contagion (Brief & Weiss, 2002). For example, Barsade (2002) tested the impact of emotions on groups by randomly assigning 94 business school undergraduates to 29 groups. Each group, consisting of three to five members, was asked to participate in a management simulation where they had to allocate bonuses for hypothetical employees. Each person in the group was acting as a manager in the simulation and had to advocate for his or her own employee. In addition, they were told that if they could not come to agreement within a certain amount of time, nobody would receive a bonus. This type of simulation creates a stressful group experience that often generates rich dynamics for research purposes. To complicate matters even further, there was a confederate or conspirator in each group secretly demonstrating a certain emotional state. Barsade (2002) instructed confederates to exhibit one of four emotional states (cheerful enthusiasm, hostile irritability, serene warmth, or depressed sluggishness) as shown below.

Each of the group sessions was videotaped and viewed by outside reviewers. Observers and group members alike confirmed the hypothesis that the positive emotions of a group member positively affected the emotional state of other members. Similarly, the negative emotions of the confederate created negative feelings in others. Furthermore, positive contagion affected group performance leading to higher levels of cooperativeness, ability to resolve conflict, and perceptions of task performance.

Members influence one another in significant ways. Interpersonal dynamics can create either a positive or negative socio-emotional environment that impacts both team

Table 3.1   Types of Emotions in Teams

	High Pleasantness	Low Pleasantness
High Energy	*Cheerful Enthusiasm* Pleasant, happy, warm, and optimistic in an energetic, active, and alert way; cheerful and enthusiastic.	*Hostile Irritability* Actively and energetically unpleasant and pessimistic; behaves with hostility, frustration, impatience, anxiety, and irritability.
Low Energy	*Serene Warmth* Happy and optimistic but in a calm, low-energy way; emits warmth, serenity, and a pleasant calmness.	*Depressed Sluggishness* Unpleasant and unhappy in a low-energy way; behaves in a depressed, sluggish, dull, and lethargic manner.

performance and member satisfaction. Even when members have high levels of self-awareness and interpersonal maturity, their varied personalities and communication styles can lead to interpersonal tension. The next section will describe the common sources of conflict and explain what teams can do to turn potential team liability into an asset.

CONFLICT

According to Forsyth (2010), conflict is "disagreement, discord, and friction that occur when the actions or beliefs of one or more members of the group are unacceptable to and resisted by one or more of the other group members" (p. 380). De Dreu and Weingart (2003) define conflict as "the tension between team members because of real or perceived differences" (p. 741). Conflict is an inescapable part of working on a team. Any time individuals work together, tensions can emerge as a result of different personalities, work habits, social styles, and the stress of operating under time pressures. Conflict can be caused by any number of issues, including misunderstandings, premature conclusions, innocent mistakes, or extenuating circumstances beyond the control of the team.

Conflict can emerge from something as simple as a sarcastic comment directed toward a member who arrives late to a meeting or a difference of opinion over the color of the background on a PowerPoint presentation slide. It could stem from a struggle over the direction of the group; the breakdown of roles; the time, organization, and frequency of meetings; or any number of smaller details that people prioritize differently and for which they have different visions. The good news is that conflict can be managed. It can even bring out the best in teams, depending on whether or not members see it as an opportunity for team development.

Many people think of conflict as bad, counterproductive, and even destructive. However, conflict is an important step in group development and team performance (Behfar, Mannix, Peterson, & Trochim, 2011). Skilled leaders and mature members who know how to recognize, address, and defuse conflict can manage it before it becomes destructive. The "storming" stage of group development described in Chapter 1 is often when conflict begins to emerge. As groups struggle to find the best way to work together, differences are likely to occur. The extent to which conflict becomes a positive force, capable of contributing to productivity, creativity, and collaboration, depends upon the ability of members to communicate effectively, consider new perspectives, exercise patience, and not take things personally.

Conflict as an Everyday Phenomenon

Teams that avoid conflict may acquiesce to overly simplistic decisions and take the path of least resistance in problem solving. In fact, Lencioni (2002) identifies fear of conflict as one of the five typical problems or dysfunctions within teams. At the other end of the spectrum are teams that experience excessive amounts of conflict where every statement is challenged or questioned and discussions get bogged down in the morass of unproductive arguments. The latter type of conflict will often turn into interpersonal disputes and power struggles. Thus, we begin our discussion about conflict with the assertion that an appropriate amount of conflict is needed for team success (Parayitam & Dooley, 2011), as demonstrated in the figure below.

The Relationship Between Conflict and Team Performance

As social beings who live in community with others, we *experience, witness,* and sometimes *instigate* conflict on a regular basis. Roommate issues, romantic squabbles, and family struggles are part of everyday life. Conflict can erupt over remote controls, laptop computers, phone usage, borrowed clothes, exes, sports teams, social cliques, political leanings, and the list goes on. Generally speaking, conflict can be difficult because it forces us to consider different points of view, to understand other people's preferences and priorities, and to accommodate others when we would rather do things our own way. Also, we battle a perceived risk of "losing," because we allow our identity to be tied to our opinions, preferences, and desires, and then become too stubborn to compromise or concede. Too often we revert to a fight or flight response in the face of interpersonal conflict, which rarely is the best option.

Figure 3.2	The Relationship Between Conflict and Team Performance

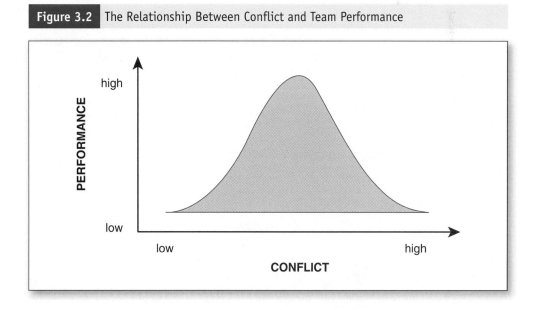

Once we are willing to view conflict as a common occurrence, it loses some of its gravity and can be approached from a pragmatic, less emotional perspective. Rather than thinking of it as a problem, or as a symptom of some bigger dysfunction, team members can view conflict as something akin to a growing pain: perhaps a bit uncomfortable, but holding the promise of development and creating just the right amount of creative friction to improve team performance.

Levels of Conflict

Conflicts, or differences among members, can emerge from any number of sources. Forsyth (2010) has identified four specific areas from which conflict can emerge. The easiest conflicts to resolve are those involving a dispute over facts or data. In those cases, there is empirical evidence that can be examined in order to help resolve the disagreement. Differences of opinion regarding how teams should accomplish their tasks or how they define the purpose of the group are a bit more difficult to resolve. Ultimately, conflicts that involve differences in values or beliefs are the most difficult to resolve because people are less likely to compromise their core values. Forsyth describes these potential sources of conflict as levels of conflict, explained below.

Level I: Facts or Data. Level I conflict involves conflict about facts or data. For example, either the attendee was late or wasn't late, either it's raining outside or it's sunny, either the experiment resulted in a statistically significant difference or it didn't. Arguments can occur, though, when members don't have all the data, or they interpret the data they *do* have in different ways. But at least members have a starting place from which to begin a conversation (i.e., the data), in order to attempt to reconcile their differences.

Level II: Processes or Methods. Level II conflict occurs when group members disagree about *how* something should be done. As groups work on various tasks, *how* they do it can become a source of tension. By defining ground rules, policies, and expectations, teams can deal with potential differences in an open and transparent way. This set of standard operating principles, along with a detailed project plan, can minimize misunderstandings and establish mutual accountability. For example, teams can agree upon ground rules, such as the ones listed below, to guide their interaction and minimize unnecessary conflict.

Sample Ground Rules

1. Be on time for meetings.

2. Put cell phones and unneeded laptops away.

3. Take risks by sharing true thoughts and innovative ideas.

4. Participate freely and fully.

5. Appreciate other points of view even if you disagree.

6. Have fun.

Level III: Goals or Purpose. Moving from *how* to *why* becomes a bit more complicated: *Why are we here? Why are we working on this? What is the ultimate objective of our coordinated effort?* Without a unified vision, team members can begin pulling against one another, and power struggles can erupt. And when a team is working under tight deadlines, as most teams are, they cannot afford such inefficiencies. Because people tend to invest themselves in the team's overall direction, they can hold on tightly to their opinions and argue less rationally than in Levels I or II. Problems can become drawn out, contentious, and thorny.

Level IV: Values or Beliefs. Level IV conflict is the most deeply rooted and difficult to resolve because it is tied to who we are. The values of group members are inextricably linked to their identities, so unless they are willing to admit that they might be wrong, the conflict is nearly permanent. As teams move from Level I through Level IV, the source of conflict becomes less tangible. They move from the concrete to the abstract; thus, coming to an agreement is more difficult. Resolving Level IV conflict depends upon both parties' willingness to consider new perspectives, ask reflective questions, and depersonalize the exchange as much as possible.

When a team is in the midst of a conflict, it can be helpful to identify in which level the disagreement is rooted. Then members can be more aware of the source of tension in order to be more efficient in resolving it. And in some conflicts, such as differences in goals or values, members might just have to agree to disagree and move on.

Task Versus Relationship Conflict

Conflict can be advantageous for teams, but it can also hinder performance (Greer, Saygi, Aaldering, & De Dreu, 2012). When disagreements revolve around work tasks and do not become personal, conflict can stimulate information processing, increase cognitive flexibility, and improve creative thinking (De Dreu & Weingart, 2003). But conflict can also immobilize teams and distract members from their work. In order to distinguish between productive and unproductive conflict, team researchers categorize conflict as either task-based or relationship-based. In general, moderate levels of task conflict can improve team performance, whereas relationship conflict almost always has a negative effect on outcomes. And both types of conflict have a negative effect on member satisfaction (De Dreu & Weingart, 2003).

Task or substantive conflict includes disagreements about the team's tasks and goals. In many cases, groups can use this type of conflict to increase creativity, make better plans, and solve complex problems more thoughtfully (Bradley, Postlethwaite, Klotz, Hamdani, & Brown, 2012). Cross-functional teams or teams made up of members with different professional backgrounds bring divergent perspectives together to offer new perspectives and ways of thinking. These deliberate differences can be catalysts for innovation. In the case of the *Survivor* teams, choosing a place to camp is an important decision that requires deliberation and thoughtful consideration. Those discussions might get heated, but they are still important to have. It is only when arguments get personal that they become problematic for the teams.

Relationship or affective conflict includes disagreements among two or more group members based upon differences in personal tastes or interpersonal style. It may come in the form of a rivalry, old grudges, perceived disrespect, or a situation in which two personalities just do not get along. In addition, relationship conflict tends to have a strong

emotional or affective component. Group members who are experiencing this type of conflict tend to have strong negative feelings toward the person with whom they are in conflict. Unfortunately, this type of conflict is fairly common and rarely useful (Chen, Sharma, Edinger, Shapiro, & Farh, 2011). According to Morrill (1995), 40% of group conflict is rooted in conflict among individuals that is *unrelated* to group goals.

Though it may seem like a good solution, forced cooperation often aggravates relationship conflict. For example, in order to resolve racial conflict as portrayed in the movie *Remember the Titans*, the coach made his players room with their racial counterparts, the people with whom they had intense interpersonal conflict, in order for them to get to know one another. Breaking down assumptions and stereotypes among conflicted parties is a reasonable solution, but one that often makes matters worse before they get better. We will discuss productive conflict management at length in the coming sections.

If conflict is managed correctly, it can improve the quality of group decisions, stimulate creativity, and build cohesion and trust within a team. Conflict can be positive, but only insofar as it is appropriately addressed and managed. According to Kruglanski and Webster (1991), even task conflict that is initially productive can turn into relational conflict when a group fails to reach a consensus on group decisions. Members can respond negatively to individuals who challenge the status quo and "slow down the process" too much. Another way task conflict can turn relational is when members are oversensitive and take things too personally when they are challenged or disagreed with. Each person has a different way of responding to conflict; this can impact whether team conflict is productive or problematic, as described in the next section.

Conflict Management Styles

Individuals respond to conflict in different ways. Some are averse to it, while others relish the opportunity to banter and argue. Kilmann and Thomas (1977) created a conflict styles model that builds upon the work of Blake and Mouton's (1961) Managerial Grid presented in Chapter 4, on leadership. There are five basic ways of responding to conflict based upon an individual's levels of assertiveness and cooperativeness, as depicted in the figure below. Assertive behavior is defined as an attempt to satisfy one's own concerns, while cooperative behavior is an attempt to satisfy the concerns of others.

A high level of assertiveness combined with a low level of cooperativeness describes a competing conflict style. Conflict of this nature is more likely to occur in groups where

| Figure 3.3 | Five Conflict Management Styles |

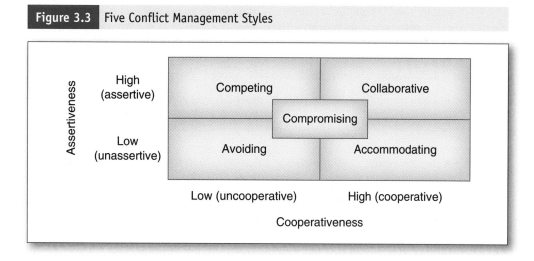

resources are scarce, as seen in the television show *Survivor*. People regress to deceptive and aggressive tendencies in competitive situations where there is perceived to be a clear winner and a loser. These social contexts create a zero-sum gain in which assertiveness outweighs cooperativeness. When people perceive that another person's success constitutes their own failure, a hostile environment ensues.

A low level of assertiveness combined with a low level of cooperativeness generates an avoiding conflict style. People with this style tend to be disengaged and try to avoid conflict at all costs. For various reasons, conflict is an extremely uncomfortable experience that takes a heavy emotional toll. Yet, when individuals and groups avoid interpersonal tension and strong differences of opinion among members, issues are not addressed and problems go unresolved.

Team members who have a low level of assertiveness and a high level of cooperativeness have an accommodating conflict style. They are quick to give in to others and do what the group wants in order to keep the peace. Often seen as ideal team players because of their pleasant personalities, they are reluctant to share their own ideas for fear of confrontation and challenge. They also have a difficult time communicating their frustrations directly.

Competing is not necessarily bad, and accommodating is not necessarily good. In most cases, collaborating is the optimal conflict style because it is an attempt to satisfy everyone's concerns and often yields the best long-term results. But if a team cannot resolve a conflict in a collaborative way, compromising is the best alternative. When a group compromises, nobody is completely happy, as everyone has to give up a little in order to resolve the differences.

For example, when a group of eight friends goes out to dinner, there may be a difference of opinion about how to split the check. Just when the waiter is about to take everyone's order, a person with a competing conflict style who is about to order an expensive meal might say, "Guys, there are so many of us, why don't we just get one check and split it eight ways?" As this is a predictable pattern his friends have seen before, the tension at the table begins to build. There are a number of options for splitting the check with certain options favoring some more than others. Here are some possible ways to make the decision:

- *Equity method:* "Contribution-based distribution" in which each person is responsible for what he or she has ordered.

- *Equality method:* "Blind justice" in which everyone pays one-eighth of the tab.

- *Power method:* "To the victor go the spoils" in which the dominant person gets to decide.

- *Need method:* "Welfare-based justice" in which the tab is settled based on ability to pay.

- *Responsibility method:* "Robin Hood justice" in which the money is taken from the richest person and given to the neediest.

Different conflict styles will respond in different ways. Someone with an accommodating style will be quick to agree with the equality method even though he or she was not going to order much food. Someone with an avoiding style is not going say anything in hopes that the tension will pass, while someone with a collaborative style wants to put all the options on the table and evaluate them. How members address the tension depends upon their level of assertiveness and desire to cooperate. If nothing is done, and the group accepts the initial suggestion to split the check eight ways, people might get frustrated and relationships may become strained. Addressing the conflict and coming to a reasonable resolution is a much better option.

Negotiation and Conflict Resolution

Conflict travels a natural course from *confrontation* (conflict comes to existence), *escalation* (it grows in intensity), and *resolution* (a tolerable outcome for the parties is reached). In their seminal work, *Getting to Yes: Negotiating Agreement Without Giving In*, Fisher, Ury, and Patton (1991) of "The Harvard Negotiation Project" designed an interest-based approach to resolving conflict in a collaborative way. They based their work on four principles:

1. Separate the people from the problem

2. Focus on interests, not on positions

3. Invent options for mutual gain

4. Insist on objective criteria

Separate the People From the Problem

As noted earlier, task conflict can easily become personal. In the midst of an intense discussion about a critical team decision, members can get angry and frustrated with one another. The first step in resolving the conflict is for members to separate the people with whom they disagree from the actual points of disagreement. On a personal level, it's important for members to be aware of their own feelings and judgments of others. They have to be willing to be honest about their anger, frustration, and feelings of resentment. Perhaps it was a fear of failure or a fear of rejection that caused them to react. Perhaps they didn't think others were giving them an appropriate amount of respect. Maybe they resented the team for not using their ideas on a specific task or decision. Once members are hijacked by the strong emotional feelings, it is easy to project negative motives and unfair assessments onto others.

Once strong negative feelings have been identified, it may be helpful for members to go to a trusted friend or mentor to get some perspective on the situation. An objective third party can help determine what went wrong and how to correct it. After processing the situation, members might need to go to the person with whom they have the interpersonal conflict in order to clear the air. That often includes trying to understand the other person's perspective, communicating one's own, asking for forgiveness, and gaining a commitment to work for the betterment of the team.

One student described the following ritual to keep team problems from getting personal. At the beginning of every volleyball practice, his team members lined up with their feet outside the court and listened to the schedule for the day. When they crossed the line to begin practice, they committed themselves fully to the team and left everything else off the court. At times, players would get heated and become aggressive because they all desperately wanted to win a state championship. But at the end of every practice, they all lined back up and walked off the court together, leaving the conflicts on the court.

Focus on Interests, Not on Positions

Fisher, Ury, and Patton describe the focus on interests as a way to find commonality. The authors point out that people often entrench themselves in certain negotiating positions, and that those positions necessarily lead to suboptimal outcomes for both parties. For example, consider a boy who threatens to take his ball home if he doesn't get to play quarterback in the after-school scrimmage with his friends. His position, "I want to play quarterback," might be posed against another boy's position of wanting to play quarterback. Either the second boy has to "give in," or everyone on the field "loses" because the first boy will take his ball home in protest. If they are able to focus on their *interests*, which might be that they want to play football and how can they work this out, then they can give themselves the intellectual space, free of emotion, to find creative solutions to the problem. By focusing on common or respective interests, participants free themselves from distracting emotions and complicating feelings so they can be creative, collaborative, and innovative in their approach to reaching a solution.

Invent Options for Mutual Gain

Inventing options for mutual gain is the process of identifying potential solutions that resolve the conflict and satisfy the needs of all parties. Once the overarching goal or interest has been articulated, the group can brainstorm possible options to achieve that goal.

Emotion is again a complicating factor here. Unless negotiators first separate the people from the problem, and then focus on interests rather than positions, they will have difficulty inventing options for mutual gain.

As described in the previous example, the two boys squabbling over who gets to be quarterback can come up with a number of mutually beneficial and acceptable options. Perhaps the boys could take turns every other play or on every other possession; perhaps they could play a series of short games that would allow a number of people to play quarterback. By backing away from the entrenched position of "if I don't get to play quarterback, then nobody does," negotiating parties have room to propose creative solutions and invent options.

Insist on Objective Criteria

After the conflicted parties have invented a number of options to resolve the dispute, they must make a decision and execute the best choice. Objective criteria are those things that, when freed of emotional weight or implication, can serve to guide the decision-making process to a mutually agreeable outcome. The way to determine objective criteria, according to the authors, is to address the issue openly and directly. What is a fair outcome? What is the best way to achieve our interests and objectives? Are there data available to support various options? In order to find the best solution to any given conflict or problem, members need to agree on the facts of the issue and then have an objective framework for making decisions. Chapter 7, on decision making, will discuss these frameworks in detail.

These four criteria offer a template for negotiation and conflict resolution across many social contexts. They can help resolve conflict in personal relationships, work out tense negotiations within project teams, or equip leaders in all environments with a basic set of skills for maintaining perspective. In principled negotiation, team members refuse to react. Instead, they reflect. They look past individual positions to find common interests that lead to reasonable solutions.

EMOTIONAL INTELLIGENCE

One of the main influences on the interpersonal dynamics of a team is the emotional and social maturity of the leader and team members. In the last few decades, a number of social psychologists have emphasized the importance of emotional and social intelligence and its relationship to interpersonal dynamics and team effectiveness (Ghosh, Shuck, & Petrosko, 2012). Upon returning to his class reunion at Harvard University, Dan Goleman (1995) noticed that the most successful graduates had an interesting combination of emotional maturity and social savvy. After collecting and analyzing data to test his hypotheses, he soon created a model for emotional intelligence. In a subsequent book, Cherniss and Goleman (2001) describe the personal and interpersonal competencies that are strong predictors of personal and professional success. As seen in the following table, their findings suggest that the most effective team members are able to recognize and regulate emotions in themselves and others.

Table 3.2	Emotional Intelligence

	Self **Personal Competence**	**Other** **Social Competence**
Recognition **(awareness)**	**Self-Awareness** Emotional self-awareness Accurate self-assessment Self-confidence	**Social Awareness** Empathy Service orientation Organizational awareness
Regulation **(management)**	**Self-Management** Self-control Trustworthiness Conscientiousness Adaptability Achievement drive Initiative	**Relationship Management** Developing others Influence Communication Conflict management Leadership Change catalyst Building bonds Teamwork and collaboration

SOURCE: Adapted from Cherniss and Goleman (2001).

A growing research base suggests that emotional intelligence is just as important to professional success as cognitive intelligence (Cherniss & Goleman, 2001). For team projects, emotional intelligence may even be more important, given the interpersonal nature of teams (Chang, Sy, & Choi, 2012; Ghuman, 2011). Group members bring various experiences, goals, and attitudes to their groups. Differences inevitably emerge because no two people are exactly alike. As a result, group experiences have the potential to trigger interpersonal tensions. Interpersonal maturity and emotional intelligence help minimize potential tensions among members. Leaders who have these skills are at an advantage because they can model and facilitate appropriate interpersonal behavior on their teams (McKee, Boyatzis, & Johnston, 2008).

COHESION

Early theorists defined cohesion simply as the force that attracts members to one another (Dion, 2000). Recent theorists acknowledge that cohesion is a complex, multidimensional construct that influences both group performance and member satisfaction (Chang & Bordia, 2001; Evans & Dion, 2012; Gully, Devine, & Whitney, 2012). Simply stated, cohesion is the level of member commitment to the goals of the group (task cohesion) and to the other members of the group (social cohesion). It can also be defined as the relative measure of the closeness among group members and the strength of those connections. A cohesive family, for example, is one that has regular contact and strong loyalty among members.

In cohesive groups, members are highly motivated to achieve their collective goals and, at the same time, have a great deal of respect and concern for one another. Cohesion acts as a lever to strengthen teams and propel them toward greater adherence and commitment to group norms (Cohen & Bailey, 1997). Military organizations have long known the importance of cohesion. Soldiers certainly fight for their countries, but perhaps more important, they fight for one another (Henderson, 1985). The importance of unit cohesion is introduced in boot camp and reinforced in subsequent training in order to prepare members for actual combat, where cohesion can be a matter of life or death.

Creating cohesion or building "team spirit" requires deliberate attention. Groups that are primarily task oriented may neglect this important aspect of their work. Allowing members to participate in defining the goals and structure of their group will help create both cohesion and commitment. The following suggestions can also help create cohesion:

• *Information-sharing*: Teams develop trust when members know one another (Purvanova, 2013). Thus, members develop confidence in one another by acquiring background information and observing current behavior. Members can do this by providing information to the whole group or by sharing information in smaller pairs or subgroups and then reporting back to the rest of the group. Cohesion is enhanced when members identify with one another in terms of similar experiences, backgrounds, ideas, or opinions. It is also built upon trust, which emerges when members feel valued and respected (Janss, Rispens, Segers, & Jehn, 2012).

• *Team identity*: Cohesive groups move from a collection of individuals to a single entity with its own identity and unique characteristics. Simple activities like identifying a team name or constructing a vision for the group may help members see themselves as part of a greater whole. Not surprisingly, members of highly cohesive groups have the tendency to use more plural pronouns than personal pronouns when talking about themselves and their accomplishments (i.e., "We closed the deal").

• *Competition*: Competition can be a strong catalyst in motivating members and helping them commit to a common task. Between-group competition is a well-known strategy in "rallying the troops," building momentum, and stimulating group commitment.

When teams are cohesive, they have the potential of achieving greater results and, at the same time, providing a more meaningful experience for members. This holds true for groups in general but especially for sports teams (Pescosolido & Saavedra, 2012). In an article written for *Sports Illustrated*, Chris Ballard (2010) studied interpersonal behavior within professional sports teams. He examined data that compared the number of instances of encouraging physical contact such as high-fives, chest bumps, head pats, and butt slaps with a team's winning percentage. The data revealed that championship teams had significantly greater numbers of these "positive" or "encouraging" behaviors than did other teams. In fact, there was a statistically significant positive correlation between the number of touches between teammates and the number of team wins. The "high-five" actually serves two purposes. It demonstrates a teammate's appreciation of a job well done, and it also is a means of picking up a struggling comrade. This gesture of goodwill builds cohesion and positively impacts both team process and team performance. When team members encourage and support one another, they are not only more motivated, they also perform at a higher level (Hüffmeier & Hertel, 2011).

LEADERSHIP IN ACTION

Conflict is a normal part of group functioning. When people work together in teams, there are bound to be tensions, challenges, misunderstandings, miscommunications, and a whole host of pet peeves that get triggered. As described in this chapter, conflict has its origin in the differences among members: differences of expectation versus reality; of message sent versus message received; of implication versus inference; of varying work styles, social styles, and communication styles; of competing visions or understandings of an assignment, and so on. Whether the group is a team on a sports field, a team in a classroom, a team on a backpacking trip, or a team in a professional setting, these differences lead to conflict.

In order to manage conflict productively, there are a few values that must be established early in the life of a group. This happens superficially during the forming stage, which is one reason why storming eventually happens. One way to help minimize the discomfort and duration of the storming stage is to encourage the team to discuss goals during the first meeting. Are some members working primarily for personal gain? Are others committed to the collective success of the team? Are still others just wishing to do as little work as possible? Questions like these will bring important information into the open so that it can be addressed in a proactive way. This, in turn, will prepare the team for any "storming" that occurs because there will be an established set of values to which they can refer. Without a shared value system, teams run the risk of drifting away from their purpose and compromising their potential.

A next step in this process involves asking questions about work styles. Are there some people who are very concerned with everyone arriving on time? Are there some who have challenging schedules? Are there some who need a lot of structure, while others prefer to figure it out as they go? When it comes to scheduling, are there some who have unavoidable conflicts? As for structure, it may be helpful to suggest formal roles and responsibilities (e.g., logistics, note-taking, research lead, meeting facilitator, etc.) to avoid ambiguity, social loafing, and the risk of overlooked details. These types of questions will help the team avoid unnecessary conflicts down the road.

As teams work together to accomplish a common objective, differences of opinion about how to get the work done are almost guaranteed. One of the roles of a leader is that of mediator. To do that, one can call upon the guidelines from Fisher, Ury, and Patton (1991). First, separate the people from the problem. Then, focus on interests, not on positions. Third, invent options for mutual gain. And, finally, insist on objective criteria. These four characteristics of effective negotiation can help teams save time, energy, and relationships as they achieve results by limiting the potential damage of interpersonal conflict.

You can separate the people from the problem by reminding yourself to focus on the data and not on the actor. This is essentially depersonalizing the environment and moving from an oppositional dynamic to at least a neutral one. When combined with active and reflective listening skills and "I" statements, you can isolate problems and deal with them objectively.

Once you isolate the problem, it is much easier to focus on interests. Positions are largely emotional. Interests, however, are much more substantive. Perhaps one team member is interested in doing her best, another is trying to juggle multiple projects, and yet another is interested in being promoted to a leadership position. Until you identify their respective interests, you will find yourself and your teammates struggling to collaborate and, perhaps, even be in conflict with one another. You can avoid much of this by establishing a climate and culture of candid communication within your group from the first meeting.

Inventing options for mutual gain is a fun and exhilarating process. Having isolated the problem and trained your attention on interests, your team is free to creatively explore options that are valued by every member. Note: The options must be *invented*, so push your team to be creative and innovative. This is about exchanging value, so work to find things that are valuable to each member. If someone needs more free time, find a way to offer that in exchange for some other investment on their part. If a member wants to ensure a top-quality product, consider exchanging ownership of the project for something else.

None of this is possible without objective criteria. "Objective criteria" means that either something *is* . . . or it *isn't*, and the judgment-free, empirical data will allow your team to operate from a position of shared understanding, equal footing, and agreed-upon standards. To do this effectively, you will have to define a common set of criteria to which everyone agrees and work diligently as a team to adhere to the standards.

Interpersonal dynamics and conflict is more than just managing differences of style and opinion. Rather, a major portion of team leadership and interpersonal management has to do with building community, affiliation, and cohesion. Team-building efforts create an environment for members to establish common bonds based on shared interests, shared experiences, shared hardship, and a shared commitment to one another and to the team. Team performance can be improved by spending time together in various nonwork activities. Perhaps the team could benefit from an afternoon of laser tag, paint ball, or bowling, or by participating in a Habitat for Humanity building day, or by volunteering at a local homeless shelter. These common experiences and shared investments lay a foundation of trust, familiarity, and mutual concern.

KEY TERMS

Descriptive norms 45

Injunctive norms 45

Ongoing self-evaluation 47

Ethical standards of behavior 47

Analytic social style 48

Driver social style 48

Expressive social style 48

Amiable social style 48

Competing conflict style 56

Avoiding conflict style 57

Accommodating conflict style 57

Collaborating conflict style 57

Compromising conflict style 57

DISCUSSION QUESTIONS

1. In order to assess the socio-emotional environment of a group, an observer might ask a question such as "Do members seem to enjoy working together?" Name two more questions you might ask.

2. Explain the difference between descriptive norms and injunctive norms. Describe the four ways norms can develop.

3. Group members can be classified into one of four social styles. Name and describe each of the styles.

4. Describe the interpersonal circumplex and the two dimensions associated with it.

5. Describe the six types of interpersonal challenges identified by the Inventory of Interpersonal Problems.

6. Sources of conflict can be found in any one of four distinct levels. Name and describe the levels and give a personal example of each.

7. Name and describe the five conflict styles. Which is the most ideal, and why?

8. Explain how information-sharing, group identity, and competition may help to facilitate group cohesion.

GROUP ACTIVITIES

EXERCISE 3.1 FEELING THE BURN

The interpersonal dynamics among team members can be challenging, especially when deadlines loom, personalities clash, and tempers flare. This exercise is designed to study the effects of tension in a group setting and to explore ways of coping with frustration.

Every member of the class should receive three strips of paper, a marker, and a strip of masking tape. Each strip of paper will have one of the following prompts:

- *I feel frustrated when my teammates* _____.
- *I show my frustration by* _____.
- *If my teammates were frustrated with me, I would feel* _____.

You are to write down your first response to each prompt without censoring your thoughts or minimizing your true feelings. After you've written your responses down, tape each of the strips in a public place such as a wall, whiteboard, or desk so everyone can see them. Please write your responses clearly so that classmates will be able to read them. Take a few minutes to read the responses that other people have posted.

Form groups of four to six students and process your reactions to everyone's responses. Come up with a list of the typical reasons why people become frustrated with one another and the best ways to deal with it.

EXERCISE 3.2 IDEAL TEAM NORMS

Form groups of four and create a list of ideal team norms. In order to get a more comprehensive list, complete the following statement: "I work best in teams when _____." Record your answers on the board. Rank-order the list from norms that are easiest to follow to norms that are hardest to follow. Include a plan of what a team should do if a member violates one or more of the norms. In other words, how can a team enforce group norms?

CASE 3.2: DISSIDENCE AMONG THE RANKS

A project team member in one of your classes is not showing up for meetings and doesn't pay attention when he does attend. Instead, when he shows up, he is texting and browsing on Facebook. However, he is very talented and would be a great asset to the team if he would earnestly engage. He is a charming, charismatic, and popular guy on campus who could be a great presenter for the final project that is due at the end of the semester. Already, though, people on your team are getting frustrated and talking behind his back about what a bad teammate he is. Finally, your teammate, April, is pushed to the breaking point during a team meeting and slams her booked down on the table, unleashing a tirade on him because he's not paying attention. April also rips him for coming late to meetings and for not following through on a recent, key responsibility that will cost the project team valuable time. She tells him, "If you don't want to be here, we don't want you here. Why don't you just do us all a favor and drop the class?!" As soon as she finishes, James, another one of your teammates, says, "Chill out, April. It's not that big a deal. Let's just get back to work." The rest of the team falls silent and clams up.

- *You're the leader of this team . . . what would you do?*

CHAPTER 4

Leadership

$\mathbf{T}$eam leadership is the practice of enlisting and overseeing others in the pursuit of shared goals. In contrast to management, leadership seeks to inspire others to the highest levels of individual, team, and organizational performance. Whereas managers focus on planning, organizing, and controlling, leadership involves vision, networking, and consensus-building (Kotter, 1998). While good leaders will possess good management skills, the converse is not always true. Leaders must be able to foster communication, cohesion, and commitment within their teams. After looking at a brief overview of management trends in organizations, we will survey the major theories of leadership, discuss the five practices of exemplary leaders, and describe how leaders can influence and persuade others. We conclude with specific strategies for conducting effective meetings.

CASE 4.1: COGENT HEALTHCARE

Brentwood, Tennessee, is home to a health care company that specializes in hospital medicine, an emerging specialty with an impressive year-over-year increase in demand. This company has experienced 24% compounded annual growth and has recently doubled in revenue and headcount. With over 1,100 physicians employed in over 130 hospitals and clinics across the United States and fewer than 200 employees running the corporate headquarters, this business relies on a distributive leadership model to make sure that the clinical services and business operations run smoothly, efficiently, and up to the highest standards.

From the executive suite down to the hospital or "program" level, the company is broken down into leadership "dyads" of a clinical leader and an operations leader. The chief operating officer and chief clinical officer distribute leadership responsibility over regional chief operating officers and regional chief medical officers, who in turn divide responsibility for program managers and program medical directors. This "role-player" model has proven successful with world champion sports teams, on paramedical teams, and within military Special Forces teams. A vital component of this model, however, is training, team-building, and the establishment of trust.

One of the key differentiators for this rapidly growing company is the investment it makes in the ongoing development of its human capital. It is one of the few health care companies of any size with a dedicated Organizational Development (OD) department, which has developed an academy model that is designed to meet the advancing needs of the corporate staff, the field support staff, the clinicians, and the hospital program and regional leadership teams. The academy model is self-buttressing, meaning that it supports itself by cross-referencing courses and training different program-level role players in unison. For example, in the initial "level 1" training program, the operations leadership and the clinical leadership team members learn the same fundamentals, laying a foundation for understanding, trust, and interdependence across the footprint of the company. This uniformity helps everyone who has attended the level 1 academy speak the same language, share the same expectations, and understand the baseline knowledge.

As they advance, the leaders participate in more specialized skills training that complements the work they do. Whether that training focuses on managing finances or managing physician performance, these team leaders are trained to be fully competent and on the cutting edge of their own specialization, and to understand the language of their counterpart. This ensures ongoing communication and transparency between co-leaders of very high-pressure, high-stress program sites, which prepares these leadership teams for the daily demands of the volatile hospital environment.

The advanced leadership training, the third level of the academy model, is designed around a "live case" structure, which requires the leadership "dyad" to bring an actual problem that is facing its hospital team—such as floundering patient satisfaction scores or a strained relationship with the hospital administration—to the training event. Each team's "live case" is used in every module or session in the training in order to lend context to the material and to create a bridge between theory and practice. The academy takes each team through a series of sessions about managing culture, relationships, conflict, and performance (to name a few), and each session involves table exercises designed to force the teams to develop a change initiative to resolve the problem. By the end of the seminar, each leadership team weaves together an integrated and multifaceted change plan, complete with milestones. These detailed plans are shared with the regional leaders for the sake of accountability and follow-through, improving the execution and implementation of those initiatives.

It is estimated that the company invests almost $10,000 per year on the development of each of its top leaders, not including the money allocated for "continuing medical education" (known as "CME") credits. The figure decreases for employees who bear less responsibility, and while it is a significant amount of money that surprises many business leaders across industries, it has proven valuable in driving business performance and retention of the company's "top talent." In the time that these academies have been instituted, average length of physician tenure has doubled, the company-wide turnover rate is the best it has been in the company's history, and the quality-based incentive bonuses that programs earn have increased across the company. Given the annual revenue of the company, the decreased costs associated with turnover, and the training of new employees—not to mention the intangible value of improved client satisfaction and industry reputation—the investment in leadership development has more than justified itself.

Case Study Discussion Questions

1. What common needs exist on teams in health care, sports, business, education, and the military? How do you think leadership addresses those needs?

2. How does Cogent Healthcare justify its investment in leadership development? What are the tangible short- and long-term benefits?

3. What is the best way to train leaders? Describe the Cogent Healthcare leadership development model.

For generations, leaders and supervisors have used their positional power to issue commands and control subordinates' behavior. They relied largely on the promise of reward and the threat of punishment to manage and motivate employees. This business model was designed by powerful men such as J. P. Morgan, Andrew Carnegie, and John D. Rockefeller Sr. in the early 1900s to run their growing companies (Kayser, 1994). As the United States transitioned from an agrarian to an industrialized economy, factories and organizations sought raw material and human labor to an unprecedented extent. To meet their needs, companies hired thousands of employees who, subsequently, needed to be managed and organized. Supervisors and foremen had almost total power to hire, fire, reward, and punish those who worked for them. Workers were given direction, evaluated, and then either rewarded or punished based upon their performance (Edwards, 1979). But today's competitive and fast-paced global economy requires a new organizational model that shares power and capitalizes on the collective wisdom of groups and teams (Guillen, 1994; Senge, 1990).

SELF-MANAGED WORK TEAMS

The most successful organizations are flexible, innovative, and collaborative in order to maximize the strengths of an increasingly educated and diverse workforce. Hierarchical command and control systems that emphasize authority and compliance are out of fashion and, ultimately, ineffective in the long term (Pfeffer, 1992). Some authors have coined this new autonomy-granting phenomenon as the second industrial revolution, postulating that it may represent as profound a change as the first industrial revolution of the eighteenth and nineteenth centuries (Fisher, 2000).

Self-managed work teams (SMWTs) are more than groups of people working together to accomplish tasks defined by their managers. SMWTs are, as their name implies, truly self-managed. These teams hold responsibility for the entire process: goal-setting, creating a project plan, dividing up the tasks, assigning responsibilities, and allocating compensation. For example, W. L. Gore and associates, the company that produces GORE-TEX, makes significant use of self-directed work teams. Job titles do not exist at Gore. Rather, every employee is known as an "associate," and when it comes to compensation, the associates are evaluated by their entire team.

SMWTs share power by allowing members to participate in important decisions and to volunteer for leadership opportunities (Oh, 2012). When individuals are empowered and motivated, they are more committed to the team's success and feel a greater sense of involvement in the process (McIntyre & Foti, 2013). In these types of teams, discussions tend to be more dynamic and innovative as members share different perspectives and work collaboratively to find the best answers and solutions (Bergman, Rentsch, Small, Davenport, & Bergman, 2012). Members realize they can use their personal power to influence group behavior and improve team performance. Shared power, then, allows individual members to exert their opinions and positively influence group decisions and actions. As Johnson and Johnson (2006) suggest, "The effectiveness of any group is improved when power is relatively mutual among its members and power is based on competence, expertise, and information" (p. 240). Shared power based upon competence as opposed to position grants all members the opportunity to contribute to team success.

LEADERSHIP AND GENDER

For most of human history, men have occupied positions of power and have enjoyed privilege in nearly all its forms. Indeed, most of the storied leaders around the world are men, and most of today's revered CEOs and titans of industry are men. However, in a 2010 article from *The Atlantic* magazine entitled "The End of Men," author Hanna Rosin wonders if the golden age of male leadership is coming to an end.

Rosin's exposition on the advancement of women leaders is based in the argument that "the postindustrial economy is indifferent to men's size and strength. The attributes that are most valuable today—social intelligence, open communication, the ability to sit still and focus—are, at a minimum, not predominantly male. In fact, the opposite may be true." Rosin argues that the historical or traditional roles and strengths of men and women are social constructs more than they are biological ones. Her conclusion, therefore, is that the dominance of males—even in leadership positions—is on the decline. She states, "As thinking and communicating have come to eclipse physical strength and stamina as the keys to economic success, those societies that take advantage of the talents of all their adults, not just half of them, have pulled away from the rest." If physical strength and size no longer command attention and respect, it follows that people with the greatest skill in the most valuable areas (in Rosin's argument, these areas are thinking, communicating, perspective-taking, and social intelligence) are the ones who will ascend to leadership positions.

Leaders are only effective to the extent to which they can influence their environment and their team. These factors may, indeed, have been influenced by certain social constructs or constraints in the past, but the world is in transition. The knowledge, skills, and abilities that lead to success are based upon communication, cooperation, and collaboration. And these can be developed, refined, and acquired by men and women alike.

THEORIES OF LEADERSHIP

Leadership is a hotly contested subject in academic and organizational settings. Not everyone agrees on what constitutes effective leadership. Kotter (1985) makes a strong argument that as the workplace continues to become more competitive and complex, issues of leadership, power, and influence will become increasingly important. Work teams today are also contending with the ever-increasing pressure to solve complex, multidimensional problems at lightning speed. The typical team leader today must manage "thousands of interdependent relationships—linkages to people, groups, or organizations" (Kotter, 1985, p. 23). Though relatively straight-forward tasks and goals can usually be accomplished through simple structures and concrete role assignments, solving more complex problems is a more difficult process. Teams have to figure out how to generate, evaluate, and implement innovative solutions to new and unforeseen problems. Leadership models that can catalyze and monitor this process while empowering and developing team members are at the very heart of effective leadership (Pfeffer, 1992).

Blake and Mouton (1961) created the Managerial Grid to graphically represent the balance between task and relationship. Their model suggests that the best leaders have a high concern for both people *and* production or results.

| Table 4.1 | Managerial Grid |

	High	Country club management		Team management
Concern for People	Medium		Middle of the road management	
	Low	Impoverished management		Authority-compliance
		Low	Medium	High

Concern for Production (task)

SOURCE: Adapted from tBlake and Mouton (1961).

When leaders are more concerned with people than production, their style is friendly and nonconfrontational. When production is given priority over the value of people, the use of authority to enforce compliance is the norm. When leaders are passive and detached from both the people and tasks of their team, the management style is impoverished. The ideal leadership style in this model is to value and invest in people while simultaneously creating accountability and the expectation of task achievement (Arana, Chambel, Curral, & Tabernero, 2009). The following section describes some of the most common models of leadership.

Trait Theories

In the early 1900s, leadership researchers assumed that great leaders had a consistent set of innate traits that set them apart from followers. Researchers believed that once people knew which personality traits were associated with success, they could identify potential leaders and put them into positions that would maximize those traits. According to this reasoning, identification was crucial because the personality traits associated with effective leadership were only present in extraordinary people and could not be developed in people lacking such traits. Although this was a reasonable and systematic approach at the time, researchers were disappointed when they were not able to identify a common set of traits present in successful leaders. Research by Mann (1959) and Stogdill (1948) shattered the illusion that great leaders are born with certain characteristics; the data simply did not support that position.

More recent research has used characteristics of the five factor model of personality (openness, conscientiousness, extraversion, agreeableness, and neuroticism) to examine leadership qualities. Traits within the five factor model tend to be relatively stable throughout life and are thus categorized as personality traits rather than learned behavior or transitional states. Using this model, leadership researchers found significant differences between leaders and followers. The most effective leaders, on average, exhibit higher levels of extraversion (outgoingness and assertiveness), conscientiousness (diligence and work ethic), and openness (flexibility and creativity) (McCrae & Costa, 1987). Not surprisingly, the most effective leaders work well with others, get things done, and find innovative ways to solve problems.

Contingency Theories

As behavioral researchers were observing leaders in various settings, they found that a consistent style of leadership did not always work for every situation. In other words, certain styles of leadership work better depending on the specific task, composition, and context of the group. Out of these observations emerged a theory of leadership that posits the importance of matching leader behaviors with the context. Contingency theories rest upon the assumption that leadership styles must adapt to changing team conditions in order to be most effective.

Situational leadership is a well-known contingency theory of leadership developed by Blanchard and Hersey (Blanchard, Zigarmi, & Zigarmi, 1999; Hersey, 1985). This theory suggests that leaders are defined by two things: the amount of direction they give and the amount of support they give. A team leader who is highly directive gives detailed information to members about what needs to be done and how they should do it. Leaders who are supportive give a lot of encouragement to others and empower them to figure out the best way to get their job done. There are four possible leadership styles, depending on the amount of direction and support a team leader gives: directing, coaching, supporting, and delegating.

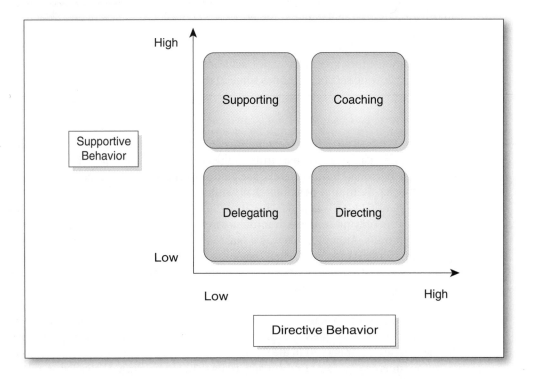

While individual leaders might have a preferred style of leadership, Blanchard and Hersey believe the most effective leadership style depends on the team.

Situational leadership theory asserts that leadership style must be fluid and dependent on the developmental level of team members (DeRue, Barnes, & Morgeson, 2010). When teams are in the forming stage of development, members are not exactly sure how they will contribute or how the team will function together. The team is in an early developmental stage exhibiting characteristics of low competence as a team but high commitment. At this stage, members respond best to a leader who provides a lot of structure and uses a directing style of leadership. As the team develops, members increase their level of competence but lose some of their initial motivation for the task. Thus, the leader must maintain a high level of directiveness while also providing high levels of support and encouragement. This style of leadership is called coaching. As members become competent in their abilities, they require less direction but still need support. Thus, the supporting style helps maintain high levels of commitment to the task. Finally, as members develop competence and internal motivation, the ideal leadership style is delegating. At this stage, members are able to accomplish the tasks they are assigned with little support or direction. This variable style of leadership is well suited to the changing needs of developing groups. Situational leaders start with a directing style and end up with a delegating style.

Transformational Leadership

Transformational leadership is a theory of leadership that describes the process by which leaders transform a group of individuals into a cohesive team that is committed to the highest levels of success (Bass, 1998). It relies upon the ability of leaders to inspire others to go beyond mere compliance by encouraging them to take ownership of a task or project and to identify with the results. Transformational leaders are visionaries who empower others to accomplish great feats. They lead by example and are able to enlist others to take on great challenges. Transactional leadership, in contrast, focuses on the management of tasks and is defined as the transaction between a manager and an employee. It relies upon structure, accountability, and a reward system to ensure that work is getting done.

Transformational leaders use influence strategies such as inspirational appeal, consultation, and personal appeal to garner the highest levels of commitment. Similarly, they use referent or expert bases of power to motivate others, as opposed to coercive or legitimate power, which may foster resentment. These leaders would rather have members volunteer for tasks than force them to comply. Thus, transformational leadership tends to generate a deep sense of loyalty to the team and commitment to the task.

Steve Jobs is an example of an inspiring, transformational leader. There are certainly tales of his occasional heavy-handedness and slavish dedication to a singular vision, but shortly after his death in 2011, many of his former colleagues and direct reports shared detailed stories of how he brought out the best in his employees. He had an appealing genius about him, according to many, and he was uncompromising in his pursuit of innovative solutions, user-friendly designs, and exceptional results. The teams that survived the intensity of his style were fiercely loyal to Apple, its mission, and to Jobs himself. The result, obviously, has been a series of historic and influential products including the iPod, iPad, and iPhone that have revolutionized technology and communication.

Primal Leadership

Primal leadership is a theory of leadership that emphasizes the emotional and social maturity of the leader (Goleman, Boyatzis, & McKee, 2004). Emotional intelligence, as we have discussed in Chapter 3, on interpersonal dynamics, begins with the ability to recognize and manage one's own emotions. Being aware of feelings such as anger or irritation and being able to manage those feelings is the foundation of emotional intelligence. If leaders are not aware of their own feelings and do not have an accurate understanding of their own strengths and weaknesses, they will not be able to manage their teams effectively. In this regard, healthy self-esteem is not thinking too highly of oneself, and it's not thinking too poorly of oneself; it's thinking accurately about oneself.

The second half of emotional intelligence is the ability to understand and manage relationships. Leaders must have social awareness and the ability to accurately read others. More specifically, they need to recognize how they are personally affecting their team members. This allows leaders to evaluate their effectiveness and make changes, if necessary. One of the reasons why the fictitious character Michael Scott, from the award-winning TV show *The Office*, is so funny is that he has absolutely no idea how foolish he appears to others. He has neither self-awareness nor social awareness, which can be quite humorous as he tries to lead his team. Ultimately, effective leaders need emotional intelligence in order to know themselves and to inspire others. Furthermore, when interpersonal tensions build, leaders need social maturity to accurately diagnose the situation and to intervene with a level head.

Leadership Development Plan

1. Where am I now?

2. Where do I want to be in the future?

3. What do I need to do to get there?

Most of us have had irritable, moody managers or supervisors who made our working lives miserable. Bosses can have a significant impact on the atmosphere of a team. Not only are emotions subconsciously perceived on a neurological level, they tend to be mirrored by others (Goleman, Boyatzis, & McKee, 2001). The mood or emotions of a team leader often generate similar emotions, either positive or negative, in the rest of the team. For this reason, Goleman and his colleagues suggest that leaders need to be aware of their emotions and how their moods impact their teams. They assert that if team leaders are to be consistently successful over a long period of time, they need to regulate their moods while still being authentic and genuine. If they are angry, stressed, or upset but try to act superficially playful or artificially positive, the team will know. It is better for them to be aware of their emotions and deal with them in an appropriate setting than to cover them up and pretend that nothing is wrong.

Another distinguishing characteristic of primal leadership is its emphasis on intentional leadership development. Goldman and his associates believe that leaders can be developed by following a specific process. First, individuals need to know their strengths and weaknesses. They can either gather data informally or they can participate in a more structured 360 degree assessment in which feedback from multiple perspectives such as peers, supervisors, and direct reports is solicited. Once leaders have an accurate understanding of their strengths and weaknesses, they can create specific goals about the kind of leader they would like to become. The final step in the leadership development process is to create a concrete action plan to achieve those goals. Starting with where they are now and moving to where they would like be, emerging leaders create a detailed, written action plan to get there. Once a plan is constructed, discipline and diligence are needed to carry it out. One of the best ways to stay committed to the process of personal development is to enlist a coach, which is one of the primary characteristics of our next leadership theory.

Resonant Leadership

The theory of resonant leadership is closely related to primal leadership, but with some distinguishing differences. Boyatzis and McKee (2005) argue that it is the relationship between the leader and his or her direct reports that is the key determinant of team success. Relationships that are positive and empowering lead to feelings of trust and growth. Conversations and meetings with resonant leaders leave members feeling excited about being a part of the team and encouraged about their role (Baran, Shanock, Rogelberg, & Scott, 2012). This is what Boyatzis calls interpersonal resonance. Conversely, when the relationship with supervisors generates feelings of fear, anxiety, or distrust, the result is dissonance. Dissonant leaders may be smart, competent, and hard-working, but they are not able to build meaningful connections with their team; thus, they will not be able to maintain sustainable success.

Leaders are often under a tremendous amount of pressure. They carry an emotional burden that can wear them down over time. If leaders are not managing stress effectively, they lose the ability to relate to others in a positive way and become disconnected from or dissonant with their team. The solution is to practice regular habits of rest and renewal. In particular, Boyatzis recommends mindfulness to slow the body down and to focus the mind. With mindfulness, leaders regularly set aside time for quiet reflection and peaceful relaxation. It is often during times of this mindfulness or increased self-awareness that the full creative capacities of our brains are utilized. It also creates feelings of hope and good-will toward others, which can lead to resonance with team members.

Another way leaders can experience renewal is to mentor and coach their team members with compassion (Boyatzis, Smith, & Blaize, 2006). This coaching experience not only has the potential to impact the development of team members, it can also be an extremely meaningful endeavor for the leader. The practice of compassionate coaching occurs when the leader is truly interested in the well-being of others and not just interested in what they can contribute to the organization. Thus, resonant leaders see one of their primary roles as developing the potential of their team members. Simply put, they are invested in helping team members achieve their own goals. Coaching appointments can foster resonance by asking team members the following questions:

1. What do you want to achieve personally and professionally?
2. How can I help you achieve those goals?
3. Are you open to me giving you specific feedback and suggestions for growth?

The answers to these questions can be used as the groundwork for future meetings where goals and plans are discussed more specifically. Again, this type of coaching is beneficial to both the leader and the team member and is one of the key characteristics of resonant leadership.

FIVE PRACTICES OF EXEMPLARY LEADERS

Trait theories, contingency theories, and transformational theories of leadership all have something to contribute to the discussion about leadership. Each perspective emphasizes certain criteria or conditions that lead to effective leadership. Another model of leadership that incorporates many of the salient components of these models is described in *The Leadership Challenge,* by Kouzes and Posner (2007). Used in many corporate leadership training programs, this popular leadership model is grounded in 30 years of research and includes data from over 3 million leaders. The authors have identified five characteristics of exemplary leaders. These include the ability to do the following:

- Model the way

- Inspire a shared vision

- Challenge the process

- Enable others to act

- Encourage the heart

The theory suggests that if individuals learn to use these five practices on a regular basis, they would be more effective as leaders. The five practices are easy to understand and, with practice, can be mastered by almost anyone. The rest of this chapter will describe each of the five practices in detail.

Model the Way

Kouzes and Posner assert that exemplary leadership begins with character. After surveying people on six continents, a clear consensus of admired characteristics emerged. The most admired leaders are honest, forward-looking, inspiring, and competent. The following chart highlights the percentage of people from their 2007 survey that identified each of these top four characteristics.

First and foremost, people want to follow leaders who are honest and authentic (Hannah, Walumbwa, & Fry, 2011). The most effective leaders establish credibility through high ethical character. Honesty, authenticity, and integrity foster trust and provide the foundation upon which effective leadership is established. Leaders who speak the truth and do what they say they are going to do engender loyalty in their followers. With that foundation in place, a leader can become a role model and example to others.

| Table 4.2 | What People Want to See in Their Leaders |

Admired Characteristic	Percentage of Respondents
Honest	89
Forward-looking	71
Inspiring	69
Competent	68

SOURCE: Adapted from Kouzes and Posner (2007)

From the first contact, team members are observing leaders to assess their character and to determine whether or not their behavior matches their words. When a leader is modeling the way, they not only verbalize their core values, they demonstrate them as well. The first step in becoming an effective leader is to identify, develop, and live consistently with one's core values. The following questions can help clarify one's personal and professional values:

- What are my core values?
- When am I at my best and my worst?
- What are the most important things to me?
- What do I want for my life?
- What do I think about my team?
- What do I believe about our task?
- What do I believe about the larger organization?
- What do I think is the best way to work with others?

Values are most effectively demonstrated by aligning actions with words. That being so, if a leader wants the team to be passionate about a certain task, she or he must be visibly passionate about it. If a leader wants to create an open environment that questions the status quo, he or she must be open to critique and refrain from defensiveness when challenged. Obviously, leaders are expected to be able to articulate their core values when asked, but they must also live them out consistently in order to establish credibility.

Inspire a Shared Vision

In order to inspire a shared vision, one must have a compelling goal for the future. As mentioned above, the most respected leaders are visionary, forward-looking individuals; they know where they are going. Visionaries live in the present but are looking to a better future. The more detailed and comprehensive the vision, the better.

In addition to having a goal or vision for the future, effective leaders are able to enlist others to join him or her in the pursuit of that goal. In order to inspire others, one must be able to communicate a compelling picture that motivates people to action. For example, Martin Luther King Jr. was a master communicator who not only had a dream for a better future, but was also able to communicate that vision and motivate others to adopt it as well. His famous "I Have a Dream" speech not only engaged an entire generation but continues to inspire us today.

Inspiring others often means communicating the vision in a way that excites the passions of others. To do this, effective leaders tend to be excellent storytellers. They use anecdotes, illustrations, and colorful language to paint a vivid picture of what the team can accomplish if everyone gets on board. Furthermore, the best stories are able to align the shared goals of the team with the personal goals of its members. That way, when the team is successful, each member personally benefits as well.

Challenge the Process

Challenging the process begins with a critical assessment of what is not working within a team or organization. It requires tenacious honesty to evaluate current practices and make changes, where necessary. Change can be a threatening process for many. Identifying areas for improvement and making changes to short-term strategies or long-term goals is often met with resistance. Regardless, the best leaders regularly evaluate team structure and operating procedures to identify weaknesses and possible blind spots. They challenge their teams to settle for nothing less than the highest levels of excellence.

The most effective leaders are not satisfied with the status quo and constantly look for innovative ways to improve performance. When something has not worked as planned, they challenge team members to learn from the experience and make improvements. This model of continuous improvement helps teams find the most effective strategies to achieve their goals. As leaders model an attitude of accountability and challenge, norms will develop within the team, and members will adopt these characteristics as well. Instead of relying solely on the leader, effective teams are those in which all team members look for ways to improve individual and team performance.

Enable Others to Act

Enabling others to act includes the ability to foster collaboration and strengthen others. It first begins by establishing a collaborative environment that fosters trust and an open exchange of information. In order to be effective in this practice, leaders must embrace a humble and relational posture. They must be willing to admit mistakes, ask for feedback, and defer to the wisdom of the group. In addition, they need to take a genuine interest in others and attempt to get to know each member of the team on some level. Building rapport can often be established by making simple statements such as "How was your weekend?" or, "Is there anything I can do to help you on this task?" Team members can sense if a leader is genuinely interested in them and their success, so the attempts to connect interpersonally must be sincere. When there is an atmosphere of trust and mutual respect, members will be more interested in making a meaningful contribution to the team.

Enabling others to act also includes the ability to coach members and help them develop competence and confidence. Leaders often play the role of player-coach on a team. They are a contributing member of the team but also have responsibilities to help others develop their skills and abilities. Since they often have more experience and expertise than others on the team, they are a great source of wisdom. Coaching includes giving real-time feedback, instruction, and informal training on various tasks or skills. In addition, coaches hold team members accountable for their particular role on the team, which communicates the belief that the team member can successfully complete the task. When members show progress or demonstrate competence, exemplary leaders will then encourage the heart, as described in the next section.

Encourage the Heart

Finally, Kouzes and Posner suggest that effective leaders recognize individual performance while at the same time creating an environment that celebrates collective effort. When a team member has made a significant contribution, that person should be recognized for his or her efforts. To do so, leaders can adopt a philosophy of looking for reasons to applaud team members instead of trying to catch them doing something wrong. As the old adage goes, "You can catch more flies with honey than with vinegar." This practice, however, can be overused. While some members need encouragement in order to stay motivated, others do not. It is up to the leader to determine the needs of each team member. But even if a member is not particularly responsive to public recognition, the leader is creating a positive, encouraging atmosphere and reinforcing the norms and expectations for ideal member behavior.

High-performing teams work hard to reach their goals and celebrate their victories with equal verve. Leaders who have pushed their teams to strive for success are quick to reward their teams for their effort. Various awards such as trophies, trips, cash bonuses, or other perks can be used to recognize excellence. When teams have faced adversity and overcome obstacles to achieve a goal, they develop a strong bond. Those experiences should be reflected upon and celebrated. For example, the 1980 U.S. hockey team overcame great odds to win a gold medal at Lake Placid, New York. Imagine the thrill and team pride shared by the players as they stood *together* on a platform in front of thousands of people as the "Star Spangled Banner" was playing. The blood, sweat, and tears that it took to get to the champion circle were swallowed up by the thrill of victory in that one moment.

FIVE BASES OF POWER

In his book *Power: A New Social Analysis*, the famous philosopher Bertrand Russell (1938) suggests that "the fundamental concept in social science is power, in the same way that energy is the fundamental concept in physics." Power is the capacity to influence one's environment and the people within it. But where does power come from? There are times when power is inherent in a position or job title. Other times, it is not the title, but a particular quality or circumstance that allows the individual increased influence and power within a social setting or organization. This section will explore French and Raven's (1959) five bases of power including reward, coercive, legitimate, expert, and referent power within a team setting.

Reward power is established when a member of a team possesses sufficient means to reward other members for positive behaviors. Rewards can take many forms, from verbal encouragement to financial compensation. If the reward is perceived as valuable and the request is reasonably attainable, individuals will comply. The drawback to this type of transaction is that member behavior may only be sustained as long as the rewards are offered. In other words, the work and ultimate purpose of the group may not be fully internalized by members (Pink, 2009). Furthermore, if rewards are promised but not delivered, resentment and distrust may follow and can compromise motivation for future tasks.

Coercive power stems from the power to punish others. The power holder has the capacity to issue negative consequences when requests are not followed or rules are broken. The degree of the consequence may range from the mild (sending a bad review to the member's superior) to the extreme (eliminating a member from the team). Individuals with this type of power can threaten, constrain, block, or interfere with others, and thus use fear to control their behavior.

Legitimate power is associated with the implied power of certain roles in a group or organization. For example, team leaders might be given a certain amount of authority over their group. Members obey the requests of the group's authority figures out of a sense of duty, loyalty, or moral obligation. While leaders can command compliance due to their position, those who provide the reasons for their requests enhance member commitment.

Expert power is awarded to members who are perceived as having knowledge that is particularly useful to the group. One of the earliest pioneers of management theory, Peter Drucker, speculated more than 30 years ago that modern employees would need to be "knowledge workers" (Davenport, 2005). The strongest assets these workers bring to teams and organizations are their knowledge, intellect, and ability to solve complex problems. Their expertise in various subject matters helps teams critique ideas and make better decisions.

Referent power is a source of power that is established by those who are charismatic and well-liked by others. They may not have the best ideas or suggestions, but they garner a lot of support because they are so likeable. Members want to please them and gain their approval, rendering them quite influential over individual members, in particular, and the group process, in general.

Some sources of power are more valuable in particular contexts than others. Naturally, groups tend to value those sources that are most applicable to their identity and purpose. For example, Krause and Kearney (2006) conducted research on power bases in hospitals, schools, orchestras, and corporations. They found that the use of legitimate and expert power were most prominent in hospitals and orchestras; this is not surprising, since those organizations value achievement and expertise. Status and power are embedded in titles such as "doctor" or "conductor." In contrast, coercive, reward, and legitimate power were strongly operational in schools. Teachers regulate school performance by distributing grades (reward power) or punishment (coercive power). Teachers and principals are granted respect in most cases because of the legitimacy of those roles. Lastly, in corporations, referent and expert power were most highly valued. Their organizational success depends on how well people work together and the amount of knowledge those individuals bring to the team. This research shows that the importance of power bases across contexts depends on their value to that particular set of circumstances (Schriesheim & Neider, 2006).

Group members respond differently to different sources of power. Coercive power can generate resistance or reluctant compliance, whereas reward or legitimate power often results in a more positive response. However, it is referent and expert power that engender true commitment (Yukl & Falbe, 1991). When members are voluntarily enlisted through rational persuasion rather than force, and inspirational appeals rather than positional power, they are far more likely to be committed to the task.

Not surprisingly, people with multiple sources of power have an even greater capacity to influence the behavior of others. For example, after successfully overseeing the merger of Compaq Computer and Hewlett-Packard, Michael Capellas joined MCI/WorldCom in December 2002 as president and CEO. Despite its position as the world's largest telecommunications company at the time, MCI/WorldCom was embroiled in an accounting scandal and forced into bankruptcy. Using his impressive business acumen, Capellas brought the company out of bankruptcy in early 2004 and successfully negotiated its sale to Verizon Business a year later. His possession of the five bases of power clearly contributed to his success. He had the power to reward competent and highly motivated employees and remove those who were less than stellar. In addition, his position at the top of the organizational chart garnered respect and obedience. But Capellas was more than a typical high-level executive who understood balance sheets and reporting structures; he was an expert in the field of information technology and an avid reader of information about technology development and future trends. He knew his stuff. Furthermore, he was likeable and very relational. He inspired hundreds of thousands of discouraged MCI employees to commit to a vision that would turn the company around and reassert its global presence. By most accounts, he was completely successful.

INFLUENCE STRATEGIES

While leaders have access to different power bases within a group, they also have choices as to how they will exercise that power. **Influence tactics** are the means by which people influence the attitudes and behavior of others. The choice of which tactic to use is based upon available resources (i.e., the power bases one possesses), the willingness to invoke a power base (based upon personal values, social norms, and possible costs associated with each tactic), and the resistance one expects from the target (Bruins, 1999; Kipnis, 1976).

Yukl and associates originally identified nine influence tactics (Yukl & Falbe, 1990, 1991; Yukl, Kim, & Falbe, 1996; Yukl & Tracey, 1992), and their most recent research has identified two additional tactics (Yukl, Chavez, & Seifert, 2005). Most of the methods can be used by either leaders or members and, thus, fit well within a self-managed team environment. The following table describes each of the 11 tactics.

Not all influence tactics produce the same results. According to Yukl and Tracey (1992), three core tactics (rational persuasion, inspirational appeals, and consultation) were found to be the most effective at gaining task commitment and were strongly related to successful leadership as evaluated by their superiors. Committed members, as opposed to merely compliant members, understand the value of the requests being made; thus, they tend to

| Table 4.3 | Eleven Primary Influence Tactics |

Influence Tactic	Definition
Rational persuasion	The person uses logical arguments and factual evidence to persuade others that a certain position is the best course of action.
Inspirational appeal	The person makes a request or proposal that arouses enthusiasm by appealing to values, ideals, and aspirations.
Consultation	The person seeks others' participation in planning a strategy, activity, or change and is willing to modify a proposal based upon their concerns and suggestions.
Ingratiation	The person seeks to get others in a good mood or to think favorably of him or her before making a request.
Exchange	The person offers an exchange of favors, indicates willingness to reciprocate at a later time, or promises a share of the benefits if help is given.
Personal appeal	The person appeals to feelings of loyalty and friendship.
Coalition	The person garners the aid and support of others before making a request for someone to do something.
Legitimating	The person seeks to establish the legitimacy of a request by claiming the authority or right to make it or by verifying that it is consistent with existing policies, rules, practices, or traditions.
Pressure	The person uses demands, threats, or persistent reminders to influence the attitudes or behavior of others.
Collaboration	The person offers to provide relevant resources or assistance if others will carry out a request or approve a proposed change.
Apprising	The person explains how others will benefit by complying with the request.

SOURCE: Adapted from Yukl, Chavez, & Seifert, 2005

carry out their tasks with enthusiasm, initiative, and persistence. The most ineffective influence tactics identified in the study were pressure, coalition, and legitimating (Yukl & Tracey, 1992). While these strategies may elicit compliance, overuse can produce resistance. Furthermore, compliance only guarantees that members carry out their duties, not that they exhibit any more than minimal to average effort.

In another study, Falbe and Yukl (1992) asked 95 managers and nonmanagerial professionals in a variety of private companies and public agencies to evaluate their reaction to 504 influence attempts made upon them. Each attempt was categorized as one of the nine original influence tactics and associated with a resulting response of resistance, compliance, or commitment. The following table describes the results.

Hard tactics such as legitimating, coalition, and pressure often produce resistance and rarely engender commitment. Leaders will have significantly better long-term outcomes if they use softer tactics such as consultation, inspirational appeals, or ingratiation

| Table 4.4 | Effectiveness of Various Influence Tactics |

Influence Tactics	Outcomes		
	Resistance	Compliance	Commitment
Inspirational appeal	0%	10%	90%
Consultation	18	27	55
Personal appeal	25	33	42
Exchange	24	41	35
Ingratiation	41	28	31
Rational persuasion	47	30	23
Legitimating	44	56	0
Coalition	53	44	3
Pressure	56	41	3

SOURCE: Adapted from Falbe and Yukl (1992).

(Falbe & Yukl, 1992). Feedback and skills training can help team leaders develop influence tactics that are most effective. Seifert, Yukl, and McDonald (2003) found that multisource feedback and the use of a feedback facilitator can help leaders and managers become more aware of their own strategies and develop more effective ways to motivate subordinates and peers.

PERSUADING OTHERS

This section describes specific things a team leader or influential member can do to ensure that his or her voice is not only heard, but heeded. We've already talked about the importance of voicing one's opinions and positions in group settings, but how do you make sure that those opinions are given the consideration they deserve by the rest of the group? Conger's (1998) research identifies four components of successful persuasion: (a) establishing credibility, (b) finding common ground, (c) providing evidence, and (d) making an emotional connection. The best and most persuasive arguments include all four components.

Establish Credibility

In order to be persuasive, group members must have credibility and respect from their peers. The ideas of a low-status or marginally committed member are not likely to be heard, even if they are brilliant. It takes some measure of status and personal power to be taken seriously. According to Conger (1998), credibility comes from intellectual competence, interpersonal competence, and personal character.

Intellectual competence is demonstrated every time a member makes a significant contribution to the group. When a competent member speaks, others believe that what is being said is worth listening to because ideas from that member have been credible in the past. In short, competence is a characteristic that engenders trust and is established when members have proven themselves to have sound judgment and valuable knowledge.

Credibility is also enhanced when a member has interpersonal competence and quality relationships with others. The ability to work collaboratively with others will go a long way toward building relational trust. When members are seen as "team players," they are appreciated by the group. This type of credibility is acquired when members are perceived as likeable, agreeable, and enjoyable to work with.

Finally, members are highly valued when they demonstrate honesty, consistency, and reliability—personal character. Honesty and fairness are admirable characteristics that earn the respect of others. Furthermore, those who consistently follow through on their commitments are highly regarded as well. Meeting deadlines with high-quality work is a sure way to win over colleagues. Another characteristic that is admired on teams is work ethic. If a person is willing to work hard and shows commitment to team success over personal gain, he or she has earned the right to be heard.

Find Common Ground

In addition to having credibility, effective persuasion requires the ability to frame suggestions in terms of their benefit to the whole group. Unfortunately, when people are overly attached to a certain perspective or position, they lose sight of the group's interests. Discussions can become personal and competitive, and members can feel compelled to win at all costs. A potential power struggle ensues with members going on the attack and attempting to pressure others to agree with them. It is not uncommon for these negative patterns of interaction to emerge when others refuse to comply. To avoid this from happening, members should keep in mind that the best arguments are tied to the ultimate goals and success of the group.

According to Conger (1998), an understanding of the audience is a prerequisite for finding common ground. The most effective persuaders are students of human nature who seek to understand the concerns and interests of others before advocating their own agenda. They are active listeners who collect data through conversations and meetings. This allows them to construct arguments that emphasize issues of mutual concert and mutual benefit.

Finding common ground also allows for compromise and collaboration. Those who wish to influence the group will be more successful if they stay open to the concerns and perspectives of others and are willing to adapt and modify their own position. When met with resistance, these individuals listen, paraphrase, and ask probing questions to better understand the issues of concern. Influence tactics such as consultation, collaboration, and apprising can be effective in identifying shared benefits and building a common framework from which to work.

Provide Evidence

As the name suggests, data-based decision making is a practice in which groups make decisions and create plans based upon careful calculations of the best data available to them.

Setting measurable goals and correctly analyzing problems help groups uncover the necessary data that can guide their efforts. Solid numerical data provide the reasoning and justification for group decisions and direction.

Before putting forth an argument, a member should anticipate the question: "What evidence do you have for your position?" Argyris (1994) describes this process as coming down the ladder of inference because members provide the data and reasoning upon which a decision, conclusion, or argument was based. When a person has already established credibility, providing strong empirical data that support a certain perspective makes for a compelling argument.

Knowledge is a source of power, and sharing it empowers the rest of the group. This principle is the basis for using trend data, which, while not perfect, give approximate projections of what is likely to occur in the future. For example, if a marketing team responsible for selling nutrition bars is trying to create a marketing plan for the next five years, it will use data from the previous five years, along with information on current market conditions, to project sales and create a strategic plan.

While numbers and data are important, they do not tell the whole story. Statistics and graphs are most effective when they are presented with vivid language and concrete examples. Stories can be powerful tools that bring numbers to life and persuade others to arrive at certain conclusions. Analogies, anecdotes, and metaphors can also be used to make data more concrete, interesting, and tangible. Instead of making an argument based solely upon past performance and current market trends, a customer testimonial describing how his or her quality of life improved after buying the company's product may provide the emotional dynamic that rounds out a strong case for more aggressive growth. Consider Subway, the fast-food sandwich giant whose marketing team designed an entire campaign around "Jared," a man who lost over 200 pounds in one year by eating nothing but Subway food. The ad campaign not only included data in terms of the number of pounds that Jared lost, but it also tied the numbers to his own life story.

Connect Emotionally

While rational arguments can foster agreement, establishing an emotional connection is often needed to ensure commitment. Inspirational appeal is the most effective tactic for generating commitment because it engages people on an emotional level. When it is done effectively, people rarely resist. In a study conducted by Falbe and Yukl (1992), inspirational appeals resulted in commitment 90% of the time and compliance 10% of the time, and they never generated outright resistance. Connecting emotionally requires that members demonstrate their own emotional commitment and passion for the position they are advocating. In addition, they must be able to accurately read the emotions of their audience to know whether or not the listeners are receiving the message enthusiastically.

With credibility, common ground, strong data, and relevant examples, members can persuasively advocate their position. But they must be convinced of the legitimacy of their own ideas, or their efforts will be in vain. People can see through a polished argument devoid of passion. If group members cannot tell that the member behind the delivery is thoroughly convinced, they, too, will likely be unconvinced. Yet too much emotion might create the impression that a person has lost objectivity or is too invested in a certain decision. Thus, members who wish to influence others should demonstrate an appropriate amount of conviction to champion a given position by taking into consideration the comfort level of the audience. Each group environment will dictate the optimal level of emotional expression.

Conger (1998) warns against underestimating the importance of being able to assess the emotional state of the audience. Presenters must be able to judge whether they are being well received or even understood. This can be achieved by observing nonverbal messages and reading between the lines of questions and comments. In spite of the stated importance of rationality in organizational settings, emotions play a strong role. Thus, those who are effective at persuading can judge the emotional reactions of others and adjust their comments accordingly.

Influential members who are effective at persuading colleagues establish credibility, find common ground, provide compelling evidence for their position, and connect emotionally with the group. If members want to be active and influential in their groups, they can utilize these methods to increase their effect on group decision making.

CONDUCTING EFFECTIVE MEETINGS

Meetings are a critical component of group work; most of the important work of teams takes place in a forum where members communicate with one another face to face or through some computer-mediated space (Kauffeld & Lehmann-Willenbrock, 2012; Scott, Shanock, & Rogelberg, 2012). Unfortunately, many people experience the typical meeting as inefficient and even unpleasant (O'Neill & Allen, 2012). In his book *Death by Meeting,* Patrick Lencioni (2004) reports that the most common complaint about meetings is that they are both ineffective and boring. Although meetings are the lifeblood of teamwork, they can be quite frustrating, especially as teams grow in size. Hence the dictum that the larger the team, the greater the potential for inefficiencies and process losses. In order to combat these shortcomings, Whetten and Cameron (2007) have identified several strategies that teams can implement to make meetings more effective, which we discuss below.

1. *Purpose:* The reason for holding a meeting should be explicitly clear. Meetings are generally called in order to share information, build commitment to a project, provide information, give or receive feedback, and/or problem-solve.

2. *Participants:* It is important to pay attention to the number of people in attendance. Meetings of more than 10 people should be used to report information as opposed to being an open discussion of ideas. Also, group composition is an important consideration: How similar are members in terms of backgrounds, personalities, knowledge, and the like? Are they competitive, or do they prefer cooperation? Are they task or process oriented? These are important questions to ask. For example, discussion may be difficult in a large group of people. And groups that are not very diverse may not be able to generate a wide variety of creative perspectives and solutions to a particular problem.

3. *Planning:* Setting the agenda is a key task for the meeting facilitator. The agenda should be distributed to attendees prior to the meeting, and should inform participants of

what to expect, any contributions they are required to make, and the duration of the meeting. Agenda items should be written with action verbs like "approve minutes," rather than "minutes," and organized into three phases: old business, new business, and closing thoughts. Then the group needs to stick to the agenda and begin and end on time.

4. *Participation:* After paying careful attention to ensure that the right people are present, it makes sense to focus on their participation. Begin meetings with introductions so that all members begin to feel comfortable with one another. Leaders can encourage participation through various communication strategies such as asking open-ended questions, making eye contact, paraphrasing comments, linking comments together, and summarizing discussions.

5. *Perspective:* Perspective involves analyzing the meeting in hindsight. Leaders who regularly reflect on the quality of their meetings not only improve their own skills, but also improve the overall productivity of the team. In the same way, it is often helpful to get the perspective of the participants as well. Direct questioning and the use of anonymous surveys are both effective ways to collect feedback on what went well and what changes should be made in the future.

LEADERSHIP IN ACTION

The five practices of exemplary leaders can make anyone a better leader. We just need to look for opportunities to serve as a positive role model, inspire a shared vision, productively challenge the process, enable others to act, and encourage the hearts of teammates. These practices, though, will require a certain amount of reflectiveness. Leaders in training must be willing to step back from team experiences and think critically about their own role, the variables at play, and the fine and nuanced dance between them and their team. Strong leaders are not only aware of their own perceptions, but are also inquisitive and responsive to other people's perceptions and needs. So much of leadership is about managing information, personalities, and perceptions. To do this well, leaders need to be constantly observing their own behavior and that of their teammates.

These five practices are not necessarily performed in order. Rather, they are a dynamic list of tools that can be employed any time a situation warrants them. The more they are used, the more effective they become. At first, it may feel strange to try to "inspire" colleagues, but those skills will develop over time and with practice. A good starting place is to lead by example by showing up early, arriving prepared, staying engaged, and bringing a positive and encouraging attitude to team meetings. Then, as credibility increases, emerging leaders can add in such practices as offering productive challenges and enabling others to act by giving feedback and suggestions for improvement.

The key to developing leadership skills is to be intentional about it. After every team experience, leaders should reflect (think critically) on what happened, what worked well, and what the leader might have done differently to improve the outcome. Essentially, these five practices need to be exercised on a regular basis so they become internalized and part of one's identity. Leaders in training should model the positive and productive habits they wish to see within their teams. They should encourage team members who demonstrate positive behaviors and challenge those who don't. They should hold their team accountable to the highest standards of excellence and create a culture in which team members challenge one another to work harder. Developing these skills requires a significant amount of trial and error. New practices will be far from perfect at first, but over time they will pay rich dividends. Successful leadership development requires courage, discipline, self-reflection, and intentionality.

KEY TERMS

Self-managed work teams   69

Situational leadership   72

Directing style of leadership   73

Coaching style of leadership   73

Supporting style of leadership   73

Delegating style of leadership   73

Influence tactics   81

Intellectual competence   84

Interpersonal competence   84

Personal character   84

DISCUSSION QUESTIONS

1. Over the last century, the dynamic between managers and workers has changed. Describe those changes and discuss how those changes have affected teams.

2. Describe French and Raven's five bases of power and give an example of each.

3. Describe the three influence tactics you think are most effective for team leaders.

4. Describe the four leadership styles within the situational leadership model. Give examples of each.

5. Discuss the difference between transactional leadership and transformational leadership. What are the outcomes of each?

6. What are the five practices of effective leaders? Name and describe each.

7. How do most effective leaders establish credibility?

8. What are the four components of successful persuasion? Create a hypothetical case study in which a team leader is trying to get members to be more committed to the team.

GROUP ACTIVITIES

EXERCISE 4.1 INSPIRATIONAL LEADERS

Get into groups of four to five people to talk about your past experiences with leaders, supervisors, and bosses.

- Create a list of qualities of the best leaders you have observed.

- Create a list of characteristics associated with the worst leaders you have observed.

- Who is the leader your team admires most? Provide a detailed rationale for your answer.

Appoint a spokesperson to present the results of your discussion to the rest of the class.

EXERCISE 4.2 PRACTICING EXEMPLARY LEADERSHIP

You have been selected to be on a nomination committee to identify viable candidates for student body president. In groups of four to five students, discuss the characteristics of a successful student body president and choose someone from your class as a possible candidate. The nominee doesn't have to come from your group but does have to be a member of this class. While you are having this conversation, practice one of the five practices of exemplary leadership described in this chapter (model the way, inspire a shared vision, challenge the process, enable others to act, or encourage the heart). Be relentless. Continue to use the same practice over and over again, no matter how silly or contrived it might feel. At the end of the exercise, try to guess the practice that each person was practicing.

CASE 4.2: OUTLINING LEADERSHIP STRENGTHS

You've been working at your company, *Galactic Enterprises, LLC*, for three years and have developed a good reputation for getting things done. Your boss, who refers to you as his "go-to person," has called you into his office to talk about a project team whose leader unexpectedly took a new job with a rival company, giving only two-weeks' notice. When you arrive at the meeting, your boss is sitting there with three other managers. He asks you to describe for the group your leadership philosophy and to lay out the approach you would use to lead the project team out of confusion and back on plan.

- *Using content from the chapter, create an appropriate, semi-formal presentation to describe how you would lead this team and why you are the right person for the job.*

Communication

Verbal and nonverbal communication among group members defines much team life. Individual goals, team goals, structure, and norms are evident in the communication patterns that develop among members. Tasks are accomplished and relationships managed through interpersonal interaction. Yet not all communication is positive, and as a result, team performance can be compromised. This chapter describes communication skills and patterns that lead to team success. It also identifies specific strategies members can adopt to improve their ability to communicate effectively. The chapter ends with a discussion about virtual communication and the benefits and challenges of virtual teams.

CASE 5.1: *THE APPRENTICE*

The TV reality show The Apprentice *first aired on NBC during the winter of 2004 and quickly became the hit that it is today. At the beginning of each season, 16 contestants are divided into two teams that compete against each other for the ultimate prize of becoming the president of one of Donald Trump's companies. Every week the two teams face off in various challenges, ranging from selling lemonade on the streets of New York City to organizing charity events. The project leader of the losing team must face Trump in the boardroom and explain why the team did not succeed. Trump then identifies a member of the team who, in his opinion, was most responsible for the loss and issues his now famous decree, "You're fired."*

In week two of the first season, the two teams, Versacorp (all men) and Protégé (all women), were given the task of designing an advertising campaign for a private jet service. Each team chose a project leader and began to structure the task. The men made a strategic error when they decided not to conduct customer interviews. Not knowing the distinguishing characteristics or the desires of the customer proved to be fatal and led to Versacorp's downfall. In addition, one of the more eccentric members of the team, Sam, talked excessively during planning sessions, frequently getting off topic. In one of the meetings, when he spent valuable project time lying on the floor of a conference room taking a nap, his credibility was compromised. As a result, when he later tried to interject his ideas and influence other members, he was interrupted by the project leader, Jason, and marginalized.

In contrast to the men, Protégé met with the customer and eventually decided upon an advertising campaign that used sexual overtones in its print ads. However, not all the members were comfortable using that approach, as it risked offending the customer. In the process of discussing options and making decisions, a number of members had different opinions, and tempers flared. Even though the women won the competition, it became obvious that there were serious interpersonal problems on their team. Two of the members, Omarosa and Ereka, had engaged in a number of arguments, and other members of the team were concerned that their dislike for each other would hurt the team's performance in the future.

For this challenge, Trump asked Donny Deutsch, the principal of a successful advertising agency in New York City, to decide the winning proposal. Deutsch and his two associates were torn between the men and the women. The sex appeal in the women's presentation may not have been appropriate for an actual print campaign, but it showed that they were more creative and willing to take risks. Ultimately, those qualities persuaded Deutsch to declare the women victorious. In addition, he commented that their presentation was sharper and more persuasive than that of the men. Their ability to communicate their ideas with passion and enthusiasm connected well with Deutsch.

After losing the task, Jason, the project manager for the men's team, identified Sam as the team's biggest problem. Jason explained to Trump how Sam failed the group by literally falling asleep during the project and not caring about the team's performance. Sam told Trump that Jason was just an average leader who made many mistakes, including not meeting with the customer. He added that because the team did not take the time to thoroughly understand the customer's needs, the project plan was flawed from the start. Thus, Sam didn't respect Jason's leadership and became passively detached. In the end, Trump held the team leader, Jason, responsible and fired him; Sam was spared. However, the group members became so frustrated with him that they decided to make him team leader for the next project in an effort to get him to "put up or shut up." While this may have been a strategic move to deal with Sam, the team suffered, losing the next competition. Although the women's team was winning competitions, interpersonal conflicts began taking their toll. Hostility and mistrust among members began to compromise the team's ability to perform.

Case Study Discussion Questions

- What should the men do about Sam? How do you view members who don't exactly fit in with the group? Is Sam a resource or a liability to the team? Explain.

- Two of the women strongly dislike each other. How would you handle that situation?

- What do you typically do in group situations when people are angry and start attacking one another? What do you do when others challenge you?

- What communication skills are needed in the men's group? In the women's group?

In an article in *Business Communication Quarterly,* Kinnick and Parton (2005) describe the results of a content analysis they performed on all 15 episodes from the first season of *The Apprentice.* They examined the following communication skills in each of the episodes: oral and written communications, interpersonal communication, teamwork skills, intercultural communication, negotiating skills, and ethical communication. In addition, they examined Trump's view of how those skills influenced individual and team performance. Trump and his associates identified poor communication skills as a factor in 5 of the 15 team losses. Poor communication was also cited as a factor in more than half of the individual firings. The last five players in the competition at the end of the season were considerably more likely to be praised for their communication skills than were the first five who were eliminated.

Communication skills are foundational for individual, team, and organizational success (Kinnick & Parton, 2005). For example, oral communication and interpersonal skills are often cited as the most important criteria in evaluating job candidates. Interpersonal skills were mentioned more frequently than any other competency listed in classified ads for entry-level jobs in 10 major metropolitan newspapers. Not surprisingly, the U.S. Department of Labor has identified communication and interpersonal skills as core requirements for future workers. Colleges work hard to prepare individuals for professional success by helping them develop these skills through team-based learning activities and class projects (Kalliath & Laiken, 2006). And once employees are hired, organizations invest significant resources to enhance their communication skills. According to one study, 88% of U.S. companies provide communication skills training for their employees (*Industry Report,* 1999). The importance of communication cannot be overstated. Thus, it is important to thoroughly understand this powerful interpersonal process.

ENCODING AND DECODING MESSAGES

Communication is the exchange of thoughts, information, or ideas that results in mutual understanding between two or more people. The process requires at least one sender, one receiver, and a message that is transmitted within a communication medium. It begins with an idea or concept in the mind of the sender. He or she encodes the idea into meaningful symbols in the form of words, pictures, or gestures (i.e., language). The sender then selects a medium to transmit those symbols so the receiver can access them through one or more senses. The medium can be a face-to-face conversation, a piece of artwork hanging in an

Figure 5.1 Sending and Receiving Messages

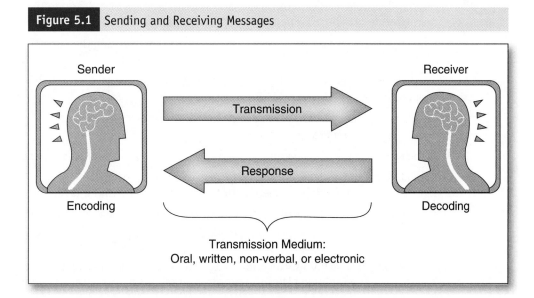

art gallery, a text message, or any growing number of electronic transmission media. When the receiver receives the message, he or she must decode the symbols in order to interpret the message and understand the intent of the sender, as depicted below.

Meaningful communication takes place when the receiver accurately understands the message transmitted by the sender. However, this does not always happen perfectly. A multitude of potential problems can hinder the process and block understanding. The rest of the chapter examines the many ways in which a message can become distorted or misunderstood; it also suggests ways to minimize the potential for communication missteps.

VERBAL COMMUNICATION

The use of verbal statements is one of the most common ways individuals communicate with one another. As team members work together to understand problems and manage projects, hundreds, if not thousands, of verbal comments are exchanged. A team member might be communicating a message at face value, or he or she may be implying hidden meanings or even multiple layers of meaning in a single statement. Because members do not always know the exact intent of one another's comments, there can be multiple interpretations and frequent misunderstandings. In the early stages of group development, team members have to learn the most effective way to interact with and understand that particular group.

Wheelan and her associates have developed a classification system called the Group Development Observation System (GDOS) as a way of categorizing and analyzing the verbal interactions that take place among group members (Wheelan, Davidson, & Tilin, 2003). The GDOS classifies statements into one of eight categories, and while statements can sometimes fit more than one category, trained observers are in agreement 85% to 95% of the time. The eight GDOS categories are as follows:

- *Dependency statements* are those that show an inclination to conform to the dominant mood of the group and to solicit direction from others.
- *Counterdependency statements* assert independence by resisting the current leadership and direction of the group.
- *Fight statements* directly challenge others using argumentativeness, criticism, or aggression.
- *Flight statements* are attempts to avoid work and demonstrate a lack of commitment to the group.
- *Pairing statements* are expressions of warmth, friendship, and support toward others.
- *Counterpairing statements* demonstrate an avoidance of intimacy and interpersonal connection by keeping the discussion distant and intellectual.
- *Work statements* are those that represent goal-directed and task-oriented efforts.
- *Unscorable statements* include unintelligible, inaudible, or fragmentary statements.

After observing 26 task groups in various stages of development, researchers identified 31,782 verbal statements made during one meeting for each of the groups. Wheelan,

Davidson, and Tilin (2003) found that established groups utilized twice as many task-related statements as compared with newly formed groups. In the early stages of group development, for example, there are more fight, flight, and dependency statements communicated among members than in later stages (Wheelan, 2005). Interestingly, they found that the number of pairing statements remain relatively stable. Approximately 17% of the statements made at any stage of development are supportive of others and meant to engender positive relationships (Wheelan, 2005).

The verbal statements of members of any group can be evaluated to determine whether or not members are committed, compliant, resistant, or disengaged from the team at any given time. Observing a member's consistent pattern of verbal statements over time is one possible way to determine that person's commitment to the task and people of the group. Dependency statements suggest compliance, whereas counterdependency and fight statements suggest resistance. Flight and counterpairing statements often indicate disengagement. Finally, pairing statements suggest commitment to other group members, while work statements suggest commitment to team goals.

NONVERBAL COMMUNICATION

As verbal messages are being communicated, an equally important process of communication is taking place on a nonverbal level. Nonverbal cues from a speaker such as smiling, eye contact, or fidgetiness help listeners interpret the meaning behind the words a person is using to communicate a message. Listeners perceive these messages subconsciously and often have a difficult time articulating why they arrived at a certain understanding of a person's message. As the title of Malcolm Gladwell's (2005) book *Blink: The Power of Thinking Without Thinking* suggests, this process of rapid cognition takes place in the blink of an eye and often outside of awareness. For instance, although the words are the same, the message below may be interpreted as having entirely different meanings based upon the nonverbal cues associated with it:

Table 5.1 Using Nonverbal Cues to Interpret Messages

Verbal Message	Nonverbal Cues	Possible Meanings
We need to be more prepared for the next project.	The speaker scans the group and gestures widely. Her facial expression demonstrates sincere pleading as she emphasizes the word *need*.	The speaker is desperate. For her, there is a lot riding on the success of the group.
We need to be more prepared for the next project.	The speaker emphasizes the word *prepared* as she looks intently at and leans toward a particular member. Her brow is furrowed and she appears frustrated.	The speaker is blaming one of the other members for the group's recent failure and hopes to shame that person into doing better in the future.
We need to be more prepared for the next project.	The speaker says this in a monotone voice with no energy, facial expression, or hand gestures. Her body is facing slightly away from the group.	The speaker is disengaged, does not actually care whether the group sees improvement, and does not plan to put in any extra effort.

Mehrabian's (1981) seminal research on the importance of nonverbal communication suggests that messages, especially those that express feelings, are overwhelmingly understood through nonverbal cues. The following percentages represent the relative contributions of the verbal and nonverbal components that a listener uses to interpret a message:

- 7% from verbal cues (words)

- 38% from vocal cues (volume, pitch, rhythm, etc.)

- 55% from facial expressions (smiling, frowning, etc.) and other body movements (arms crossed, eye contact, etc.)

Nonverbal cues such as physical appearance, facial expressions, level of eye contact, body movements, vocal qualities, and the physical space between members all contribute to the way a message is interpreted. An accurate perception of nonverbal communication helps the listener understand the intent of the speaker and is strongly related to social intelligence and interpersonal sensitivity (Goleman, 2006). So while an individual's "words" can be difficult to understand, nonverbal cues are even more subject to personal interpretation as listeners use their own subjective frame of reference to interpret the nonverbal expressions of others.

Nonverbal cues not only help members interpret verbal messages, they also help regulate the flow of conversation (Goleman, 2006). For example, when members want to interject a comment into a discussion, they may use any number of nonverbal prompts such as leaning forward, clearing their throats, making direct eye contact with the current speaker, or posing a facial expression that indicates a desire to speak. Additionally, if speakers receive positive nonverbal feedback from others while they are speaking (i.e., head nodding, eye contact, or smiling), they will continue with confidence that they are being heard. Speakers signal the end of their comments by relaxing their body posture, reducing verbal volume, or leaning back in their seat. These cues prompt others to respond or add their own thoughts. A more direct invitation might be to nod or gesture toward a particular member with an open hand, palm facing upward. Effective group facilitators frequently use these types of nonverbal cues to move members in and out of the conversation and to otherwise regulate the discussion.

POSTURING

Individuals use both verbal and nonverbal means to establish credibility and communicate ideas in a persuasive manner. Because people desire to be understood and respected, the use of posturing is common. Posturing and the use of identity markers are used to influence the perception, opinion, and approval of others and to bolster one's status within the team (Polzer, 2003). According to Polzer, "We do not communicate identity-relevant information solely for the benefit of others. . . . When we bring others to see us in a favorable light, we tend to boost our own self-image as we bask in their approval" (p. 3). Identity markers might include the following:

- *Physical appearance:* This includes how people are dressed, whether they have a well-groomed appearance, or their fitness level.

- *Personal office or room decorations:* The presence or absence of plaques, framed diplomas, photographs, or other indicators of success.

- *Body posture:* How much space a person takes up, whether their arms or legs are crossed, whether they stand up straight or slouch, the direction they are facing, strength of eye contact.

- *Demeanor:* Loud voice or soft, smiles or frowns, engaged or withdrawn, warm or cold, attentive or aloof.

- *Explicit statements:* Success stories that are shared verbally, statements of one's strengths, subtle references to past accomplishments.

The communication and utilization of these markers is driven by the need for self-enhancement. The **self-enhancement** motive relates to the desire to present oneself in a positive light to garner respect and admiration from others. This is commonly demonstrated on college campuses, for example, by identity markers such as fraternity or sorority T-shirts, sweatshirts, and accessories to identify as a member of an elite social group or by clothing, automobiles, and vacation trips to communicate wealth and social status. Leaders need to be attuned to both the subtle and blatant attempts of members to promote themselves. Self-promoting behavior can intimidate others and restrict the free expression of ideas, and it can be off-putting and hinder the development of trust and cohesion. It might also signal a strong need for recognition and admiration on the part of those who employ such tactics.

Unfortunately, members posture and perform for others in order to gain their respect and admiration at the expense of authenticity. Teams can become like families in which the members (siblings) compete for the approval of the team leaders (parents). This type of "sibling rivalry" in which the members compete for the favored child status can be a distraction for the team. One way a leader can help minimize this dynamic is by establishing the norms of authenticity, honesty, and transparency early on in the life of the team by sharing his or her own mistakes or weaknesses. This sends a strong message that members do not need to compete with one another for performance-based status but, instead, will be valued for their genuineness and humanity.

COMPONENTS OF EFFECTIVE COMMUNICATION

Communication skills, such as active listening and assertiveness, help make information processing more transparent. Actively trying to understand and interpret the verbal messages of others takes work. Simply asking another person to provide the evidence that led to certain conclusions can be very enlightening. Similarly, it is helpful to others when we describe the specific data and interpretation of that data that led to our conclusions. Advocating our ideas in a confident and comprehensive way is demonstrated in the practice of assertiveness. In a typical workgroup setting, assertiveness can take many forms such as promoting a new idea, lobbying for a policy change, or publicly supporting one method of resolving a problem over any number of alternatives. The following section describes the communication skills of active listening and assertiveness in detail.

Active Listening

Active listening is the key to accurately understanding what another person is saying. It requires effort and discipline. Yet group members are often preoccupied or distracted, and thus do not give 100% of their attention to one another (McKay, Davis, & Fanning, 1995).

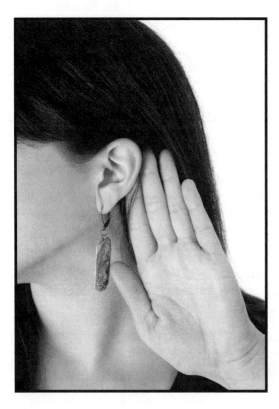

Instead, listeners may be busy comparing themselves with the speaker, mentally rehearsing what they will say next, daydreaming about a past experience, or wishing they were somewhere else. They might also be speculating about what is going on in the mind of the speaker (mind reading), filtering out parts of his or her message, or jumping to conclusions and offering premature advice. It is also all too common for some listeners to be more focused on debating and critiquing than actually hearing what is being said. In contrast to the benefits reaped when a person feels heard, contentiousness can elicit either a defensive reaction or passive detachment, compromising meaningful dialogue.

An accurate understanding of others is needed before a meaningful response can be made. Effective listeners suspend judgment in order to first understand the perspective of the speaker. This advanced developmental skill requires listeners to attempt to "get into the shoes" of the speaker and see the issue through his or her eyes before responding (Kegan, 1994). The comments of others will make more sense if understood from within that person's perspective. Paying attention to posture, paraphrasing what is heard, and probing for deeper meaning are skills that facilitate this type of perspective taking and lead to a more accurate understanding of the messages that are communicated.

First, active listeners pay attention to their *posture*. Specifically, they use their physical posture to help them focus on what is being said. It also creates an interpersonal dynamic that signals to speakers that the listener is paying attention. The acronym **SOLER** describes five specific behaviors that encourage a listening posture:

S—**Square:** Face the person squarely.

O—**Open:** Keep an open posture without crossed arms or legs.

L—**Lean** slightly forward to communicate interest and engagement. Head nods and verbal encouragers like "uh-huh" and "yes!" are also effective.

E—Eye contact: Maintain direct eye contact according to appropriate social norms.

R—Relax: Stay relaxed. Listeners should be comfortable with silence where appropriate and allow the conversation to unfold without force.

By following these guidelines, listeners will be perceived as engaged and interested in what is being said. This approach helps the speaker to feel more comfortable in sharing information.

Paraphrasing is a powerful listening skill that validates others, builds trust, and invites deeper levels of disclosure. A paraphrase restates the message that was communicated in order to clarify and confirm an accurate understanding of that message. For example, in the following dialogue, Mary responds to her roommate's comments regarding the cleanliness of their room without appearing defensive or minimizing the problem. In this way, the paraphrase is an attempt to understand the roommate's concern before responding to it.

Sue: I hate that our room is constantly a mess. We can't live like this! I try to keep my side of the room clean, but yours is always a mess. I want to hang out with friends here, but I can't because I don't want them to see this place!

Mary: Okay, I understand that you're feeling frustrated with our room and the way it looks, and you're even embarrassed to have friends here because you don't want them to think you're sloppy. Am I hearing you right?

This paraphrase invites Sue to elaborate on her frustration because Mary has neither become defensive nor has she discounted Sue's concern. At this point, Mary is simply listening and gaining a better understanding of the issue. Thus, the paraphrase ensures an accurate understanding of the situation, maintains a peaceful interaction, and affirms Sue that she has been heard before moving to the problem-solving phase of the conversation.

Probing is the third skill that facilitates active listening. In order to understand the ideas, opinions, and perspectives of others, a listener may need information beyond that which the speaker has already provided. A good question is often the catalyst to an information-rich response. Open-ended questions lead to a deeper understanding of the issues at hand because they stimulate reflective thinking and can be used to identify underlying assumptions. Once an accurate paraphrase has been communicated, probing questions can be used to solicit more specific, useful, or otherwise relevant information. Returning to the example of the messy roommate situation, Mary's response might include some of the following probing questions:

- What do you consider the messiest parts of our room?

- When were you thinking of having friends over?

- What are some realistic expectations for both of us?

- How can I be more sensitive to you in the future?

- What do you need from me right now?

These questions can be used to address issues and create meaningful dialogue. Instead of avoiding difficult issues, probing questions address them directly. Additionally, they validate the speaker by showing genuine interest or concern on behalf of the listener.

Probing with *open-ended questions* is an excellent way to gather information about someone's priorities, beliefs, and concerns because you give the respondent complete control over the content of his or her response. The material on which the respondent chooses to focus is likely the material most pressing or important to that person. Open-ended questions often begin with the words *how, what,* or *why.* Examples may include "What motivates you?" or "How could this process have been improved?" Open-ended questions can also come in the form of an invitation for the speaker to provide more detail. For instance, one might begin with "Describe for me . . ." or "Tell me in your own words . . .".

Hypothetical questions give insight into the state of mind of the speaker as well. These types of questions allow you to discover the nuanced thought process of your respondent and/or his or her comfort level with a given skill. Respectively, examples may include "Suppose you were the project manager on this task. How would you proceed?" or "If I were to give you the lesson plans, would you feel confident teaching the class tomorrow morning?"

Unlike the types of questions that we have discussed thus far, *closed-ended questions* aim to gather specific information, facts, or details. The range of responses available to your question's recipient is quite small, and his or her answer is likely to be short and to the point. Examples of closed-ended questions include "Did Kevin complete the spreadsheet for the meeting?" or "What is the fastest route to 6th Avenue?"

Finally, *forced-choice* questions call upon the respondent to make a choice. The answer to one of these questions will demonstrate the respondent's priorities and may guide a decision about how to move forward in a given scenario. Consider the following example: "The printing company is wondering whether or not it should go ahead and ship the signs with the typo. Would you rather the signs arrive on time, or that they are printed accurately?" Forced-choice questions are also frequently used in a negotiation if one is trying to limit the other person's options.

While the previous types of questions can all be productive within certain discussions, the following, however, are not. Leading questions, loaded questions, and multiple questions asked in rapid fire make it challenging for a recipient to respond productively. Instead, recipients are likely to feel challenged, intimidated, and confused. Leading and loaded questions often use harsh language and make unflattering assumptions in order to embed an accusation within a question. An example may be "Do you always pawn off your work onto other people?" or "How long have you been wasting the company's time dealing with personal issues at work?" Obviously, questions like these will be perceived negatively by the recipient and have the potential to compromise trust and goodwill in the relationship. It is rarely beneficial to make enemies, so questions should not be used as weapons.

Multiple questions refers to a string of questions asked in rapid progression that, while they may be related to the subject at hand, confuse and disorient the recipient. The following is an example of multiple questions: "How could the team have missed the deadline, and how do you know, and what are the consequences that we now face, and did you notify everyone, and who was supposed to have been keeping track of this?" By the end of this five-question series, it would be difficult for the responder to decide where to begin or to which question the asker truly wants an answer. Stressful situations can instigate the use of multiple questions. Therefore, when intensity mounts, it is helpful for members to slow down their speech and make discrete, productive, and answerable questions.

Assertiveness

Assertiveness is the ability to express oneself directly and honestly without disrespecting or dishonoring another person. Assertive people are able to stand up for themselves and communicate their ideas firmly without bullying, patronizing, or manipulating others. Because group discussions can move quickly, teams frequently arrive at conclusions that are not well thought out or supported. Thus, it is important that members speak up either to promote other perspectives or to challenge ideas that are ill-conceived. Assertive members, therefore, are actively engaged in group discussions and avoid the extremes of being either too passive or too aggressive.

Baney (2004) suggests that assertiveness can best be expressed by including the following three components: I think, I feel, I want. The first step in this assertiveness formula is to describe one's thoughts about a particular situation. For example, a member of the team is often late for meetings, so the project leader might say something like: "I've noticed that you've been late to most of our recent meetings." Next, the leader describes his or her feelings about the situation: "It's frustrating to be interrupted when you arrive, and I never know if I should stop and bring you up to speed." Finally, the assertive person would make a respectful request: "Do you think you could make it a priority to arrive on time from here on out?" This interchange shows respect for the other person but also values one's own needs. According to the social style framework, drivers and expressives do much better at advocating their positions than do analytics or amiables.

When making a point in a group setting, especially when responding to a particularly complex or important set of questions, assertive communicators pay attention to the introduction and conclusion of their comments. To start, a brief overview of their position will let others know what to expect. For example, an explanation of one's position may begin with "I'd like to discuss a few key areas where I think that the team could have been more organized." At the end of the comments, a concise summary can be given to reinforce the main ideas. Returning to the example at hand, a person might end his or her comments with "and I believe that these were the problem areas that led to the poor performance of our team." Opening and closing with clarity are useful practices that reinforce effective communication.

It is often beneficial to provide specific examples or anecdotes to give texture and nuanced understanding. Some people are more likely to remember interesting statistics or quotes, for example, than general concepts. Memorable stories or illustrations not only reinforce the main concepts, they also help listeners remember the main concepts. In addition, supporting comments with data and examples not only makes the argument more interesting and informative, but also credible. However, there is a difference between this tactic and attempting to establish credibility by overusing confusing jargon that others do not understand. This can alienate others and decrease their desire to engage in meaningful dialogue.

At times, strong, assertive statements will provoke negative responses or questions from others. As discussed, an initial overview at the beginning of a response can be a useful tool in rephrasing and perhaps softening the nature of the question. For this reason, this strategy is an excellent one to employ when asked a leading or loaded question. If faced with multiple questions, the speaker can slow down the pace of the conversation by calling attention to the multitude of questions and acknowledging the desire to answer the questions one at a time. For example, an appropriate response to a hostile barrage of questions might be, "You clearly have a lot on your mind and are looking for some clarity. Let me see if I can explain my position, beginning with your first question." Finally, it is perfectly acceptable to acknowledge feeling ill-prepared or uncomfortable answering a question and, instead, choose not to respond at that particular time. For example, if one team member pushes another team member into making a commitment about a certain problem, he or she might need to say something like "There are several aspects of this situation about which I know very little, and I do not want to speculate. Can you give me a few days to think about it and get back to you?" In that way, he or she can buy time and formulate a more thoughtful response.

CENTRALIZED VERSUS DECENTRALIZED COMMUNICATION

Group researchers have observed that one of the most important features of group communication is the level of centralization (Brown & Miller, 2000). When one or two members do most of the talking and comments are routinely directed toward these members specifically, the group is said to have a centralized communication structure (Huang & Cummings, 2011). Conversely, when groups exhibit more balance in terms of who speaks and with what frequency, the group has a decentralized communication structure. In a decentralized structure, members engage in both advocacy (proposing their own views) and inquiry (exploring the views of others). Of course, due to logistical and time constraints on any given meeting, not everyone can be expected to comment on every topic. In larger groups, it can be very easy to situate oneself on the periphery and become marginally involved. In smaller groups, it is more difficult to be anonymous, and members may choose to confront those who are consistently not speaking up. Nonetheless, who speaks, how often they speak, and to whom they speak are each important characteristics of communication structure. The degree of communication centrality within a given group is influenced by the level of complexity of the group's task as well as the characteristics of individual group members.

Groups tend to adopt a more centralized communication structure if the task is relatively simple and become more decentralized as the tasks become more complex (Brown & Miller, 2000). This trend is due to the fact that task uncertainty and ambiguity lead to wider participation and a more open exchange of information. Put another way, complex tasks require cognitive flexibility and open discussions in order to thoroughly understand the issues and to make well-reasoned decisions (Roy, 2001). Relatively straightforward tasks, on the other hand, are conducive to one or two people directing the discussion and coordinating the efforts of the group. Simpler tasks benefit from the efficiency of centralized communication, allowing group discussions to be more organized, efficient, and concrete.

In addition to task complexity, individual member characteristics influence the communication structure of the group. Some members speak often and with confidence, while others tend to be more hesitant. Individual member traits such as interpersonal dominance, perceived competence, and commitment to the group's task all serve to influence the degree of centrality in group communication. People with high interpersonal dominance have a strong need to be in control. Even if they are not the designated leader, they may attempt to take charge and direct the group. When members acquiesce and allow plans and meetings to be controlled by their dominant teammates, the communication becomes centralized. But sometimes members resist. When faced with dominant members, some group members form alliances or subgroups in order to create a balance of power and, thus, ensure a decentralized communication pattern where everyone's voice is heard.

During the "forming" stage of group development, members assess one another's knowledge, skills, and competencies. This is done partly to see how they might compare with their new teammates, but it is also done with the intent of taking inventory of the group's resources. Those who are perceived as competent and who possess important abilities are allotted greater amounts of influence over the decisions, direction, and dynamics of the group. However, the criteria used in this assessment are not always related to the task at hand. Sometimes members are given status based upon characteristics such as gender, physical attractiveness, education level, or professional success. For example, when medical doctors are given too much status while nurses or other health care professionals are marginalized, patient safety is compromised (Lingard et al., 2004). As a result, the health care industry has gone to great lengths to improve the quality of communication on health care teams (Brock, Abu-Rish, Chiu, Hammer, Wilson, Vorvick, Blondon, Schaad, Liner, & Zierler, 2013).

Once a member is perceived to have high levels of competence, regardless of the reasoning behind this perception, and is granted status in the group, members will naturally direct their questions and comments to him or her. Members who perceive *themselves* as having competence are also more likely to speak up in discussions. Interestingly, there is a slight tendency for men to overestimate their knowledge and abilities (Lemme, 2006), possibly explaining why men tend to be more frequent contributors in mixed-gender groups (Dindia & Canary, 2006; Krolokke & Sorensen, 2006).

Commitment to the group's tasks and goals will also affect the level of member engagement. Highly motivated members will tend to be more active and contribute more frequently to discussions. They are more invested in the group's success, and will subsequently seek to be involved in major decisions. At the same time, there may certainly be members who are very committed to the task but withhold their comments and ideas from conversations. In these cases, other personal or circumstantial variables have intervened to reduce their perceived involvement. In order to establish balanced communication within the team, leaders have to figure out the reasons for poor participation and help low talkers become more active.

As group members interact, each establishes his or her place in the group relative to other members. A systems view of groups suggests that individual communication styles will depend upon the particular group composition within which members find themselves. For example, a dominant member might take over if there are no other dominant members in the group. As that member exerts control, submissive or passive members become more passive, in turn encouraging the dominant member to become even more dominant. Each member reacts to others in a reciprocal fashion. If there are a number of dominant members in a group, control and management of the group may be shared. Similarly, if no particular person has a great deal of competence in a given area, a member with moderate competence will likely be forced to become an active participant. The assessment of one's own competence is related to the perceived competence of other members. The same holds true for commitment to the group's task. If nobody is passionate about the goal or interested in taking charge, a member who normally does not take a leadership role might find him or herself doing just that. Each group has a unique configuration that influences how people act, interact, and communicate with others in that particular group. For this reason, the tasks and interpersonal roles that people fill will vary with each new group they experience.

The process of communication is complex and highly idiosyncratic. Different people can hear the same message but have completely different interpretations. The practice of reflection can help group members slow down the interpretation and evaluation of messages to improve the accuracy of understanding and thoughtfulness of responses. In addition, certain listening skills (posture, paraphrasing, and probing) can increase the likelihood that accurate understanding is taking place.

Group members can also learn to express themselves more intentionally. They can become more aware of how they are communicating observations, thoughts, feelings, or needs. Members can provide the data and reasoning that led to certain conclusions. In addition, members can enhance their ability to communicate by avoiding mixed messages and becoming more assertive. Assertiveness is a form of communication that respects the opinions of others while directly stating one's own thoughts and perspectives.

Effective communication requires members to suspend their assumptions and judgments of others in order to stay open to new ideas. Members can learn to minimize their reactivity even when dialogue becomes spirited or difficult. In the most effective groups, members feel comfortable to freely express their views and engage in a balanced level of participation. When this happens, communication contributes to the effectiveness and efficiency of group processing and team success.

VIRTUAL COMMUNICATION

Virtual teams bring geographically dispersed members together though electronic information and communication technologies to accomplish organizational tasks (Powell, Piccoli, & Ives, 2004). The use of technology can significantly improve team efficiency and increase productivity, but they need to be actively managed (Hertel, Geister, & Konradt, 2005). Technology has become such an integral part of organizational life that some teams never meet face to face; they only exist in a virtual environment. Virtual teams and the technology that drives them offer the following benefits: (a) team compositions that increase quality and outcomes, (b) efficiency of communication, and (c) the development of intellectual capital.

Putting the right mix of people together without regard to geographic location allows managers to maximize knowledge, skills, and abilities (Blackburn, Furst, & Rosen, 2003). These types of diverse and specialized teams are especially necessary to solve complex

organizational problems and tasks. For instance, a team of school principals and district administrators working on educational reform might be able to benefit from the experience and knowledge of parallel committees in other states. The team might also benefit from the perspective of a curriculum specialist at a university who consults with school districts.

Virtual teaming allows diverse members to collaborate in ways that were heretofore difficult if not impossible. Virtual teams allow team members in various locations to interact without the need for face-to-face (F2F) meetings. Scheduling and attending meetings may be easier when workers can stay at their own desk (wherever that may be) and participate in virtual meetings instead of flying in from various places around the world to meet in a central location. Since physical spaces and other arrangements such as travel and accommodations are not necessary, organizations can save both time and money. While virtual meetings may not be as efficient as F2F meetings (Levenson & Cohen, 2003), the financial and logistical benefits are attractive. Without the benefit of nonverbal clues, group communication can be ambiguous and cohesion can be difficult to build. These obstacles, however, can be overcome by effective leadership.

Improved Knowledge-Sharing

When geographical obstacles are removed, teams have access to subject matter experts from all over the globe. But those experts might live in different time zones and have technological limitations that prevent them from engaging in virtual meetings. Knowledge management systems assist members in capturing, storing, and cataloguing what they know so that others can access that knowledge and experience. Knowledge-sharing links team members together through a virtual repository of expertise. For example, Proctor and Gamble (P&G) has an electronic network that links 900 factories and 17 product development centers in 73 countries. In the past, it was difficult to know what new products were being developed in different locations, centers, and departments around the world. To address this issue, P&G purchased collaborative knowledge-sharing software that permits product developers to search a database of 200,000 existing product designs to see if a similar design or process already exists in another part of the company. As a result, the time it takes to develop new products has been reduced by 50% (Ante, 2001).

Buckman Labs, a chemical manufacturing company, has effectively pooled the expertise of 1,400 employees in over 90 nations through an electronic knowledge base (Buckman, 2004). For example, when one of its customers has an outbreak of a bacterial contamination that threatens production in a paper mill in Brazil, the local Buckman engineer in that part of the world can access the company knowledge base for possible solutions based upon the knowledge and experiences of engineers at other locations. In this way, problems can be solved more quickly and effectively than when field offices operate independently from one another. This type of quality customer service earned Buckman Labs the 2005 MAKE Award (Most Admired Knowledge Enterprise) from a panel of leading knowledge management experts.

Inherent Problems

Virtual teams are not without their problems; they tend to be abstract and ambiguous, and, by their nature, are challenging to manage. Davis (2004) found that problems within virtual teams take longer to identify and solutions longer to implement. The distance inherent in virtual teams may serve to (a) amplify dysfunction, (b) dilute leadership, and (c) weaken human relations and team processes. Virtual teams can be especially difficult to manage in terms of goal definition, task distribution, coordination, and member motivation.

Teamwork requires interdependence. Members need to have a level of trust that their teammates are equally committed to the goals of the group and will do their part to achieve those goals (Aubert & Kelsey, 2003). In organizational contexts, trust is built by assessing the ability, benevolence, and integrity of other group members (Mayer, Davis, & Schoorman, 1995). In virtual groups the lack of face-to-face interaction makes it difficult to carry out this assessment. Therefore, virtual teams struggle to gain a level of trust that maximizes group potential. When group members interact in person, they are able to observe one another and draw conclusions about a number of variables including intellectual ability, past experiences, interpersonal style, and personality type. Virtual members have less information from which to make assessments. Thus, virtual environments can be more tenuous and less trusting (Gibson & Manuel, 2003).

In addition to developing trust, virtual groups may also have a difficult time creating a shared vision. Shared vision includes not only an understanding of the group's goal but also a shared commitment to achieving it. In a virtual environment, it can be difficult to assess commitment levels. Because virtual members typically interact less frequently and with less perceptual richness, they do not have the opportunity to observe interpersonal characteristics such as vocal tone, body language, and facial expressions. Thus, it is difficult to determine who is invested in the success of the group.

Communication Challenges

Communication is more of a challenge in virtual teams than in F2F teams (Martins, Gilson, & Maynard, 2004). Since trust is difficult to achieve, members are more reluctant to express their opinions in virtual discussions (Baltes, Dickson, Sherman, Bauer, & LaGanke, 2002). Contributions in a virtual environment lack the nonverbal and social context to understand others accurately and to be understood. Teams take longer to make decisions and arrive at a shared understanding. In an F2F meeting, an idea can be acknowledged and agreed upon

through nods, smiles, or verbal responses. Puzzled looks, shrugs, and raised eyebrows signal a lack of understanding and a request for more information. Even the most sophisticated computer-mediated communication channels are not able to capture the richness of F2F exchanges (Driskell, Radtke, & Salas, 2003).

Obviously, it is more difficult to communicate complex information by phone or e-mail than it is in person. Even video conferencing has its limitations. For example, consider the experience of going to a college football game or hearing an orchestra perform a symphony. Live action includes the sights, smells, sounds, and various intangibles that cannot easily be put into words. Even watching a game or musical performance on TV does not capture all the details of the experience. Listening on the radio or reading a *New York Times* review does even begin to convey the nuances of a live performance. Likewise, virtual environments are limited in capturing all the detail and "feel" of F2F meetings.

Virtual teams, by nature, tend to be more diverse than F2F teams since they often span multiple geographic locations. Greater geographical distances can translate into differences in regional, national, and organizational cultures. Diversity introduces the potential for increased creativity and problem-solving, but it also creates a context for miscommunication and misunderstanding. Therefore, in addition to the challenges noted above, virtual teams also have to contend with the lack of a common set of assumptions and social norms that facilitate effective communication (Hinds & Weisband, 2003). Members may not even be communicating in their native language. Yet even with a common language, different words and phrases have different meanings from culture to culture. It is easy to see that the potential for miscommunication and misunderstanding is great.

LEADERSHIP IN ACTION

In many team discussions, there is too much talking and not enough listening. To test this hypothesis, try monitoring your next interaction with friends, family, or colleagues. People are often more interested in delivering a message than receiving one. This is certainly true in meetings where emotions are running high. What happened the last time you had a disagreement with someone or were in a tense or stressful situation? Why did your voice rise in volume and pitch? Why did your words hasten? It was probably because you wanted to make sure you got your point across before it was too late. This chapter emphasizes the fact that communication is critical when it comes to leading people, working in teams, and facilitating interpersonal dynamics.

Team leaders can model active listening and manage the dialogue so that understanding takes place and everyone feels heard. It is amazing how much can be accomplished when members are invited to participate and feel validated when they do so. Because leaders want to encourage a high standard on clear, concise, and well-supported dialogue, they might need to push members to explain their position and to develop their ideas more completely. While leaders will have their own position on various subjects, they should not discount the value of open dialogue or minimize the contributions of others. Effective communication involves members verbalizing their ideas clearly *and* listening carefully to the ideas of others in order to create a fertile environment for understanding, exploration, and innovation.

So, the next time members are locking horns with one another, try using an engaged posture, probing questions, and paraphrases to help them explain their perspectives and arrive at a mutual understanding. Once all the information is on the table and understood by the team, members will be closer than they originally thought. This nuanced and challenging skill set can be difficult to master, but with conscientious practice and risk-taking, it can be learned. And there is no better time or place to hone one's communication skills than when working on a team.

KEY TERMS

Self-enhancement   97
SOLER   98

Advocacy   102
Inquiry   102

DISCUSSION QUESTIONS

1. Name and describe the eight GDOS categories of verbal communication. Give an example of each.

2. Compare and contrast verbal versus nonverbal communication.

3. What impact does nonverbal communication have on a conversation? What are some examples of nonverbal cues?

4. Name and describe the SOLER acronym. What is this communication strategy designed to do?

5. Recall a time when you either misunderstood a message or were misunderstood in a group atmosphere. What were the repercussions?

6. What are the three skills of active listening? How can you apply these in group situations?

7. Describe the difference between advocacy and inquiry. Create three examples of each.

8. What are the benefits and challenges of virtual teams? As a leader, how would you address some of the inherent challenges?

GROUP ACTIVITIES

EXERCISE 5.1 THE OLD RUMOR MILL

We have all played "Telephone." This exercise is designed to illustrate distortions that can occur as information is relayed from one person to another.

The instructor enlists the help of six volunteers. The rest of the students remain to act as process observers. Five of the six volunteers are asked to leave the classroom so they can't hear the class discussion. One remains in the room with the instructor and the observers.

The instructor reads an "accident report" (or a detailed account of an event) to the first volunteer. One of the volunteers who is waiting outside the room comes back in the room and the first volunteer reports the details of the story to him or her. The process observers record what information was added to the original story, what information was left out of the original story, and what information was distorted.

A third volunteer returns to the classroom and the second repeats the story that was reported from the first volunteer. Again, the process observers write down what was added, deleted, or distorted. The process is repeated until all the volunteers are back in the room. The last volunteer will write the details of the event on the board. Compare that version with the original version.

Class observers should report their observations and identify where the message went awry.

EXERCISE 5.2 HIGH TALKER/LOW TALKER EXERCISE

Place yourselves into one of two similar-sized groups: high talkers (people who are more expressive) and low talkers (people who are quieter). Make sure that everyone agrees with who is in which group (some high talkers do not see themselves as high talkers, and vice versa). Adjust groups accordingly and form a circle with the low talkers in the middle and the high talkers in the outside circle. *Note: high talkers and low talkers are just labels—one group is not better than the other.*

The goal of this exercise is for low talkers and high talkers to gain a better understanding of one another's experience. When one group is talking (the group in the fishbowl or inner circle) the other group (the group on the outside of the circle) is to remain quiet.

Ask the low talkers the following questions:

- What is it like to be a low-talking member of this class?

- What would you like the high talkers to know about what it is like to be a low talker in this class?

- Have the high talkers paraphrase what they heard. Then have the low talkers either confirm or clarify.

Have students switch places (the high talkers are now in the fish bowl and the low talkers are on the outside of the circle). Remind the low talkers that they cannot speak while they are on the outside.

Ask the high talkers the following questions:

- What was it like for you not to be able to speak?

- What did you hear the low talkers say about their experiences as low talkers?

- What would you like the low talkers to know about what it is like to be a high talker in this class?

- Have the low talkers paraphrase what they heard. Then have the high talkers either confirm or clarify.

After everyone has returned to his or her original seat, discuss what you learned from this experience.

CASE 5.2: ENEMY LINES AND FRIENDLY FIRE

It's the third week of the semester and you have met with your class project team several times. You've already noticed that two of your teammates, Sam and Alex, seem to be very friendly with each other. On e-mails, texts, and in person, this duo strikes you as fun, light-hearted, and occasionally flirtatious. After the next team meeting, Sam and Alex are the last two people left in the meeting room. As they are walking out the door, Sam turns to Alex and says, "Hey, Alex, I really enjoyed getting to know you these last couple of weeks. With Homecoming next weekend, I'd love to hang out and grab a bite to eat before we hit some of the parties together." After an awkward silence, Alex turns to Sam and says, "Gosh, Sam. That's so sweet. I'm not sure if my roommate has anything planned for us, but let me check and see. I'll shoot you an e-mail."

The e-mail from Alex never comes. Sam doesn't know what to think, but feels angry and hurt that Alex didn't follow through. At the next meeting, Sam pulls up a chair next to Alex and says, "Hey, what's up? I never heard from you." Alex curtly snips, "Yeah, I can't make it. It's not going to work out," just as the meeting was beginning.

During the meeting, Alex withdraws and takes an aloof posture. Sam is visibly agitated and very critical of everyone else's contributions. The two have spread a negative dynamic over the team. You, as team leader, pull Sam aside during the break and say, "Hey, Sam, I've noticed that you're not yourself today. What's going on?"

- *Using active listening skills from this chapter, what would you do to find out the source of the tension between Sam and Alex that has affected the team? Please write out a hypothetical conversation that might follow.*

- *If you were Alex, how could you have been more assertive in setting boundaries between work relationships and potentially romantic ones?*

CHAPTER 6

Decision Making

Decisions are continuously being made by both individuals and teams. Some decisions are made subconsciously while others are the focus of much deliberate thought and debate. Healthy discussion considers multiple perspectives and weighs their relative strengths and weaknesses before coming to a decision. This chapter is divided into three major parts. First, we discuss the way people process information. Then, we describe the typical mistakes that occur when groups make decisions. Finally, we describe a systematic model of decision making that encourages thoughtful and consistent team participation to avoid those mistakes.

CASE 6.1: WEAPONS OF MASS DESTRUCTION

In March 2003, the United States decided to launch an invasion of Iraq. At the time, fear of the possibility of Iraq having weapons of mass destruction (WMD) was widely held and received broad coverage in the media. This created a deep concern that the United States was in great danger, which buffered the president and his administration from scrutiny for the decisions they made. The perceived risk had escalated to the point that it compromised objective and critical thinking.

Though not all of the information has yet come to light, due to the fact that many records still remain sealed, there are meaningful data that suggest President George W. Bush and his cabinet fell into some of the common pitfalls of poor group decision making as they launched a decade-long war. According to the Economist *article "History's Second Draft,"*

Contrary to statements by President George W. Bush or Prime Minister Tony Blair, declassified records from both governments posted on the Web reflect an early and focused push to prepare war plans and enlist allies regardless of conflicting intelligence about Iraq's threat and the evident difficulties in garnering global support. Perhaps most revealing about today's posting on the National Security Archive's website is what is missing—any indication whatsoever from the declassified record to date that top Bush administration officials seriously considered an alternative to war. In contrast there is an extensive record of efforts to energize military planning, revise existing contingency plans, and create a new, streamlined war plan.

Some Bush officials insist the war decision was made just before the March 2003 invasion. The evidence does not support that construction. Others believe no decision was ever made. Richard Armitage, deputy secretary of state under Colin Powell, observes, "Never to my knowledge, and I'm pretty sure I'm right on this, did the President ever sit around with his advisors and say, 'Should we do this or not?' He never did it." George J. Tenet of the CIA agrees. He wrote, "There never was a serious debate that I know of within the administration about the imminence of the Iraqi threat." And again, based on conversations with colleagues, "In none of the meetings can anyone remember a discussion of the central questions. Was it wise to go to war? Was it the right thing to do?" (*Economist*, 2010)

This senior leadership team had come to believe in the presence of something that, if true, posed a catastrophic, horrifying, and unprecedented threat to America and her allies. In fact, the threat of a terrorist attack was so great that the administration overlooked contrary data that demonstrated an absence of WMDs, and that conclusion led to a decision that propelled the United States into the Iraq War. When the United States occupied Iraq and systematically searched for the WMDs and found none, the U.S. was in the position of not being able to justify an extreme act of aggression and a declaration of war.

With an influential core of determined people driving toward a single conclusion, the conditions lent themselves to a "groupthink" climate in which dissent was discouraged. If this seasoned team of subject-matter experts felt the pressure to conform to emotionally based decisions, what can everyday leaders do to ensure that the decisions their teams make are rational, evidence-based, objective, and intentional? How can they avoid similar decision-making mistakes? While the stakes will almost certainly be much lower and, therefore, easier to manage than the variables at play in the decisions leading up to the Iraq War, what can leaders do to maintain impartiality, encourage critical reflection on processes, and allow for enough consideration of questions like, "Are we making the right decision?"

Case Study Discussion Questions

1. In teams, who is ultimately responsible for making the decisions? Why?

2. If you were present in the cabinet meetings that made the decision to invade Iraq, what would you have said or done differently?

3. Other than fear, what other factors influenced the group's decision-making practices? Which do you think were the most pertinent?

4. Describe other examples involving high-stakes decision making. How do they compare to this case? How do they differ?

There are many advantages to group decision making. The collective wisdom of groups can be far superior to the knowledge and decision-making ability of a single person (Suroweicki, 2004). Groups will often have more information about any given subject than a single individual does. Furthermore, the process of group discussion and deliberation can foster critical analysis and reflection that can lead to high-quality decisions. But groups can also make terrible decisions. As a matter of fact, some very disastrous decisions, such as the U.S. decision to go to war with Iraq over the suspicion of weapons of mass destruction, have been made by groups as opposed to individuals.

INFORMATION PROCESSING

Information processing is the series of cognitive processes that make sense of incoming sensory data. Words and nonverbal cues are perceived through the five senses and ascribed meaning. This raw data are interpreted and evaluated based upon idiosyncratic as well as shared frames of reference. Past experiences, current assumptions, and the surrounding social context are used to decipher incoming messages. Argyris (1994) describes the process of perceiving and interpreting data as the Ladder of Inference, depicted below. Each step or "rung" describes how information is perceived and processed, beginning at the bottom of the ladder and moving up (Cannon & Witherspoon, 2005).

Perception and information processing occur unconsciously at the lower rungs of the ladder and become more conscious as one moves up the ladder. However, over time, repetitive patterns of processing become ingrained and automatic. For example, learning to drive a car initially requires great concentration and effort, but eventually the process becomes routine, making conscious thought no longer necessary.

Figure 6.1   Ladder of Inference

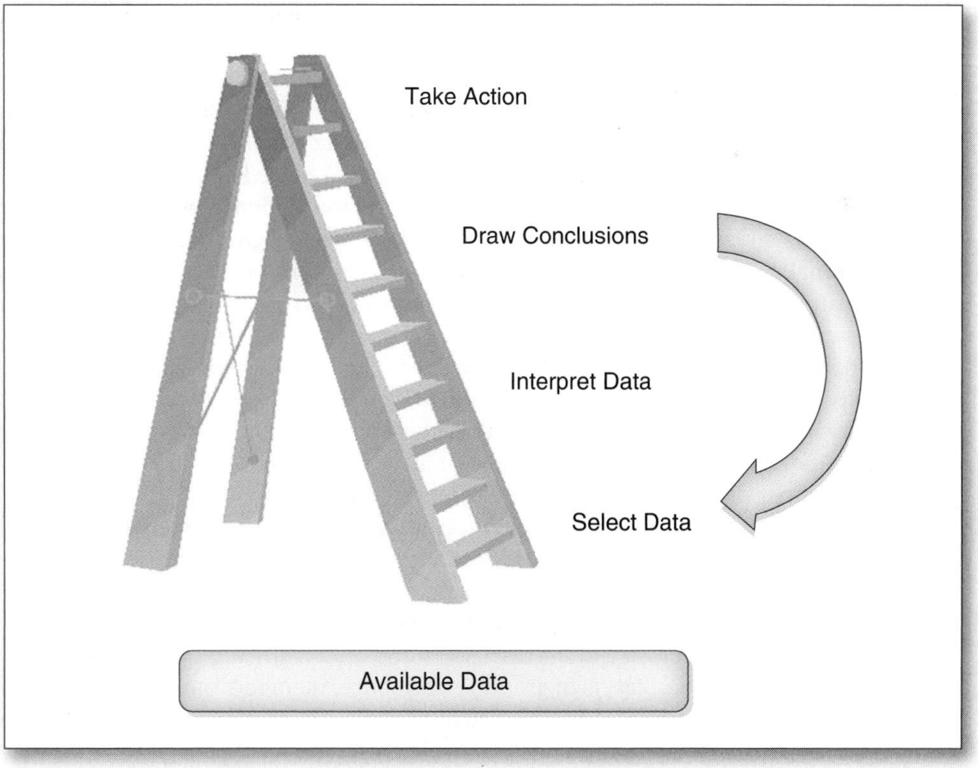

Take Action

Draw Conclusions

Interpret Data

Select Data

Available Data

In order to process incoming information quickly, individuals make assumptions and draw inferences based upon the perceptual data's similarity to past experiences. Thus, deliberate, conscious reflection is often neglected in favor of a preprogrammed response that is made in accordance with memories and tendencies associated with comparable past experiences. It would be inefficient for people to experience all new data as if it were their first time seeing, hearing, smelling, tasting, or touching that phenomenon. The benefit of this process is that people can respond quickly to stimulus without much conscious thought; the downside is that not all new experiences fit neatly into our database of previous experiences. Conscious reflection, whether done as an individual or in a group setting, is a practice that can help evaluate and revise old patterns of thinking as well as assumptions that are either outdated or limited in perspective.

Selecting Data

Human beings only have the capacity to pay attention to and process a limited amount of incoming data at one time. While some may have a greater capacity to "multitask" than others, the limit exists for all of us and requires us to select specific pieces of information or data on which to focus. For example, the first meeting of a group with a large number of participants convening in a new location will contain literally hundreds of pieces of perceptual data, including seating arrangement, lighting, room temperature, verbal messages, nonverbal messages, and interactions among members. Because there is simply too much information to attend to at the same time, we choose that which is most important to us.

The internal process of selecting information to interpret and then "present" to our conscious minds is not unlike that in which video editors engage. Although reality TV producers film hours of video footage, they air only a small percentage of the total interactions that occur among show participants, carefully selecting the pieces they wish to show the viewing audience. In the documentary *Secrets of Reality TV Revealed,* producers describe how they edit and manipulate data (scenes) in order to lead the audience to certain conclusions and make the show more entertaining. In a similar way, it might be said that people have an "internal producer" that selects, screens, edits, and interprets data. Since it is impossible to pay attention to all available data, certain pieces of information are eliminated from awareness. For the sake of continuity and stability, people tend to look for evidence to confirm expectations and assumptions. Thus, the selection of data is influenced by existing assumptions, biases, and stereotypes. This reflexive loop leads people to see what they both want and expect to see, in turn reinforcing those beliefs and making it more difficult to see things in a different light. This confirmation bias is the tendency to search for and interpret information that supports first impressions and preconceived notions.

People are also more likely to attend to information that is perceived as important. For example, if a group is having a discussion about whether or not to request a deadline extension for an existing project, some members may have strong feelings about the issue, causing them to sit up and pay close attention. Members who are ambivalent about the topic may choose not to engage in the discussion and only halfheartedly pay attention. In order to achieve the highest levels of group performance, members must continually ask themselves what they might be missing. Realizing that perception is limited and potentially flawed is the first step in opening up to new perspectives and seeing things that have yet to be discovered. Increased awareness and appropriate data selection comprise the first rung of the Ladder of Inference.

Interpreting the Data

Once data have been selected for processing, individuals must interpret that information. We interpret data by comparing the current situation to past experiences, which have been summarized and cataloged into core beliefs and assumptions called schemas (Griffith, 2004). **Schemas** are the internal dictionaries or rule books that are used to interpret incoming data quickly and efficiently. For example, a red light at an intersection is automatically interpreted as a symbol for "stop," triggering a certain response by the driver of a car. The interpreted stimulus and resulting response is deeply ingrained as a habit that requires little to no awareness or conscious attention. Similarly, group members may hear a particular word or interpret a certain nonverbal gesture as a "red light" (danger) and disengage from the conversation. Under stress, people tend to revert to the deeply embedded primal responses of fight or flight, both of which can be counterproductive to meaningful communication. When tensions are running high, group members can easily default to emotionally laden reactions instead of thoughtful, reasoned responses.

Biases, assumptions, and stereotypes include generalizations about groups and can be based upon any number of variables including gender, age, race, or geographic background. For instance, after meeting a distant relative from New York City who talks fast and is very direct, one might create an internal stereotype about all New Yorkers. Thus, future interactions with anyone associated with New York can potentially be influenced by that initial experience. The generalizations about New Yorkers, in this example, have been created prematurely and with limited data, and thus are likely to be inaccurate and unfair. Yet we do this all the time. It is all too easy to discount a person's message because of the label we have put on him or her.

Vague messages that have less concrete information to aid in interpretation are, consequently, more prone to misunderstanding. For example, if a male project leader told a female member that she was not pulling her weight in the group, she could internally respond to that statement from a variety of interpretive frameworks, including those related to the following:

- Her view of her own competence ("I know I am competent")

- Her view of leaders ("Leaders are never satisfied")

- Her view of men ("This is a typical male power play")

- Her view of the organization ("Women can't get ahead in this organization")

- Her view of other members of the group ("They're all threatened by me")

- Her view of groups in general ("I knew this would happen; I hate working in teams")

If she is not open-minded and reflective about the possible ways to interpret this statement, she may choose an interpretation that has very little to do with the intended message of the team leader. Instead of a thoughtful response or a request for more information, she might respond with a preprogrammed reaction.

If an individual is operating from an incorrect interpretation or assumption and responds accordingly, misunderstandings and interpersonal problems that hinder group functioning are likely to result. Therefore, it is important for members to be aware of their own existing schemas and to combat tendencies to make unsupported inferences. Active listening skills, which we will discuss later in the chapter, can go a long way in preventing misinterpretations and can lead to a more accurate understanding of what others are saying.

Drawing Conclusions

After a message has been interpreted, conclusions are drawn. Obviously, it is difficult to arrive at an accurate conclusion if the data have been misinterpreted. Beck (1995) has found that when inaccurate conclusions are made, the mistakes leading up to the conclusion are remarkably similar across circumstances. The following list describes common mistakes people make when receiving and responding to messages:

- *Overgeneralization:* Conclusions are based upon a limited number of past experiences. Example: "Recycling programs don't work; we tried that once before."

- *All-or-nothing thinking* (also called dichotomous or black-and-white thinking): Viewing a situation as "all-or-nothing" without considering other possibilities or recognizing that most hypotheticals exist on a continuum. Example: "We should make a decision today, or we should just forget about it."

- *Catastrophizing:* Assuming that a current negative experience will undoubtedly produce a devastating effect. Example: "I bet I failed the test; I'm probably going to fail the course and flunk out of college."

- *Personalization:* Speculating that the comments or behavior of others are related to you in some way. Example: "Bob didn't sit next to me in the meeting today. I'm sure he's mad at me. I must have said something to offend him the last time we met."

- *Emotional reasoning:* Strong feelings about an issue or a person cloud one's ability to hear other perspectives. Example: "She may have a good argument for the policy change, but I still don't trust her, and I'm not going to go along with it."

- *Mind reading:* A person attributes motives to others and speculates on what they are thinking. Example: "He was intentionally trying to hurt me by not calling last night."

These common tendencies lead to inaccurate conclusions that translate into misguided actions. It is difficult to create an effective action strategy based upon poorly formed or distorted conclusions.

A common problem in interpreting interpersonal behavior is the **fundamental attribution error**, which is an assessment of others that attributes behavior to personality traits and underestimates social context. For example, a group member named John has become quiet and disengaged because he is annoyed by the lack of structure in the group's meetings. Observing this quiet behavior and noticing a scowl on John's face, another member might make the fundamental attribution error and conclude that John is angry by nature. From then on, this observer will likely select and interpret data about John based upon that assumption, and thus confirm that bias. Other possible explanations, such as whether or not the meetings *were* in fact poorly run, or whether the individual was under some unrelated pressure for time, may not have been given enough consideration. Once judgments have been made, it can be difficult to step back and reverse the process. The fundamental attribution error is a frequent information processing mistake that creates blind spots in perception and misunderstandings in communication.

Taking Action

When a verbal message is received, nonverbal cues and assumptions are used to interpret and evaluate it. Then, the receiver takes action or responds to the message. No two people will process information in exactly the same way. In group situations, leaders increase the level of mutual understanding by regularly summarizing what has been said and agreed upon. Another strategy is to ask group members to reflect upon the content of a discussion. This approach serves the same purpose as the summary but involves the perception of more members of the group instead of relying solely on the leader's understanding. Many groups record minutes to document the details of a discussion; those minutes serve to reduce the ever-present potential for future misunderstandings and the need to rehash old discussions. Good minutes record not only the decisions themselves, but also the reasons and support for those decisions.

Boardroom scenes in *The Apprentice* are often quite interesting as Donald Trump asks project leaders and team members to explain their actions. He is basically asking them to describe their reasoning: What data or information did they use to make sense of the challenge given to them? How did they interpret that data? What conclusions did they draw that led to the actions they took? This process is known as "moving down" the Ladder of Inference and helps explain how a person or group approached a problem or dilemma. Once the thinking process is made transparent, individual and group behavior make more sense. It also identifies where the reasoning may have been inaccurate or short-sighted. For example, in the first challenge of season one, Trump asked the two teams to sell lemonade on the streets of New York. The women's team focused on the fact that location would be important (select data). In addition, the members chose Midtown Manhattan, where a lot of men would be present who would potentially be attracted to the women selling the lemonade (interpret data). Finally, they set a reasonable price point of $5.00 per glass but included a kiss with the purchase, which they thought would win over customers (draw conclusions). They executed their strategy (take action) and, in the end, beat the men's team by a margin of 3 to 1. The men, in contrast, chose a poor location and, in desperation, tried to sell glasses of lemonade for $1,000 each. Since this strategy did not have any data or logic to support it, it was doomed to fail. While some teams capitalize on the collective wisdom of the group, others make very poor decisions. How can such smart and competent people can make such bad decisions?

COMMON DECISION-MAKING MISTAKES

Groupthink is one of the most common decision-making problems in groups. According to Janus (1982), groupthink is "a mode of thinking that people engage in when they are deeply involved in a cohesive ingroup, when the members' striving for unanimity override their motivation to realistically appraise alternative courses of actions" (p. 9). Thus, groupthink often occurs in highly cohesive groups that have strong norms of cooperation and agreement. Decisions are initiated by high-status, influential members who generate momentum for a certain position. Because it is frowned upon to question the direction of the group, members are reluctant to speak up. In addition to highly cohesive groups, teams that are under pressure to make quick decisions can also fall prey to groupthink; a few individuals can promote a certain idea and then pressure others to agree for the sake of time and expediency.

When groups make decisions, it is easy for them to demonstrate **overconfidence** in their conclusions (Kerr & Tindale, 2004). Without fully considering the depth or complexity of the problems that they are trying to solve, groups can draw superficial and ill-conceived conclusions. Even when groups are initially unsure of the decisions they make, they become more confident over time. After they have made a decision and initiated a course of events, they can be overly committed to their plan and unwilling to acknowledge the possibility that they made a mistake.

Another common problem in group decision making is the tendency of groups to make **premature decisions.** When faced with a decision, groups often consider only a few options before making their decision. For example, in a class where students are asked to identify a problem on campus they would like to address during the semester, teams often consider only a handful of options before making a decision. When forced to use a structured brainstorming process in which each individual takes 10 minutes to create a list of ideas before combining them into a larger list, teams generate 50 to 60 unique ideas instead of a mere 5 or 6. Another problem with premature decision making is that groups rarely have a deep and nuanced understanding of the issues upon which they are deciding. They simply have not had enough time to consider how the issues are embedded in larger organizational and institutional contexts.

Confirmation bias occurs when members look for information to confirm a decision that, for the most part, has already been made (Nickerson, 1998). Group decisions are often made on an emotional level and only afterward do members look for data or reasoning to support their decision. This happens more frequently than we might care to admit. When confronted with a decision, group members have an initial reaction or response that leads to a potentially short-sighted decision. After coming to a conclusion, members then look for evidence to justify their positions. This common practice can greatly reduce the overall quality of decisions that are made by a group. A similar problem is when members are reluctant to voice unique information, as seen in the following decision-making mistake.

Shared information bias is the tendency of group members to spend most of their time discussing information that is already known by most members (Baker, 2010; Boos, Schauenburg, Strack, & Belz, 2013). In other words, it is easier for members to discuss information that most people already agree upon than it is to bring a new and novel perspective to the discussion. In some cases, members may not feel that what they know is important and, therefore, are reluctant to contribute. Another possible deterrent to speaking up is the possibility that a member's perspective will be challenged by the group. In order to avoid the discomfort of being an outlier, they remain silent. In either situation, potentially important information is not considered in the decision-making process.

Group polarization is the tendency for groups to make more extreme decisions than any individual member of the group would make. When a certain idea or concept starts to gain momentum in a group discussion, it can take on a life of its own. It can grow to the point that no member would endorse it individually, but collectively, it appears that the group fully supports it. Examples of this dynamic are abundant in today's political landscape. During budget talks, Republicans and Democrats become more entrenched in their positions and are unable to arrive at a compromise with one another. When a decision is time-sensitive and under pressure, movement toward the extremes can be difficult to slow down; someone has to be willing to break ranks and suggest that perhaps the group has gone a bit too fast and too far on any given decision. While groups benefit greatly from such a deviant role, not many individuals are willing to play it.

At times, groups make decisions that produce ineffective or adverse results. But even as mounting evidence confirms a poor decision, groups can experience an escalation of commitment to that course of action (Moser, Wolff, & Kraft, 2013). Group decisions often require the investment of resources such as time, money, and effort in order to achieve the desired results. When the results are not forthcoming, groups can be reluctant to "cut their losses" and choose another course of action. Instead, they "double down" and decide to put more resources into a failing proposition. Gambling in the face of significant losses, continued investment in long-term conflicts such as the Vietnam War, and the subprime mortgage crisis that produced the global recession of 2008 are all examples of an escalation of commitment. The next section describes a structured framework that can help groups avoid making bad decisions.

FUNCTIONAL MODEL OF DECISION MAKING

In light of the potential for groups to make poor decisions, a functional model of decision making allows groups to be more deliberate, thorough, and systematic in the decisions they make (Forsyth, 2006). Many of the shortcomings of group decision making can be addressed by establishing a system that challenges premature consensus and encourages diverse perspectives. Poor decisions can be avoided by implementing a structured decision-making process that includes orientation, discussion, decision rule, and implementation.

Orientation

When groups are given a problem to solve, there is a strong temptation to start proposing various solutions before appropriately defining the problem and planning the decision-making process. The orientation phase of group decision making begins with a thorough understanding of the problem to be solved. Group members are well advised to understand the task at hand from multiple perspectives before launching into problem-solving mode. Teams can waste a lot of time trying to solve poorly understood problems. Characteristics of a good solution should be identified and posted in a public place during the orientation process. For example, students who want to improve the dorm food on campus might need to find a solution that (a) students approve, (b) won't cost more money for the school, (c) the administration would be willing to embrace, and (d) the dining staff are capable of implementing. Those criteria need to be identified before students start brainstorming ideas about the types of food they want to see in the cafeteria, or a lot of time could be wasted.

In addition to thoroughly understanding the problem to be solved, effective groups create a process for making decisions. For example, they might set aside a specific amount of time to collect data about the problem and then meet to discuss that information. Then, they might have a session devoted to brainstorming possible solutions and identifying their three best options that address the problem. After more research on those three options, the team leader might call for a vote. Once a decision is made, the group might spend time creating a detailed implementation strategy. This type of orientation schedule helps everyone know what is expected and how the group is going to use its time.

Discussion

Discussion allows members to voice their perspectives and critically evaluate options. These conversations are a form of critical reflection in which members analyze issues and weigh the pros and cons of various decisions. Educational reformer and philosopher John Dewey described reflective thought as "active, persistent, and careful consideration of any belief or supposed form of knowledge in the light of the grounds that support it, and the further conclusions to which it tends" (1910, p. 6). In this way, the practice of reflection can help group members monitor their assumptions and critically evaluate the decisions they are considering (Griffith & Frieden, 2000).

Reflective discussions identify the facts, formulas, and theories that are relevant for supporting existing positions and for solving complex and ill-defined problems (King & Kitchener, 1994). The highest level of reflective thinking assumes that knowledge is gained from a variety of sources and is understood in relationship to a specific context. While it may be impossible to arrive at a perfect understanding of a given issue, judgments based upon conceptual soundness, empirical justification, or personal experience are a good starting place. Effective groups are receptive to a multitude of options and perspectives, but are clear about the criteria upon which they base their decisions and actions. The process of reflective discussion accomplishes the following objectives:

- To consider multiple perspectives

- To identify the assumptions for one's interpretations

- To critique the accuracy of and evidence for one's conclusions

- To evaluate the effectiveness of one's actions

Individuals who are not reflective may not understand how their behavior affects the group. For example, in some groups a small number of members can dominate discussions. They speak without listening and offer opinions without a deep understanding of what is being discussed.

Conversely, there are members who overanalyze and cautiously rehearse their responses before speaking out, causing them to miss the opportunity to contribute as the discussion moves on without them. Group members are unlikely to change until they become aware of their patterns of processing and participation. For this reason, reflecting on one's own communication patterns is an important practice.

Psychologist Carl Jung, whose ideas form the basis for the Myers-Briggs Type Indicator, asserted that the general way in which individuals participate in groups can be categorized into two processing styles (Barbuto, 1997). People are either introverted or extroverted. Introverts are energized by being alone and tend to process their thoughts internally. Extroverts, on the other hand, are energized by being with people and process their thoughts aloud. Introverts prefer more time before responding so they can pull their thoughts together and present coherent ideas and perspectives. Extroverts, on the other hand, prefer fast-moving and active discussions. They tend to do their reflecting verbally, and subsequently will offer ideas that may not have been thoroughly thought out or complete. Team leaders who are aware of the personality types of their members will seek to facilitate a conversational pace suited to all. In addition, they will monitor the amount of relative talk time among members, ensuring that all members, especially those who are introverted, are contributing equally to the discussion.

Senge (1990) warns against falling into the trap of making overly simplistic causal evaluations without consideration of the large, complex systems within which decisions exist. **Systems thinking** is an approach to problem-solving that encourages group members to resist a reductionist view of problems that can result in short-sighted solutions and unintended consequences. Ideas, decisions, and plans must be considered in light of the context within which they will be implemented. As Senge suggests, today's problems are often the result of yesterday's well-meaning but ill-conceived solutions. Groups are often guilty of taking action without fully considering all of their options and without understanding the consequences of their decisions. The individual and collective practices of reflection serve to slow down the communication process, consider multiple perspectives, and identify evidence for various conclusions.

Decision Rule

There are a number of ways that groups can come to a decision. Because there are dozens of decisions that need to be made on most projects, it is inefficient for the leader to bring all of them before the group. Therefore, some decisions are made by the leader without consulting the rest of the team. Of course, one of the tricky aspects of leading teams is knowing which decisions can be made alone and which need the input of others. Even if a leader has the authority and the experience to make a certain decision, seeking input from the team can build trust and commitment. Another decision-making strategy is for the leader to delegate the decision to one or more members of the group. In all of these options, the power to make the decision rests with the leader or with those whom he or she designates.

Some decisions need the full attention of the group, and thus include a full discussion and debate. After a topic has been exhausted or a designated amount of time has passed, someone may call for a vote. Parliamentary procedures such as *Robert's Rules of Order* provide a detailed and structured procedure for voting. One of the most common voting schemes that groups use to make a decision is majority rule. In this case, votes are counted and the option that has garnered the most votes wins. Majority vote could also mean that for an option to win, it must have more than 50% of all the possible votes. So, even within the concept of majority rule, there are some gray areas. The exact definition of what it takes to win should be determined at the beginning of a discussion before votes are cast.

Finally, some decisions are made by consensus. This can be a time-consuming process, as groups continue to deliberate until they find a solution with which everyone in the group can agree. For example, in most jury deliberations, the jury must come to a unanimous decision to arrive at a verdict (Poole & Dobosh, 2010). Because there are often multiple ways of viewing things, this may be a difficult goal to achieve. When juries cannot come to an agreement about the guilt or innocence of a defendant, they are known as a "hung jury" and the judge declares a mistrial. Consensus is an admirable decision-making goal but may not be realistic in all situations.

Implementation

After a decision is made, teams will often create an implementation plan to put the decision into action. This is the last phase of the functional decision-making model. Once a decision has been made, tasks can be assigned, deadlines determined, and schedules created. For example, teams might use some of the project management strategies discussed in

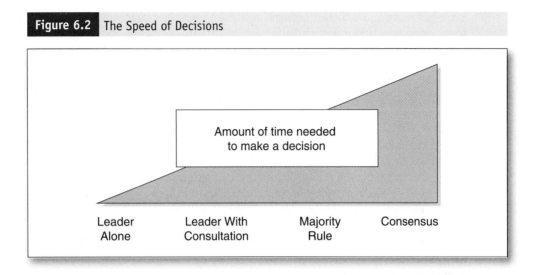

Figure 6.2 The Speed of Decisions

Amount of time needed
to make a decision

| Leader | Leader With | Majority | Consensus |
| Alone | Consultation | Rule | |

Chapter 3 to create a project plan and begin work. At this point in the process, an assessment strategy can also be created in order to measure the quality of the decision and the implementation of the solution.

INFLUENCES ON GROUP DECISIONS

The influence of powerful members and the reluctance to take a stand against the majority can compromise the collective wisdom of groups. As groups discuss options and make decisions, individual members can have tremendous influence over the direction of the group. While it can be difficult for members to question a popular idea held by the majority of the group, it is often the courage of a lone individual who is willing to challenge the status quo that saves the day. The following section will discuss the deterrents to open and balanced communication and highlight the importance of dissenting opinions.

Status and Influence

Issues of status and power are always present in group settings as members strive to influence the decisions, direction, and performance of the group (Christie & Barling, 2010). Members gain power through a number of means and use various strategies to influence others and garner support for their ideas. Social status, a concept related to power, is defined as the degree to which a group member has influence over other members of a social network (Sell, Lovaglia, Mannix, Samuelson, & Wilson, 2004). Whereas power implies force and pushing others to do something they may not want to do, group members themselves confer status upon individuals based upon an assessment of their potential value to the group (Krackhardt, 1990; Sell, Lovaglia, Mannix, Samuelson, & Wilson, 2004).

Status allocation, which can occur even before members meet for the first time, can be based upon reputation, past performance, education level, or position in the organization. Over time, status differentiation takes place and status hierarchies form. Power dynamics are most obvious in groups where there is a diversity of perspectives, open disagreement, and interpersonal conflict. Diagnosing power in groups that are homogeneous and conflict-free may be a bit more difficult, as influence strategies are typically more subtle.

So who exactly are these powerful, high-status members? In his bestselling book *The Tipping Point*, Malcolm Gladwell (2002) argues that social movements from fashion trends to attitudes about morality are instigated and perpetuated by a relatively few, yet influential, individuals. Through his analysis of phenomena such as the resurgence of Hush Puppy shoes, the influence of Paul Revere, and the spread of sexually transmitted diseases, Gladwell identifies three types of influential people: mavens, salespeople, and connectors. Mavens have specialized knowledge and information that give them credibility. Salespeople are optimistic, enthusiastic, likeable, and highly persuasive. Connectors are at the hub of communications within and among social networks. Thus, Gladwell suggests, people gain status either through (a) knowledge and reputation, (b) degree of likeability, or (c) a prominent position within communication networks.

Status is granted to those who are perceived as being competent and knowledgeable. High-status individuals are valued within organizational and team contexts because they have a reputation for getting things done (Pfeffer, 1992). When faced with important decisions or confronted by challenging obstacles, groups look to these individuals for wisdom and guidance. Krackhardt (1990) found that those with a reputation for getting things done are granted high status in organizations, and consequently are solicited for work-related advice. Furthermore, people in the study who had high status were also good at identifying others with high status. In other words, they were able to accurately assess and utilize status networks to their own advantage.

Knowledge and perceived competence aside, people who are friendly and likeable tend to have higher positions in social networks than those who are not. The reason for this is that people have a more difficult time saying no to a friend than to a stranger or to a person they don't like. This is one of the reasons why home and relationally based businesses such as Tupperware and Mary Kay Cosmetics are so successful; their marketing strategies capitalize on the importance of likability and friendships (Pfeffer, 1992). These business models rely upon friendly salespeople inviting people they know into their homes in order to present their products. Even if guests are not interested in the products, it can be enjoyable to socialize with others, and therefore relatively painless to make a small purchase in order to maintain positive social connections.

Finally, those who are at the social center of their own group and who have connections with other groups are well positioned to have high status. Being at the hub of a communications network allows one to be privy to knowledge and information that others may not have. Controlling the flow of information gives one the discretion to selectively choose which information is passed on to other members of the group. This gate-keeping role effectively establishes one's importance and ensures influence over group actions and decisions. Those who are skilled can guide the discussion in whatever direction they choose, giving them tremendous influence over group decisions and direction. Meanwhile, connections *among* groups give individuals access to a greater amount of knowledge and resources.

High-status members who have connections among multiple groups are potential power brokers who have the opportunity to create alliances and coalitions. This enables them to broker resources and negotiate solutions to complex problems. Thus, the more connections one has with other groups, the more importance and status one will have in his or her own group.

For example, one undergraduate student describes the power of social networking like this: "I am on the board of Grassroots, an umbrella service organization that connects students to other nonprofits in several different sectors (education, homelessness, hunger, etc.). It is very clear in this type of setting that those who have the highest status and respect in the group are the ones who are most involved in other service organizations around campus. This is because they are able to provide connections to other organizations and are typically the ones who have the best ideas for how to grow our organization."

Status can also be attributed to people for a number of reasons such as gender, race, physical attractiveness, socioeconomic status, occupation, and education level. These variables, known as **diffuse status characteristics,** may have little to do with the specific tasks of the team, yet they still influence how group members are perceived and judged. Take, for example, a middle-aged, male, Caucasian physician serving on a school task force charged with evaluating a school bus maintenance program. This person may know very little about vehicle maintenance or its costs, but he may be given great respect by other group members simply because he is a white, male doctor. Based on these characteristics, people assume him to be intelligent and qualified even when the task at hand lies outside of his expertise.

In contrast to diffuse characteristics, **specific status characteristics** are qualities that are directly relevant to the task or decision at hand. Returning to the bus maintenance example, a Hispanic woman in her mid-20s who works as a maintenance manager for a rental car company may be granted high status on the task force because of her specific status characteristics. This is despite her diffuse status characteristics as a young, female minority member, which can unconsciously and unfairly be judged in unflattering ways. In the world of status attribution, some people are given more status than they deserve while others are given less than they deserve. Unfortunately, those with low status can feel marginalized and detached from the group.

In contrast to low-status members, high-status members tend to speak up more and play a more active role in group discussions (Keltner, Gruenfeld, & Anderson, 2003). Active members both acquire and use their status by validating certain viewpoints, summarizing discussions, and telling others what to do (Stiles, Lyall, Knight, Ickes, Waung, Hall, & Primeau, 1997). In the presence of influential members like these, it can be intimidating to speak up and share a potentially unpopular perspective. Instead, some members just feign agreement and avoid any potential conflict.

High-status members help teams overcome inertia, make decisions, and take action. For those who wish to influence the direction of their teams, Pfeffer (1992) has identified a practical, seven-step model for applying power dynamics (p. 29):

- Decide what your goals are; what you are trying to accomplish?

- Diagnose patterns of dependence and interdependence; which individuals are influential and important in helping you achieving your goal?

- Predict what these individuals' points of view are likely to be; how will they feel about what you are trying to do?

- Determine what external power bases you will contend with; which of them will have the most influence in the decision?

- Determine your own bases of power and influence; what bases might you develop in order to gain more control over the situation?

- Decide which of the various strategies and tactics for exercising power are most appropriate; which are likely to be effective, given the situation you confront?

- Based upon the above, choose a course of action to accomplish goals and objectives.

Pressure to Conform

Group membership often requires individuals to surrender some amount of individuality in order to gain entrance and acquire the benefits associated with membership. The extent to which groups influence their members varies greatly from group to group. Some groups have rigid rules and roles for members, while others give tremendous latitude.

For members to be in good standing with their peers, they typically must conform to some concept of "normal behavior" for that particular group (Cialdini & Goldstein, 2004). And while diversity gives groups an advantage in problem-solving and creativity, conformity benefits the group by creating cohesion, predictability, and structure.

In a series of well-known experiments conducted in the 1950s, Solomon Asch gave groups of 8 to 10 college students the simple task of comparing the lengths of three lines on one card to a standard length line on another card (Asch, 1956). Simply put, students were asked to identify which of the three lines on the right was the same length as the line on the left.

Line Comparisons

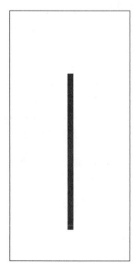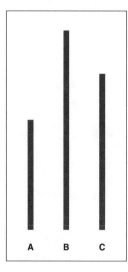

A   B   C

Even though the answer was obviously C, most students chose A or B. How could this be? The answer is in the way the experiment was set up. All but one student in the group, the real subject, were confederates instructed to give erroneous answers a majority of the time. The experimenters were interested in understanding to what degree peer pressure would affect participant responses. They found that when participants were tested individually, only 5% answered incorrectly. When tested in a group setting and exposed to a majority opinion that was incorrect, however, Asch and his colleagues were quite surprised to find that 37 out of 50 (74%) gave a wrong answer. When the majority was unanimous in its incorrect answer, subjects were even less likely to give the right answer. As subsequent studies have confirmed, it is extremely difficult for individuals to diverge from a majority opinion, especially when they are completely alone in their opposition. Furthermore, the pressure to conform is generally stronger in collectivist cultures, which place a strong emphasis on interdependence and group cohesion, than in individualistic cultures, which value autonomy and individuality (Bond & Smith, 1996).

From the classic Asch studies and others like it, social psychologists have concluded that groups have significant influence over individual members. For example, jury deliberations that determine a defendant's guilt or innocence are immensely important decisions that require consideration of all perspectives. However, 45 years of research on jury deliberation reveals that jury members followed the initial opinions of the majority 90% of the time (Devine, Clayton, Dunford, Seying, & Pryce, 2001). This evidence strongly suggests that values and norms held by a majority of group members can be difficult to resist, no matter how important the task or impactful the decision.

Divergent Perspectives

It is all too often that groups miss out on the very best ideas and fail to prevent major decision-making catastrophes because members decide not to voice their insights or objections for fear of being rejected, ridiculed, or reprimanded by the group. The effectiveness of groups is dependent, in part, on the ability of group members to banter and vigorously discuss various ideas and strategies. When members hold back or avoid sharing their perspective, the potential synergy of the group is compromised. If a group member has an opinion on an issue, he or she should be able to offer it to the group with confidence.

In an interview published by the *Harvard Business Review,* J. Richard Hackman (2009) emphasized the need to have at least one "designated deviant" in every group (p. 1). A designated deviant is a person who is assigned the role of "devil's advocate" and vigilantly questions popular assumptions, challenges the status quo, and ensures that all perspectives are considered before a decision is made. According to Hackman, "[The designated deviant's] observations can open up creative discussion—but they also raise others' anxiety level. People may feel compelled to crack down . . . maybe even knock him off the team. Don't let that happen: if you lose your deviant, your team can become mediocre" (p. 1). As long as the designated deviant is earnest in his or her efforts to question the ongoing discussions and decisions of the team, he or she is a tremendous benefit. But because this can be a tiring role to play, astute leaders should support, protect, encourage, and empower their deviant.

LEADERSHIP IN ACTION

When working in teams, you will find that the very best of human nature comes out, as well as the very worst, especially when difficult decisions have to be made. When you reach a difficult situation or challenge, automatic responses such as flaring tempers, judgmental attitudes, and impatience only serve to make matters worse. The following "Top 10" list presents some of the hard lessons we've learned from working in teams. They are reminders to us all about how to navigate the tough spots:

1: In work and life, anger and frustration never help the process.

2: In work and life, being trustworthy is a good thing.

3: In work and life, be easy on the people and tough on the problem.

4: In work and life, fairness isn't the issue . . . so avoid that bias.

5: In work and life, clear communication is the key.

6: In work and life, take your time.

7: In work and life, be open and true to your values from the start.

8: In work and life, chalk the field before you play.

9: "When you're going through hell, keep going." (Winston Churchill)

10: "An ounce of prevention equals a pound of cure."

Taking time, being reflective, and honoring the decision-making process are common themes throughout this list. Taking time to do things right the first time; taking time to deescalate feelings such as anger or frustration; taking time to communicate clearly and effectively; and taking time to define the scope of the project, meeting, or decision at hand all involve extra steps, extra effort, extra presence of mind, and extra discipline. But those little extras can yield exceptional results.

Even in the best of teams, conflict of some type is likely to emerge over contentious decisions. The decision-making process is often questioned by members, and sometimes leaders are unfairly critiqued and scrutinized. In the early stages of a group, members are inclined to go along with the opinions of influential members for the sake of cooperation. But at some point, they begin to challenge the process. If a foundation of honest and respectful communication has been established, differences of opinion can be managed in a productive way that allows all perspectives to be considered. This process, according to Tuckman, is the norming phase of group development and includes a reexamination of group processes and an appreciation for member differences. At this point, cohesion and trust are deepened and teams are ready to enter the performing phase.

Arriving at the performing stage, teams have "emerged from the darkness" of storming and "charted a new course" in norming. Teams in the performing stage have clearly stated expectations, shared rules, clarified roles and responsibilities, and a list of core values to which the entire team can be held accountable. Groups have learned how to avoid making premature, ill-advised decisions and, instead, use a systematic and thoughtful process for deliberation and problem-solving. Of course, this stage is not permanent; nor is it without risk. Leaders must be willing to identify and address issues that might lead to a second trip through storming and into norming. Teamwork is a highly variable undertaking. Sometimes it's necessary to cycle back to earlier stages in order to continually improve team functioning.

Ultimately, honesty, candor, transparency, and a willingness to resist anger, personalization, and reactivity are all great ways to harness the collective wisdom of teams. Effective leaders are willing to speak unpopular truths, ask unpopular questions, and suggest unpopular processes in order to manage the tenuous balance between support and challenge found in high-performance teams. The short-term investment might be high, but the long-term payoff is invaluable.

KEY TERMS

Information processing   115

Confirmation bias   116

Schemas   117

Fundamental attribution error   118

Groupthink   120

Overconfidence   120

Premature decisions   120

Confirmation bias   120

Shared information bias   121

Group polarization   121

Escalation of commitment   121

Systems thinking   123

Diffuse status characteristics   127

Specific status characteristics   127

DISCUSSION QUESTIONS

1. Explain the Ladder of Inference. How does it help us understand the potential problems in processing information?

2. Name the seven common decision-making problems presented in the chapter and give a real-life example of three.

3. What are the four stages of the functional model of decision making? Briefly describe the importance of each. Recall a time when you observed this process in action.

4. Gladwell (2002) identifies three types of influential people. Name and describe them.

5. Pfeffer (1992) identifies a practical, seven-step model for applying power dynamics in groups and organizations. What are the seven steps?

6. Describe the experiment that Asch (1956) conducted with college students. What do the results tell us about group dynamics and decision making?

7. Name and describe the three major influences on group decision making.

GROUP ACTIVITIES

EXERCISE 6.1 MILLENNIAL PEACE PRIZE

In groups of four to five students, imagine you are on a committee working with the Nobel Peace Prize organization. You have been asked to award a $5 million Millennial Peace Prize to the Nobel laureate who has made the biggest impact on world peace in the new millennium. The organization has already created a shortlist of previous winners for you to consider. They are Jimmy Carter (2002), Sharin Ebadi (2003), Muhammad Yunnis (2006), and Barack Obama (2009). Rank order this list from your top choice to your last choice and provide a strong rationale for the ranking. Describe your process in making this decision.

EXERCISE 6.2 THE NAME GAME

You are employees of an advertising agency that has been hired by a large automobile manufacturer to create a name for a sports car it has recently designed. Its new two-seat, hardtop convertible is capable of going from 0 to 60 miles per hour in 4.5 seconds and sells for approximately $100,000. The typical customer is a successful, male business executive who has plenty of disposable income. In groups of four to five, decide upon a name and advertising slogan for the car.

CASE 6.2: MAKING ASSUMPTIONS

In one of your classes this term, the professor has formed teams of six students to work on a class project together. She has given the teams a lot of latitude to decide what their project will be. During the first meeting, you observe the following dialogue:

- John says, "We know the professor likes projects that collect a lot of data. Let's go with that."

- Susie says, "I know exactly what we should do. My big sis at the Delta house took this class last year, so it would be stupid to do anything else. I'm sure we can all agree with this."

- Nigel says, "I think it's really important that we all get on board with the decision, so don't let me be the one to stand in the way of progress."

- Damon says, "We simply can't go wrong with this topic."

- Fran says, "Let's not take all day to get ideas on the table! We have two great topics; either one is fine. Let's just choose one and move on!"

- Which common group-decision-making mistakes did each member of the team make? And how could they make a better decision?

CHAPTER 7

Creativity and Innovation

Effective problem-solving requires creativity in order to identify innovative solutions to complex and ill-defined problems. This chapter describes groups that value unique ideas and nurture creativity. We begin by explaining why innovation is important to teams and organizations. Then we define creativity and discuss the characteristics of creative people. Next is a description of the social and organizational contexts that nurture creativity. Finally, we propose brainstorming techniques that can empower groups to think outside the box.

CASE 7.1: THE IPOD

Although Apple Computer is known for its creativity and innovation, this has not always been the case. It is difficult to maintain a consistent track record of groundbreaking innovations, and Apple has had its share of problems. British designer Jonathan Ive joined Apple in 1992, with dreams of creating new and innovative products. However, during his first few years at the company, Apple strayed from its original foundation of innovation and imagination, and it began acting as a mere imitator in the market. In essence, Apple had become a follower in the industry. The stagnant corporate culture that had emerged had a negative effect on Ive and his design team, as they were no longer free to experiment and invent. However, when Apple's founder, Steve Jobs, returned to the company after pursuing other business interests, Apple Computer reinvented itself and returned to its prior mission. According to Ive, "By re-establishing the core values [Jobs] had established at the beginning, Apple again pursued a direction which was clear and different from any other company. Design and innovation formed an important part of this new direction." With the reestablished culture supporting experimentation and creativity, Ive had the opportunity to develop a new standard in music technology.

Initially, it was Tony Faddell, a computer engineer with an interest in developing an MP3 player, who came up with the initial idea for the iPod (Kahney, 2005). Then it took a team of a dozen designers from all over the globe, including New Zealand, Germany, Italy, and England, to bring the idea to completion. But what made this team so successful? According to Ive, it was the members' "fanatical care beyond the obvious stuff: the obsessive attention to details that are often overlooked that allow for creativity to blossom." They were committed to developing a new music player that would redefine the music industry.

One of the greatest strengths of the team was its inquisitiveness (Burrows, 2006). It was this curiosity and sense of exploration that led members to consult with a wide range of people such as engineers, marketing specialists, and other manufacturers. During one of their trips to Asia, they observed the manufacturing technique of layering colored plastic over other materials that would become the signature look for iPods and iMacs. Even Jobs, CEO of Apple, contributed to the project. He met with developers on a daily basis to contribute to the product's design and interface. Jobs was obsessed with intuitiveness and ease of use, demanding that a song be accessible in less than three clicks.

Interestingly, the iPod prototype was made almost entirely from existing parts Apple bought from other companies, including the internal units from PortalPlayer, the battery from Sony, and the hard drive from Toshiba, to name a few (Kahney, 2005). The design team was able to look at the same pieces that other companies had produced and envision a different configuration that would change the industry. On October 23, 2001, at 10:00 a.m., Jobs announced the iPod's arrival—and the rest, as they say, is history. Ive and his design team helped Apple restore its image as the iconic, innovative company it is today.

Case Study Discussion Questions

1. Why has the iPod been so successful? What are its most innovative design features?

2. How did Steve Jobs create an atmosphere at Apple for creativity to flourish?

3. What was the benefit of using a team versus an individual to develop the iPod?

4. How did Steve Jobs' leadership style affect the development of the iPod?

In today's fast-paced and global economy, organizations must be innovative in order to survive (Hesselbein & Johnston, 2002). The most successful organizations are efficient, adaptable, and able to generate novel ideas as market conditions change. Innovation has become the new route to financial success (Hamel & Skarzynski, 2002). Products and services that are commonplace today, such as iPods, Facebook, and online banking, simply did not exist a decade ago. With rapidly evolving technologies driving much of the change, organizations have had to abandon the status quo and stretch themselves in order to compete in the new global market. In addition to leveraging technology, diversity has also become a competitive advantage for organizations. Diverse teams and organizations are able to take advantage of novel perspectives that result from demographic, gender, educational, or functional diversity and generate ideas that normally would not surface within a homogeneous group (Cox & Blake, 1991).

Improvisation is the ability to invent or compose something in real time with little or no preparation. For example, when well-trained jazz musicians play together, the results can be unpredictable, exciting, and spectacular. The complex and fluid interpersonal context that exists in a jazz session can be compared to the modern workplace (Kao, 1996). Just as the most exciting bands will incorporate unusual and novel rhythms into their music, the most successful businesses will utilize their diverse resources to come up with new and innovative ideas.

Complex problems that confront organizations and teams are often poorly defined and ill-structured (Van Gundy, 1984). While proven routines and formulas may be effective for simple or previously encountered problems, the more challenging and often unforeseen situations of today require thinking that is "outside the box." These unstructured problems do not have a set of proven guidelines to follow, and the problem itself can be difficult even to define and articulate. For example, how much should a manufacturing company invest in robotics in order to be competitive in the next decade? What are the most cost-effective, yet family-friendly policies to embrace as an organization? How can we use science and technology to end the cycle of poverty in Africa? In sum, diverse groups that invite creativity and integrate the creative contributions of their members have the potential to find novel solutions to complex problems that exist in turbulent times.

Creativity

Creativity can be difficult to define and even more difficult to facilitate. Thompson (2004) suggests that "[t]eam creativity is the Holy Grail of teamwork: Everyone wants it, but very few people know where to look for it or how to set up the conditions to make it happen" (p. 178). For the purposes of this text, we will define creativity as the process by which original and useful ideas are produced (Rowe, 2004; Thompson, 2004). Individuals and groups may generate unusual ideas that might even border on the bizarre; but if those ideas have no practical use, they are of limited value. Creative ideas that are original *and* usable, however, don't have to be of the magnitude of an Einstein, Picasso, or Da Vinci to be creative. The same process that creates a Mona Lisa can generate a brilliant new marketing strategy or innovative way to reduce expenses (Amabile, 1990). Creative solutions lead to innovation and change because they are able to go beyond existing perspectives (Woodman, Sawyer, & Griffin, 1993).

E. Paul Torrance, a dominant figure in the field of creativity research, is well known for the development of creativity assessments. His assessments are the gold standard in educational settings (elementary, secondary, and postsecondary) and noneducational settings alike (Baer, 1993). Torrance (1988) defines creative thinking as "the process of sensing difficulties, problems, gaps in information, missing elements, something askew; making guesses and formulating hypotheses about these deficiencies; evaluating and testing these guesses and hypotheses; possibly revising and retesting them; and finally communicating the results" (p. 47). Thus, the first step in the creative process is seeing the problem accurately. Similarly, Csikszentmihalyi (1990) argues that the way one defines the nature of a problem is one of the most important components of the creative process. After all, identifying and defining the problem determines the quality and effectiveness of the solution.

Many theorists associate creativity with divergent thinking or the ability to generate multiple perspectives and unconventional ideas (Baer, 1993). Old conceptualizations and judgments are suspended in favor of generating a variety of possibilities. Divergent thinking is expansive and resists convention; it looks for alternatives that are not often apparent at first glance (Baer, 1993). For example, when asked to identify all the possible uses of a toothbrush, the most obvious answers have to do with cleaning teeth or other surfaces because that's what we think of when we picture a toothbrush in our mind. But someone who is using divergent thinking might envision a toothbrush as a director's baton, or a paintbrush, or a back scratcher. These answers are outside the conventional "box" that is normally associated with the concept of a toothbrush and, thus, qualify as divergent perspectives.

Convergent thinking, by contrast, suggests that there is "one right way" to go about any given task and that the primary job of the team is to find that right way. Chapter 6 described a process of informational processing called the Ladder of Inference. In this model, individuals use exiting cognitive categories to make sense of incoming data. For example, based upon years of schooling, most people know what to expect when they walk into a classroom. Mental models of "proper classroom behavior" help to reduce anxiety and guide behavior. But those existing mental models can be restrictive and prevent people from seeing outside of their existing frames of reference. Thinking outside the box requires the ability to question assumptions and take risks.

Those who can think divergently have less rigid and less structured internal categories. This is important because individuals and teams that resist convention and expand their thinking have more possibilities to consider in solving any particular problem. According to Guilford (1967), there are four different ways to think divergently:

- **Fluency** is the ability to produce a large number of ideas for understanding or solving problems. For example, the iPod design team might have come up with 40 different music player platforms and delivery systems that it needed to consider before settling on the iPod.

- **Flexibility** is the ability to produce ideas in a variety of categories. The iPod designers might have considered a number of music delivery systems including hardware solutions, software solutions, and phone-based platforms. These three categories are very different from one another and demonstrate flexibility.

- **Originality** is the ability to produce unusual or unique ideas. If the design team suggested a variation of existing technology, it would not be very novel. A more original idea was for designers to think outside the box for a system that went far beyond existing MP3 players.

- **Elaboration** is the ability to develop ideas by generating details and depth. Creative ideas may not seem very usable at first glance. Elaboration is the ability to develop abstract ideas into realistic solutions that can be implemented successfully. In order to bring their product to market, the iPod designers had to create an innovative manufacturing process that advanced technology while keeping costs within reasonable levels.

The most vexing problems facing groups today resist easy answers. As Senge (1990) suggests, today's problems are often the result of yesterday's well-meaning yet ill-conceived solutions. Groups that encourage creativity are able to avoid superficial solutions by generating and evaluating a greater number of possibilities. Divergent thinking helps groups consider a plethora of possible outcomes that can lead to better outcomes. Convergent thinking can then narrow down the options and decide upon the best course of action.

CHARACTERISTICS OF CREATIVE PEOPLE

In order to understand creativity, researchers have studied the lives of creative people in a variety of contexts including art, literature, music, science, and organizations (Amabile, 1990; Dacey & Lennon, 1998; Gardner, 1988, 1993). Interestingly, Gardner (1988) found that creativity is tied to specific domains or tasks. Some creative acts require expertise in language, others require logical problem-solving ability, and still others require specialized spatial skills. Being a creative genius in one area does not mean that a person will be creative in other areas. For example, a world-renowned ballerina might not be able to apply her creativity to the world of commerce and become an innovative, successful CEO. Different tasks and domains require different types of knowledge, expertise, and skills to produce results that are truly effective and unique. Thus, domain-specific knowledge is one of the first characteristics common to creative individuals (Amabile, 1990).

Characteristics of Creative People	
1. Knowledgeable	3. Comfortable with ambiguity
2. Intrinsically motivated	4. Willing to take risks

Subject Knowledge

Creative genius is grounded upon a foundation of knowledge and technical skill. One can hardly imagine the brilliance of a Galileo or a Michelangelo without rigorous training and expertise in their disciplines. Thompson (2004) speculates that it takes 10 years of experience within any given area for an individual to gain enough expertise and understanding to make major leaps in creativity. Although existing knowledge and expertise can hinder individuals from seeing new and fresh perspectives, it is also difficult to make innovative advances without any knowledge at all (Woodman, Sawyer, & Griffin, 1993). According to Amabile (1990), this knowledge can be derived from innate cognitive abilities, perceptual skills, and both formal and informal education.

Knowledge acquisition is often influenced by curiosity and a love for learning. Albert Einstein was reported to have said that he had no special talents apart from passionate curiosity (Hoffman, 1972). Creative people acquire knowledge because they desire to understand and make sense of the world around them. Thus, the desire to learn for the sheer pleasure of learning is a trait common to creative people. They are curious about life, in general, while also being committed to their own specific discipline.

Intrinsic Motivation

For most people, creativity takes effort. The most significant creative achievements take long-term dedication and hard work. Intrinsic motivation can provide the perseverance that is often necessary to achieve results (Csikszentmihalyi, 1990). Amabile (1985, 1990) explored the relationship between motivation and creativity by enlisting 72 young adults to write two brief poems. The first poem functioned as a pretest, while the second poem was the posttest. Before writing the second poem, approximately one-third of the participants were asked to complete a seven-item questionnaire that prompted them to think about intrinsic motivations for writing a high-quality poem, such as deriving personal satisfaction or enjoyment from their work. Another third was given a questionnaire that asked questions about extrinsic motivations such as making money or achieving recognition. The final third, the control group, was not given any questionnaire. The questionnaires were used by the researchers to prime the participants and influence the type of motivation that was used to write their poems.

After each participant wrote his or her two poems, a panel of 12 literary experts rated each of the poems on a 40-point creativity scale. The initial poems of the three groups of participants were rated at about the same level of creativity, ranging from 18.18 to 18.76, as described below.

Table 7.1 The Relationship Between Motivation and Creativity

	No Prompt	Intrinsic Prompt	Extrinsic Prompt
Pretest	18.18	18.76	18.19
Posttest	18.78	19.88	15.74

SOURCE: Adapted from Amabile (1985, 1990).

Writers who were prompted by intrinsic questions demonstrated a modest improvement in creativity from the first poem to their second, but not enough for statistical significance. Interestingly, the intrinsic group performed at about the same level of creativity as the group without any questionnaire, suggesting that all the writers were intrinsically motivated at the beginning of the experiment. People, by nature, want to improve their performance on repetitive tasks. But the levels of creativity demonstrated by those who were exposed to extrinsic prompts were significantly lower than their original poem and also lower than the other two groups' second poem. In other words, the extrinsic prompts had a detrimental effect on levels of creativity. This decline may have occurred because external rewards and judgments undermine the pure enjoyment and satisfaction that can come from the work itself. The results indicate that introducing extrinsic rewards for individuals who are intrinsically motivated can have a detrimental effect on creativity.

Tolerance for Ambiguity

One of the most important traits of creative people is that they have a tolerance for ambiguity (Zenasni, Besançon, & Lubart, 2008). Innovation and creativity are often born out of confusion and sometimes even out of desperation. "An ambiguous situation is one in which no framework exists to help direct one's decisions and actions" (Dacey & Lennon, 1998, p. 98). History is replete with examples of tortured poets, musicians, and artists whose greatest accomplishments happened when they broke from convention and forged their own paths. Since there are no maps or trail markers on the road less traveled, creative individuals must be comfortable with ambiguity and the uncertainty of not knowing exactly where they are going.

In ambiguous situations, people do not have all the facts. There is no clear path upon which to embark. Rules are unclear, and existing procedures are outdated or nonexistent. For many, this produces great anxiety; the unknown can be quite unsettling. But for highly creative people it can be intriguing to attempt to make sense of the confusion and complexity (Dacey & Lennon, 1998). A tolerance for ambiguity means remaining open-minded and resilient in the face of uncertainty (Schilpzand, Herold, & Shalley, 2011). This attitude helps prevent premature and ill-conceived judgments and provides adequate time for creative ideas to emerge.

Willingness to Take Risks

Innovation and creativity require the ability to take risks. Creative individuals are recognized as such because they were willing to communicate their unconventional ideas to others. Most adults are risk aversive and prefer security to the possibility of rejection (Dacey & Lennon, 1998). Our desire to be accepted and respected often leads us to conform to the expectations of others. However, the "play it safe" principle sometimes hinders creative expression. It is unfortunate to think of the countless number of world-changing ideas, literary triumphs, innovative business plans, life-enhancing inventions, and inspirational songs that lay dormant in the heads of very talented people who were unwilling to take the risk of sharing their ideas with others.

Creative people are not restrained by social convention. They are willing to appear unusual or odd. Because they are intrinsically motivated and have a strong belief in their work and themselves, they have minimal concern for what others think. Take, for example, noted physicist Richard Feynman, who was known for his curiosity and unique way of thinking. While in high school, he reinvented his math formulas. Feynman was never afraid to question the experts, even those of the magnitude of Niels Bohr. While listening to Bohr give a lecture, Feynman was the only one in the audience to argue with and debate the scientific giant. Ironically, this garnered Bohr's respect, and he requested a meeting with Feynman. Due, in part, to his tenacious quest for understanding and willingness to take risks, Feynman went on to win the Nobel Prize in Physics for quantum electrodynamics.

Discovery Orientation

Finally, creative individuals possess a discovery orientation. Renowned creativity researcher Mihaly Csikszentmihalyi (1988, 1990, 1996) made the following observation of creative people: They have the ability to identify problems and explore possible solutions that are only vaguely recognized.

Accepting a problem as it is presented means that it "is clearly defined, has an accepted method of solution, and has a generally agreed-upon solution" (Csikszentmihalyi, 1990, p. 193). In contrast, individuals who approach a problem with a discovery orientation do not rely upon proven methods or established procedures. They are not bound by convention; instead, they consider a multitude of possibilities as they define the task in their own minds. In a study of 31 art students who had been asked to draw a picture of their choosing, Csikszentmihalyi (1990) found that those with a discovery orientation considered the widest variety of drawing materials before they started and made the most changes during the task. The drawings of students who had a discovery orientation were higher on originality and aesthetic value than those who viewed the task as a conventional problem.

Furthermore, those with a discovery orientation went on to greater levels of artistic success when evaluated 7 and 18 years later. In sum, creative individuals have the ability to see problems in unique ways in order to produce solutions that are equally unique.

THE SOCIAL AND ORGANIZATIONAL CONTEXT FOR CREATIVITY

Creative ideas are neither developed nor demonstrated in isolation; they are nurtured and expressed in social contexts. Human beings are social creatures, and human behavior can be attributed to a unique synthesis of biological, psychological, and social factors (Dacey & Lennon, 1998). While initial research on creativity focused on individual variables alone, subsequent work has broadened to include social and environmental influences (Amabile, 1990). Leading that perspective has been Mihaly Csikszentmihalyi (1988, 1990), an articulate advocate for a systems view of creativity.

While studying creativity in the traditional context of individual traits and cognitive processes, Csikszentmihalyi (1988, 1990) became convinced of the limitations of a person-centered view. In contrast, he believes that creativity is best understood as the interaction among three subsystems: the person, the domain, and the field. Creativity begins at the level of the *person*, with his or her natural and learned abilities. Those abilities are then exercised within an existing *domain*, which poses its own unique structure and expectations. For example, chess is a domain defined by certain rules, a unique set of vocabulary that players use to communicate with one another, and a reservoir of standard moves and strategies. Within every domain is a *field* of experts who define excellence and decide whether someone is truly innovative. Commentators, art critics, record executives, chess masters, and experts in every domain are part of the social context that influences what is deemed creative. Returning to our chess example, the most creative players are able to go beyond existing strategies and create their own unique style. But that style operates within a specific domain and is validated by experts in the field.

Family

Parents, mentors, significant others, and colleagues all contribute to the ability of individuals to fulfill their creative potential (Dacey & Lennon, 1998; Mockros & Csikszentmihalyi, 1999). Families are perhaps the most significant social influence on the development of creativity (Dacey & Lennon, 1998). Many of the world's creative geniuses grew up in environments that both supported and challenged them (Gardner, 1993). In interviews with 96 people noted for their creative accomplishments, virtually all of them described their childhood environments as intellectually stimulating and supportive of their talent development (Csikszentmihalyi, 1996). Raw potential is often shaped by disciplined study and practice guided by parents and mentors.

Education

Education also plays a significant role in the development of creativity. Unfortunately, education can also have an adverse effect. As Dacey and Lennon (1998) emphatically state, "Schools suppress creativity" (p. 69). Early childhood is a critical time in the development of creativity. Fueled by curiosity, children are eager to explore and learn, yet Gardner (1991) found that when children enter school, they become more cautious and less innovative. It seems that the need to conform to a structured system of externally imposed guidelines can extinguish creative imagination.

Distinguished Harvard professor and creativity researcher Theresa Amabile (1990) tells of how her own experiences in school had a lasting impact on the rest of her life. In kindergarten, to her delight, she overheard her teacher tell her mother that she had great potential for artistic creativity. Her first year of school nurtured that potential with liberal access to art materials and the encouragement to experiment. Unfortunately, her creative expression was discouraged in the first grade, when she and her classmates were given pictures of classic paintings and told to copy them. Instead of creative expression, art became an exercise in frustration as students were strictly graded on how well they replicated the paintings. Even years later, when given the opportunity to draw what she wanted, she was told by one of her teachers that she was exercising too much creativity. Sadly, this story captures the potentially negative influence of early education on wonder and creativity.

Mentors

During adolescence and young adulthood, mentors play a key role in nurturing the development of creativity (Mockros & Csikszentmihalyi, 1999). Mentors can be teachers, role models, parents, or colleagues who provide knowledge, resources, and encouragement. Observing mentors as they process information and solve problems is a tremendous benefit. In this way, the apprentice or novice is exposed to the tacit knowledge and inner processes of the mentor, which are more "caught" than taught. Ultimately, mentors provide direction and guidance that can have a lasting impact on development.

In adulthood, creativity and innovation are often supported and stimulated by colleagues and significant others. The most successful careers of creative people are aided by strong and supportive relationships. Spouses often provide both emotional and financial support to allow the development and expression of creative potential (Mockros & Csikszentmihalyi, 1999). Romantic partners can also be a source of inspiration and encouragement. Another important social influence comes from collegial relationships that provide intellectual stimulation and the opportunity for collaboration.

Organizations

Organizational settings can also have a profound effect on the development and expression of creativity. Certain organizational climates nurture creativity, while others destroy it. Amabile (1990) argues that environments that emphasize evaluation, surveillance, rewards, competition, and restricted choice negatively affect creativity. Thus, while performance-driven command and control hierarchies may improve efficiency, they also hinder innovation (Mauzy & Harriman, 2003; Van Gundy, 1984). Therefore, Woodman, Sawyer, and Griffin (1993) advocate environments that encourage risk-taking, the free exchange of ideas, legitimate conflict, active participation, and the use of intrinsic rather than extrinsic rewards. The most creative organizations have an entrepreneurial culture that empowers employees to take ownership and spawn innovation (Mauzy & Harriman, 2003).

Amabile and her colleagues (Amabile, Conti, Coon, Lazenby, & Herron, 1996) found that creativity is enhanced when the organizational environment supports the following four conditions. First, risk-taking and innovation should be nurtured at all levels of the organization. From the boardroom to the production line, all employees should be encouraged to think of ways to improve operating procedures and generate new ideas. Second, creative ideas should be critiqued and evaluated in fair and supportive ways. Most initial ideas will need to be refined and developed; yet a harsh, critical evaluation is a sure way to squelch innovation. Third, creative achievements should be rewarded in ways that validate and communicate the importance of innovation. Appropriate reward structures reinforce organizational values without suggesting that employees be innovative solely for the purpose of recognition or compensation. Finally, innovative organizations should encourage open communication and participative decision making. Collaboration and the exchange of ideas can create synergy that fosters reflection, learning, and experimentation.

Collaboration allows people the opportunity to discuss, debate, and dialogue as they work together. This free exchange of ideas creates a social environment where new perspectives are considered and innovative solutions can be discovered. Unsurprisingly, a study of 160 college students showed that their ability to produce unique ideas increased as they were exposed to the creative ideas of others (Dugosh & Paulus, 2005). Contrary to the common image of creative geniuses working in isolation, many great thinkers develop their ideas as they engage in critical dialogue with others. Proposals that are critiqued and challenged force individuals to think more deeply and to find grounds that support their ideas or position. If adequate evidence cannot be found, new ideas and assertions are constructed. When vigorous debate is done with interpersonal sensitivity, unexamined assumptions can be identified, revealing blind spots and inviting exploration. In this way, groups that encourage dissent and value a multiplicity of perspectives are especially helpful in generating creativity and innovation (Woodman, Sawyer, & Griffin, 1993).

In interviews with highly successful and creative scientists, Mockros and Csikszentmihalyi (1999) consistently heard about the value of collaboration in the creative process. For instance,

a prominent physicist and author who received both the Max Planck Medal and the National Medal of Science stated, "I was able to do creative work collaborating with other people. Most of my work is collaborative. That's how you find out how to do something which hasn't been done before. Collaboration is extremely important" (p. 205).

Another highly successful physicist who won both the Einstein and Niels Bohr Prizes said, "Usually ideas grow slowly, they're like flowers that have to be tended by reading, and talking with people . . . if you don't kick things around with people you are out of it. Nobody, I always say, can be anybody without others around" (p. 205). Reinforcing the importance of dialogue, another physicist who is a Fellow of the Royal Society and a member of the National Academy of Sciences noted, "It is only by interacting with other people that you get anything interesting done" (p. 205). These prominent scientists not only verbalize the importance of collaboration, their work demonstrates it.

Creative collaboration is enhanced when members with difference educational or functional backgrounds are placed on cross-functional teams. Cross-functional teams consist of members from different departments or areas within an organization who come together to accomplish a specific task. For example, AT&T may assemble a group of accountants, engineers, and salespeople to improve the company's website. That way, different perspectives can be considered. The benefits of cross-functional teams are their ability to act quickly, especially when dealing with complex issues, their creativity, and their ability to learn (Parker, 1994). Cross-functional teams are able to accomplish tasks quickly because the knowledge and skills required to complete the task are represented on the team. Time that would have been spent soliciting various stakeholders outside the group is reduced. Furthermore, more complex tasks are easier to address when different types of expertise exist in one group. Because each member comes from a different functional background, they bring different perspectives, resulting in greater creative potential. And because members come from various parts of the organization, it is difficult only to advocate for their own group; this helps cross-functional teams focus on customers and the larger organizational mission.

However, cross-functional teams are not the answer for every organizational task or challenge. Jehn and Bezrukova (2004) found that cross-functional groups were most effective when involved in growth-oriented tasks, or tasks that emphasize innovation and creativity. The diverse backgrounds of members bring different perspectives to team discussions that can help generate new ideas and unique solutions. In contrast, cross-functional teams did not fare well in stability-oriented tasks, or tasks that emphasized efficiency and hierarchical differentiation over innovation. Essentially, cross-functional teams can generate a wide variety of ideas to complex organizational tasks and problems. Much of their success can be attributed to a rich and unrestricted brainstorming process.

CREATIVITY THROUGH BRAINSTORMING

Brainstorming is a common practice for idea generation in teams and organizations. Early researchers such as Alex Osborn (1953) explored the circumstances under which creativity is optimally nurtured. His colleagues first used the term *brainstorm* in 1938 when he called a collaboration meeting at his company. Through systematic observation of this and many other meetings, he identified four characteristics of successful brainstorming: (a) minimal criticism of ideas, (b) frequent "free-wheeling" or free expression of ideas, (c) a large quantity of ideas, and (d) the use of proposed ideas as a catalyst for more ideas. Unfortunately, Osborn found that most brainstorming sessions do not have these characteristics. Consequently, brainstorming does not always produce the results teams are capable of achieving. Group processes such as social loafing, evaluation apprehension, and production blocking reduce the effectiveness of group brainstorming.

Social loafing is a common problem in which group members withhold their best efforts and most creative ideas because they perceive that others will do the work for them. Harkins and Petty (1982) found that participants who generated ideas collectively produced fewer ideas than the sum total of ideas that were generated by participants who brainstormed individually. However, in completing difficult tasks, participants working in a group produced a comparable number of ideas as those who were working alone. This suggests that social loafing is more common when tasks are simple and people do not feel that their work will be missed. In addition, Nijstad, Stroebe, and Lodewijkx (2006) found that groups tend to insulate individual members from feelings of failure, and do not hold them accountable. Since group members do not feel personal failure as keenly, they do not realize that they are performing below standard.

Evaluation apprehension is the reluctance to contribute to a discussion out of a fear of being judged or evaluated by others. Most people want to be perceived as competent and to garner the respect of others. So when group members are unsure of the quality of their contribution, they might hold back. In a study conducted by Camacho and Paulus (1995), evaluation apprehension due to social anxiety caused group members to contribute fewer ideas in a group setting than they would alone. Furthermore, as group size increases, individuals tend to become more intimidated and therefore withhold their opinions even more (Mullen, Johnson, & Salas, 1991).

Production blocking is the logistical reality that when one person is talking, others are blocked from contributing their ideas. In most groups, time is limited and not everyone can speak out on every topic. Diehl and Stroebe (1987) found that as members wait for their turn to speak up, they can forget what they were going to say. In addition, the discussion can move on to a different topic while members mentally rehearse what they are going to say, thus missing their opportunity. Nijstad, Stroebe, and Lodewijkx (2003) support this view with their study on delays. Nijstad and his colleagues manipulated wait delays to see how they would affect the number of ideas that were generated by participants. Unpredictable delays were found to reduce the number of idea sequences, also known as semantic clusters, because participants were distracted by the uncertainty of the timing in their chance to contribute. Long delays shortened the length of semantic clusters for the same reason.

Although there are challenges to effective brainstorming, groups can take specific steps to improve both the quality and quantity of ideas that are generated (Goldenberg, Larson, & Wiley, 2013). For instance, Paulus, Nakui, Putman, and Brown (2006) found that taking breaks during brainstorming sessions helped yield more ideas. Breaks should be taken at times when the session loses momentum and ideas have stopped flowing. The number of breaks, meanwhile, should vary with the time apportioned for brainstorming. The use of a facilitator to prompt participants was also found to be helpful. In that way, one person is guiding the process instead of focusing on generating ideas. The use of ground rules such as "stay focused on the task," "everyone's ideas are important," "keep the ideas flowing," "no critiquing of ideas until we're done," and "quantity over quality" can help improve the quantity and quality of ideas.

One particularly helpful exercise to enhance group brainstorming is "brainwriting" (Paulus & Yang, 2000). Brainwriting involves jotting down ideas on slips of paper and passing them around the group. Members read one another's ideas and add their own. A variation of this exercise is to have everyone generate as many ideas as possible by writing each on a Post-it note. Then, after a predetermined amount of time, everyone sticks their notes on a whiteboard or public medium for other group members to see. After that, similar ideas are grouped together and collapsed or combined. In this way, a group can create a shortlist of 5 to 7 strong ideas for further examination and critique. The benefit of allowing everyone in the team to contribute in a systematic and structured format cannot be overstated. In this way, a team of eight people can generate 80+ ideas on any given topic. This is considerably more than the typical 8 to 10 total number of ideas that are usually generated when the whole group speaks in an unmoderated, free-for-all discussion.

LEADERSHIP IN ACTION

Creativity and innovation help us solve problems and improve our personal and professional lives. They bring about needed change and progress. Isn't it ironic, then, that creativity and innovation are resisted by so many? Within teams, some members actively resist, while others drag their feet, becoming quiet in their reluctance to change and brainstorm new ideas. Team leaders can overcome this resistance by strategically planning for the creative process ahead of time. At the beginning of a proposed brainstorming session, leaders can present specific ground rules and guidelines for the meeting. For example, an agenda might be created that allocates 10 minutes for idea generation, 20 minutes for the systematic reduction of options, 20 minutes for evaluation of a limited number of ideas, and 10 minutes for final voting. During the idea generation phase, it should be emphasized that there will be no criticism, no sarcasm, and no explanations of how or why something *won't* work. When a rule is violated or the process compromised, the leader can simply remind the team of the rule, get it back on track, and move on.

Members have 10 minutes to generate as many ideas as they can. At this point in the process, the goal is quantity and not necessarily quality. After all of the group's ideas have been generated and publicly displayed on a whiteboard or other visual format, the team can enter the reduction phase. Members are granted a limited number of votes with which to choose their favorite ideas. This can be done by placing a check mark or sticker next to the ideas people are in favor of. After the voting, the ideas with the most votes will be critiqued more closely. If necessary, teams can revote if something is "too close to call the first time around." Sometimes, ideas are combined and expanded upon during this phase. Dialogue and "thinking outside the box" should be encouraged. Next, smaller groups are formed to evaluate the remaining ideas on the shortlist. Each group has 10 minutes to construct an argument in defense of one of the ideas. After each team has presented its proposal, a formal voting process can be used to make the final decision. Members can place stickers on the wall above each of the ideas, or take a vote by hand, or vote "yea or nay" for each idea.

For any number of reasons, members may be resistant to the creative or innovative process. In those cases, leaders may need to sit down with the resistant party one on one, and inquire about why he or she isn't contributing to the group's task. An open, investigative, or inquisitive approach is often the best strategy; this is not the time to put someone who is already defensive *on* the defensive. The leader can begin by making some observations about how he or she has perceived the member's behavior. For example, the leader might have noticed a pattern of passive behavior or lack of involvement in team discussions and is interested in getting the member's perspective. Often, the first response will be superficial and vague; but if the leader is able to listen actively, the real issues may emerge.

Active listening skills and sincere inquiry can help lead the conversation to the heart of the matter. Eventually, the leader might hear a member vent about why the team has to "change what it's doing," or "think outside the box," or "come up with new ideas." Or a member might say that he or she is just not very creative. In any case, it can be the beginning of a meaningful conversation in which the leader has a better understanding of where the member is coming from. Once the real issues are on the table, the creative process can be engaged to find a way to reenlist and reengage the resistant member. The two can brainstorm possible solutions to the problem, choose the best option, and then implement that choice. While this might be a lot of work for the leader, it can yield a higher-than-average rate of return for his or her effort. Enlisting the entire team in the creative process can be the difference between good teamwork and great teamwork. And modeling it is one of the best ways to teach it.

KEY TERMS

Fluency 136	Originality 136
Flexibility 136	Elaboration 136

DISCUSSION QUESTIONS

1. Name and describe the four ways to think divergently according to Guilford.

2. Describe how divergent and convergent thinking styles affect the process of creativity.

3. Describe the four characteristics of creative people and give an example of *each*.

4. Name and describe the three subsystems of creativity according to Csikszentmihalyi.

5. What are the four characteristics of successful brainstorming discovered by Osborn?

6. Create a hypothetical group meeting that uses an effective brainstorming strategy.

GROUP ACTIVITIES

EXERCISE 7.1 DIVERGENT THINKING

In groups of four, generate a list of all the possible uses of a red solo cup. You have 10 minutes to complete this task and will be awarded one point for every unique idea. Ideas that are on the list of two or more groups will cancel one another out. After the time is up, declare a winner and make observations about the process.

EXERCISE 7.2 BRAINSTORMING EXERCISE

Form teams of four students and assign the roles of task leader and time keeper to two of the members. The leader should follow the following instructions to identify the best business a college student could start to make money and have fun at the same time:

- **Generate ideas (4 minutes):** Each team should have a stack of Post-it notes to begin. Each member should silently write down as many ideas as possible (one per Post-it). The goal is quantity, not quality.

- **Organize ideas (10 minutes):** Post all the Post-it notes on the board and organize them into categories.

- **Create a shortlist (14 minutes):** Weigh the relative merits of each idea and determine the best idea per category.

- **Vote (4 minutes):** Vote for your top three choices by placing a check mark next to those ideas. (You can put all three votes on one idea if you feel that strongly.) Add up the votes and determine the group's top idea.

After 32 minutes, have each group present its top idea to the class. Discuss this structured brainstorming process and evaluate the quality of the results.

CASE 7.2: FROM BRAINSTORM TO THUNDERSTORM

Starways Technology is a small start-up company that has become known for attracting talented programmers to create web applications ("apps") for the iPhone. You're working there as a summer intern in "apps dev" (application development), and the company decides to spend time brainstorming and coming up with five new ideas for apps that it can develop and launch in the coming six months. You walk into the room and quietly take a seat at the back. When the meeting starts, the CEO and VP of Product Development both give a short presentation together about the goal of the meeting, at which point people start anxiously asking questions:

- "How long do we have?"
- "How many downloads are we shooting for?"
- "What's our budget?"
- "This is going to take a lot of time; what will be done about our overtime issue?"

You sense that this meeting is rapidly deteriorating into a town hall–style complaint-fest. Luckily, the CEO brings order by saying, "I know you all have questions and concerns. Right now, my primary interest is in identifying the best ideas in the room. So . . . please call them out. We will capture your thoughts and evaluate them later. Tell us, what are your ideas for apps that we can develop in the next six months?"

There is silence for a few seconds before the first idea is shouted across the room. Immediately, someone disagrees with the idea, and two new ideas are offered. Before long, it is hard to distinguish between ideas and critiques, and people begin judging the ideas using very different criteria. One group talks louder and more insistently while another starts to withdraw. Several people pull out their technology and start tapping on the screens, and it is clear to you that this has officially become an unproductive brainstorming session.

- *If this were your meeting, what would you do as the leader to improve (a) the quantity of viable of ideas, (b) the quality of those ideas, (c) the ability to capture those ideas in detail, and (d) the process to differentiate good ideas from bad?*

CHAPTER 8

Diversity

Diverse membership within teams can be a tremendous asset. At the same time, diversity tends to magnify the typical challenges present within most groups. Diverse teams must learn to appreciate their functional, cultural, and geographical differences before they can harness the power of their collective wisdom. This chapter will discuss the benefits, challenges, and potential of diversity. Unfortunately, the outcomes of diversity are not always positive. A skilled and insightful leader can be the difference between success and failure in a diverse team.

CASE 8.1: DELOITTE

As one of the most successful consulting companies in the world, Deloitte regularly shows up on lists such as Forbes *magazine's "Top 100 Employers," the "Top 100 Places to Launch a Career," and, most important to this chapter, the Diversity Inc. list of "Top 50 Companies for Diversity" (number 11 in 2013). Deloitte is an employer of choice among the top undergraduates and MBA graduates from leading business schools around the globe, competing with the likes of McKinsey, Bain, and Ernst & Young. It attracts the best and the brightest talent and is known for investing heavily in its human capital; in fact it recently invested over $300 million in a new team development and leadership development campus in Westlake, Texas, called "Deloitte University." One of the ways Deloitte has developed this stellar reputation as the top consultancy in the world is by utilizing and nurturing diverse, integrated teams of highly trained specialists, and Deloitte University is just the latest example of the extent to which Deloitte has learned to harness the power of diversity.*

Deloitte's success has not happened by accident. It has required a sustained and strategic effort to build internationally and culturally diverse teams, to create an integrated operational platform, and to struggle past the challenges of heterogeneity to a point where diverse groups can elicit the best that each member can offer. At any of Deloitte's client engagements, there is likely to be a fair amount of cultural, racial, gender, national, and functional diversity represented. In order to reach this rare level of interdependent and high-functioning effort, Deloitte holds leadership development trainings for its consulting associates from offices around the world who have been with the company for at least one year (as well as more advanced training and development opportunities throughout an associate's tenure with the company). Deloitte does this because it is dedicated to developing a cross-functional leadership pipeline that leverages diversity and ensures the future success of the company.

This training model is available to associates in either a one-week- or two-week-long seminar built around consulting cases, cohort discussions, debates, projects, and team challenges. In many instances, associates are divided into teams to tackle the cases, for example, so that these professionals can learn (or refine) how to work with other exceptionally smart, driven, talented, competitive, "type-A" leaders in a "quick-change" environment. Consultants must be able to establish trust, develop understanding, scope and scale a project, delegate responsibility, and produce solutions on very short timelines. Deloitte University equips its associates to formalize these skill sets, philosophical bases, and best practices so that the diversity of the teams becomes a strength instead of a weakness.

One way of forcing teams to learn how to adapt comes at various intervals during the case-based portions of Deloitte University's sessions. The consulting teams are given additional case information that brings unexpected changes—such as the sudden dismissal of the case company's CEO or a surprise legal investigation into some aspect of the company—and the teams have to find ways of accommodating the new information. This demands that the teams "think outside of the box" and, in many cases, calls on the full breadth and depth of the experience that all members bring, whether they are from offices in Atlanta, Singapore, London, Buenos Aires, or San Francisco; whether they are of European, African, American, or Asian descent; or whether they are men or women, gay or straight, young or old. Team members learn to work together to harness their collective capacity for solving problems throughout the workshop.

While participants share a great deal in common since they are all members of the Deloitte community, the diversity of these teams presents a valuable challenge and learning opportunity. Not only are these rising leaders able to sharpen their consulting skills, they are also able to learn lessons about how to harness the strengths other participants bring from their respective backgrounds and markets. This is more than working in teams; this is leadership development and diversity training in action. It is how Deloitte keeps its diverse talent pipeline full. For example, according to a recent DiversityInc "Top 50" list, it has double the percentage of senior leaders of black, Latino, and Asian descent than the average company. According to a May 8, 2013, press release:

> "We believe that diversity and inclusion are essential for sustainable success in today's business environment," said Kelvin Womack, Deloitte's managing principal for Diversity. "At Deloitte, by looking at our people holistically, there are more opportunities for advancement as well as a more productive work environment, resulting in greater value to our clients through a variety of experiences and perspectives."

Case Study Discussion Questions

1. Why does Deloitte think diversity is so important?

2. What is uncommon about Deloitte's approach to diversity?

3. Name three short-term and three long-term diversity issues Deloitte University might help overcome.

4. Discuss how Deloitte University might eventually lead to a sustainable competitive advantage for the company.

In her engaging and practical book on diversity, Laura Liswood (2010) introduces the concept of diversity with a parable about a mouse and an elephant. When a mouse and elephant are in a room together, the elephant is hardly aware that a mouse is even present. The elephant is powerful and strong enough that the mouse is of little concern. On the other hand, the mouse is very aware of the elephant. As a matter of fact, much of the mouse's movement is governed by the elephant. As a result, the mouse is very observant of what the elephant is doing at all times. Much of what the mouse does is determined by where the elephant is in the room and what it is doing. This makes the mouse very perceptive and aware. In contrast, the elephant is, to some degree, oblivious to the fact that there are other creatures sharing the same space they inhabit. As a matter of fact, most elephants know nothing about mice. Furthermore, because of the elephant's powerful and elevated vantage point, it can be shortsighted and slow to react to changing conditions.

Liswood goes on to say that this parable is a perfect example of how dominant and nondominant cultures exist together in organizations and teams. Members of the dominant culture are rarely aware of the perspectives of the nondominant culture. Yet members of the nondominant culture are very aware of the movements and power of the dominant culture. And as the world has gotten more unstable and complex, the mouse and the elephant need to combine their resources and work together in order to survive. They have much to learn from each other's unique perspectives and life experiences. Applied to the context of teams, team members need to understand that people have different perspectives, and that those diverse perspectives can make the team stronger and more adaptable.

VISIBLE VERSUS NONVISIBLE DIVERSITY

In order to identify how people differ from one another, some diversity researchers have classified those differences as either visible or nonvisible (Milliken & Martins, 1996). Visible forms of diversity include characteristics such as race, age, and gender. Nonvisible differences include individual variations in education level, socio-economic background, personality, and values. Another type of diversity involves differences among people based upon cultural background. The distinction is important because different types of diversity affect groups differently. Thus, a mixed-gender group with different nationalities and languages will experience diversity differently than a group of middle-class, white, male executives with different backgrounds in engineering, marketing, accounting, and human resources. In general, visible differences are more of a challenge to groups than are nonvisible differences (Mannix & Neale, 2005). However, these outcomes are moderated by the work environment within which the groups operate (Jehn & Bezrukova, 2004).

Visible Differences

With the diversification of the workforce over the last few decades, demographic changes have increasingly become a challenge for organizations. Employees tend to be more comfortable working with people who are similar to them (Mannix & Neale, 2005). Similarities among people create a sense of familiarity and security, and many of those clues about similarity and difference come from physical appearance. As a general rule, people are more trusting of those who look just like them.

Furthermore, as a result of past experiences, exposure to the perspectives of friends and family, and images from the media, individuals construct beliefs about certain groups of people that tend to be one-dimensional and overgeneralized. These broad categories are used to assess incoming data and make quick judgments. Often, people are categorized and judged by their external, visible characteristics. When this happens, superficial judgments run the risk of being unconscious, unfair, and problematic for working groups. Unfortunately, since many groups of people have unfair and inaccurate stereotypes, issues such as racial prejudice, sexism, ageism, and homophobia are not uncommon.

Nonvisible Differences

Nonvisible differences can be divided into characteristics that are either psychological (based upon personality) or functional (based upon occupation and training) (Jackson & Ruderman, 1995). The table below describes three types of diversity that can exist within organizations. While demographic differences are most often visible, personality and functional difference are not.

Psychological differences include those personality traits and characteristics that make people unique. Much of the research on personality characteristics uses the Big Five model of personality. The Big Five model is a well-established conceptual framework for psychological research that measures individuals on five dimensions: conscientiousness, agreeableness, openness, neuroticism, and extraversion (Halfhill, Sundstrom, Lahner, Calderone, & Nielson, 2005). Excluding neuroticism, each of the variables is positively correlated with team effectiveness.

Teams tend to function better when there is a variation of personality traits among members. For example, it might be helpful if a majority of team members are agreeable. If there are not enough people with that characteristic, the group can get mired down in unproductive conflict and endless power struggles. But it is also important for some members not to have that trait. Otherwise, the group is susceptible to groupthink because nobody is willing to challenge the status quo and disagree with others. A healthy balance is ideal.

Table 8.1   Different Types of Diversity

Type of Diversity	Examples
Demographic differences	Race, ethnicity, gender, age
Psychological differences	Personal beliefs, goals, past experiences, personality, interpersonal style, attitudes
Functional differences	Training, work experience, education, knowledge, skills

In the same way that psychological diversity is beneficial to teams, functional differences are also desirable when considering the composition of workgroups (Hüttermann & Boerner, 2011). For example, a team leader might want someone on the team who is technologically savvy if he or she wants to utilize regular virtual meetings. That individual's specialized training and knowledge fill a need for the group. Cross-functional workgroups capitalize on this philosophy by enlisting members with different backgrounds in education and training in order to bring a diversity of perspective to the group. Constructing teams of people with different functional backgrounds ensures that problem analysis and decisions are considered from multiple angles.

CULTURAL DIVERSITY

Culture can play a significant role in groups and teams (Zhou & Shi, 2011). Members of the same familial, geographic, or professional culture typically share similar values, beliefs, and attitudes. Of course, not everyone in a cultural group holds to the exact same beliefs in a consistent manner, but a common worldview helps foster a sense of community, mutual understanding, and communication. Stories and proverbs communicate and reinforce important values that distinguish one culture from another (Liswood, 2010). For example, Americans have the saying, "The squeaky wheel gets the oil," highlighting the importance of assertiveness and being outspoken in order to get what you want. But in Japan, a common saying is, "The nail that sticks out gets hit on the head." In a similar fashion, one might hear a grandmother in China say, "The loudest duck gets shot." The Japanese and Chinese sayings extol the virtues of conformity and quietness, in contrast to American assertiveness. Given these cultural traditions, it would be easy to imagine an American team leader becoming frustrated with Asian team members who were quiet and rarely participated in team discussions. Likewise, Asian members might be put off by American members who were loud and boisterous. Cultural differences can create misunderstandings that hinder team performance (Haas & Nüesch, 2012).

Cultural diversity can be an asset on teams because it brings fresh perspectives to discussions (Crotty & Brett, 2012), but it can also be a potential problem if members are culturally ignorant or insensitive. In order to distinguish one culture from another, Trompenaars and Hampden-Turner (1998) surveyed over 15,000 participants from 30 companies within 50 countries. They found seven specific characteristics that distinguish one culture from another. Five of those differences have to do with how people relate to one another, one has to do with attitudes about time, and one relates to perceptions of the environment.

One of the ways cultures differ from one another is in how members relate to one another. Relationship norms are modeled, taught, and passed down from one generation to the next. They govern the interaction among members and evoke various degrees of punishment if a member strays too far from acceptable interpersonal behavior. Trompenaars and Hampden-Turner (1998) have identified five general differences in the way members of various cultures define relationships. Each of those cultural norms exists on a spectrum between two opposite extremes.

Characteristics of Relationships

- Universalism versus particularism
- Individualism versus collectivism
- Neutral versus emotional
- Specific versus diffuse
- Achievement versus ascription

Universalism versus particularism describes the degree to which members adhere to societal norms and values. A universalist believes in universal rules that apply to everyone, while a particularist is willing to bend the rules based upon the circumstances and give special treatment to those who are deemed worthy. **Individualism versus collectivism** describes whether people define themselves primarily as individuals or as members of a group. Individualists give priority to the individual, while collectivists regard the community as more important than any one person. Next, cultural norms define the appropriate level of emotion in interpersonal transactions in the dimension of **neutral versus emotional**. In a neutral culture, emotions such as anger or sadness are not displayed, whereas in an emotional culture it is appropriate to show such feelings. The **specific versus diffuse** dimension describes the degree to which members include their personal lives in business relationships. Some cultures are task oriented (specific) and require little in the way of relationship-building, while others (diffuse) invite people to share their lives with one another and welcome social connectedness. Finally, **achievement versus ascription** refers to the way people within a certain culture define status. Achieved status is granted on the basis of personal accomplishments, whereas ascribed status is awarded on the basis of other attributes such as age, education, kinship, or personal connections.

Attitudes about time and environment are additional dimensions that differ among cultures and influence individual worldviews. Cultures with a *past orientation* value tradition and time-tested institutions and procedures. In contrast, a *future orientation* attempts to create a more desirable future by being progressive, innovative, and idealistic. A *present orientation* tends to minimize the value of tradition and does not necessarily strive to improve the future; instead, it focuses on present activities and enjoyments. In addition to these general orientations to time are norms regarding the role that time plays in daily life. In some cultures, for example, a 3:00 appointment should start exactly on time, while in other cultures it might mean anytime between 3:00 and 3:30.

Finally, attitudes about the environment or natural world often vary by culture. Some cultures attempt to control the environment, while others view it as something that should be honored and respected. In contrast to control-oriented cultures, those with a cooperative orientation understand events as products of powerful natural or supernatural forces worthy of respect. In other words, these cultures attribute events such as a booming economy or a catastrophic earthquake to external forces such as fate, luck, or a divine force, whereas control-oriented cultures place the source of good and bad events within human control related to effort, planning, and ability.

People from diverse cultural backgrounds have different ways of seeing the world, relating to others, and solving problems. These differences can have a significant effect on a number of group processes including communication, member satisfaction, cohesion, commitment, and decision making (Milliken & Martins, 1996). Unfortunately, members of certain groups are negatively evaluated and devalued based upon cultural differences. According to Bazerman (2006), people have a greater tendency to attribute positive characteristics to their own cultural group and associate negative characteristics with other groups. If group members are not aware of these ingroup and outgroup biases, an atmosphere of distrust and conflict can emerge, creating a suboptimal working environment. Attention must be paid to countering and minimizing internal biases and stereotypes in order to achieve optimal interpersonal dynamics and group performance.

THE CHALLENGES AND BENEFITS OF DIVERSITY

With changing demographics in the United States, organizations are becoming more diverse (Hays-Thomas, 2004; Jackson, 1992). While individual differences, or heterogeneity, make it more difficult to create a sense of cohesion and trust in workgroups, a number of trends, including the growth of multinational corporations, the increasing age gap, and the integration of female, minority, and international workers within organizations, has increased the frequency with which employees interact with persons of diverse backgrounds (Milliken & Martins, 1996).

Thus, it is particularly important to understand how diversity affects organizational behavior. To benefit from diversity, groups must overcome the tendency for interpersonal differences to divide. Group members must learn to embrace diversity and address potential problems before they begin in order to maximize the benefits of a diverse team.

Diversity in work teams can increase productivity due to the benefit of multiple perspectives and skill sets (Holtzman & Anderberg, 2011). For example, because members of cross-functional work teams have more exposure to employees outside of their particular workgroup, they have the ability to generate a wider range of perspectives and produce higher-quality solutions than do functionally nondiverse groups (Milliken & Martins, 1996; O'Reilly, Caldwell, & Barnett, 1989). However, without effective management, diversity can create problems by compromising trust, cohesion, and a shared identity (Mannix & Neale, 2005).

Diversity is a complex issue that affects organizations in various ways, both positive and negative (Jayne & Dipboye, 2004). Not all forms of diversity foster positive relationships or organizational effectiveness. Yet diversity has the potential to bring innovative and fresh perspectives to complex problems and stagnant systems when there is an atmosphere of acceptance and psychological safety (Martins, Schilpzand, Kirkman, Ivanaj, & Ivanaj, 2013). In his book *The Difference*, Scott Page (2007) explains diversity by using the analogy of a toolbox. He describes people as having different toolboxes with different sets of cognitive skills and perspectives. The more diverse a team is, the more tools it has to accomplish any given task. Page suggests that diversity based upon cognitive differences—that is the way people think and process information—is the real benefit of diversity. Diversity based upon demographic differences such as gender, race, sexual orientation, or religion may have little or no impact on team performance. In other words, when diverse perspectives are not relevant to the specific tasks the team is engaged in, diversity may not impact performance.

As groups process information and make decisions, the most innovative ideas are often suppressed. As described in Chapter 6, on decision making, group members tend to conform to the ideas of the majority. The Solomon Asch line experiments (Asch, 1956) offer convincing evidence that members are reluctant to disagree with the dominant views of the group. In these experiments, more than a third of the subjects were willing to deny their own perception in order to side with the majority. People adopt the majority view because they assume that the majority must be right and because they do not want to face possible rejection by others. But minority views are extremely important and can have a significant influence on a group (Martin & Hewstone, 2001). When dissent is voiced, members are more likely to question assumptions and consider alternatives, which increases the likelihood of groups selecting and developing more optimal solutions, products, and results (Nemeth, 1992).

Minority perspectives are viewpoints held by either one person or a small percentage of members. Minority views are generally more divergent in thought, which can lead to greater levels of creativity and innovation in group decisions (Nemeth, 1986, 1992, 1995). When groups fail to consider alternative viewpoints, they are at risk of making premature and ill-

informed decisions. Innovation and change often begin with an alternative view that is brought to the attention of a group. When members question the dominant position, the decision-making process is not only slowed down (preventing groupthink), it is also qualitatively changed. The minority position may not be adopted, but it can serve as a catalyst to help the group think more divergently, make better decisions, and improve group performance (De Dreu, 2002; De Dreu & West, 2001).

Minority dissent prevents premature consensus and promotes cognitive complexity, but because groups generally resist deviant perspectives, group leaders have a tendency to encourage, and if necessary, enforce conformity to the majority position (Marques, Abrams,

Paez, & Hogg, 2001). In the classic "Johnny Rocco" experiment done by Schachter (1961), participants were asked to decide the punishment of a fabricated lawbreaker, Johnny Rocco. A confederate was planted in each group who insisted on an especially harsh punishment, which functioned as a deviant position within the group. After some initial attempts to change the mind of confederates, groups stopped communicating with them and relegated them to low status and marginal roles. When group members were asked whom they would like to remove from the group, deviants were most often identified. It can be a very lonely and uncomfortable position to be in the minority on a group discussion.

The pressure to conform is even more salient in homogeneous groups (Marques, Abrams, Paez, & Hogg, 2001). Group members who stray too far from collective attitudes and beliefs can be judged harshly. Deviant or minority perspectives are often incorrectly perceived as weakening the social identity and cohesion of the group. Thus, alternative views are devalued, marginalized, and discounted. Groups that value diversity and invite disagreement can avoid these pitfalls. When there is freedom to challenge and debate the dominant perspective, groups are able to consider more options and alternatives (De Dreu & West, 2001). In this way, there is an increased likelihood that the worst ideas are exposed and scrutinized while the best ideas will be identified, evaluated, and implemented.

OUTCOMES OF GROUP DIVERSITY

The research on group diversity has produced conflicting results (Ely & Thomas, 2001; Mannix & Neale, 2005; van Knippenberg, De Dreu, & Homan, 2004). In an attempt to synthesize the data, Milliken and Martins (1996) surveyed the literature in 13 leading management journals between 1989 and 1994 and found 34 studies related to diversity in organizational settings. Most of the studies looked at the influence of visible demographic characteristics (race, ethnicity, gender, and age) and functional differences (educational background, occupational history, job-related knowledge, and skills) on group performance. Very few studies have focused on the effects of personality differences within organizational groups. In general, the majority of results indicate that diversity at all levels has the potential to increase the effectiveness of workgroups, but it also poses a threat to the relational connectedness and satisfaction of group members. People tend to be more comfortable with those who are most similar to them. However, groups that are diverse have a greater potential for success, especially with tasks that require innovation and creativity.

Cognitive Outcomes and Task Performance

In terms of team performance, diversity has been linked to a number of competitive advantages (Milliken & Martins, 1996). Differences of ethnicity and nationality have been shown to improve the quality of ideas and level of communication on complex tasks. Presumably, these positive outcomes occur because heterogeneous groups are able to consider a greater variety of perspectives, eventually leading to more realistic and sophisticated ways to analyze issues, make decisions, and solve problems. While it might take ethnically diverse members longer to warm up to one another, cultural differences can garner a wider variety of perspectives within the group (O'Reilly et al., 1989).

Gender diversity has been linked to higher personal productivity for women when there are high-level female executives present in the organization. If women perceive that career advancement is a realistic goal as evidenced by the success of other women, they will work harder to obtain it. Gender diversity also influences the communication structure within a group. A study by Smith-Lovin and Brody (1989) found that men were twice as likely to interrupt women as they were other men. Women were equally likely to interrupt both women and men, but were less than half as likely to successfully interrupt men.

In terms of communication networks, diverse groups have access to and communicate more frequently with members outside of their workgroup (Milliken & Martins, 1996). Because members come from varied backgrounds, they are embedded in diverse social networks. Thus, diverse workgroups gain valuable information and resources from outsiders, while avoiding insulated, limited perspectives. This increases the range of perspectives as well as the number and quality of ideas that are discussed within a group.

Results for both functional and educational diversity are not consistent across work contexts. While boards of directors, top management groups, and organizational task groups benefit from diversity, other groups have mixed results. Groups that are more functionally diverse have better links to external networks, thereby allowing them greater access to outside information. But cross-functional teams also have greater process losses because members have different ways of approaching tasks and projects. For example, engineers might approach certain tasks very differently than would marketing specialists. Yet these differences, when handled properly, can produce a more comprehensive view of issues that leads to better decisions and more effective solutions (Milliken & Martins, 1996).

Affective Outcomes and Relational Connection

While diversity has the potential to improve the quality of work within a team, it can be difficult for minority members to feel like they are accepted and valued. In general, members who are racially and ethnically different than their teammates tend to be less committed to their organizations and have higher rates of absenteeism (Milliken & Martins, 1996). Furthermore, minority members tend to have lower levels of group identification and member satisfaction, and are more likely to be evaluated negatively by their supervisors. Unfortunately, these lower levels of commitment together with lower performance ratings lead to higher turnover rates among minority workers.

Functional diversity can also be frustrating for members because it incurs higher coordination costs than those for functionally homogenous groups (Milliken & Martins, 1996). After all, it takes more effort to coordinate the work of members who have different skill sets and functional backgrounds. While it might be beneficial for engineers to work with salespeople and advertising specialists, it can also be difficult. Consequently, functional diversity has been linked to higher turnover rates and lower social integration within organizations.

The most consistent finding in the review of diversity research done by Milliken and Martins (1996) is that groups have a systematic tendency to homogenize all forms of diversity. Diverse groups have lower levels of member satisfaction and higher rates of turnover than homogenous groups typically do. These results apply to multiple types of diversity, including race, ethnicity, age, and gender. In particular, minority members are less satisfied with their groups than are other members. However, if groups can overcome the initial difficulties and predisposition toward conformity and learn to value differences, then they can experience the benefits of diversity (Watson, Johnson, & Zgourides, 2002).

CONTEXTUAL CONDITIONS FOR SUCCESS

Clearly, teams and organizations can benefit from a diverse workforce. However, some organizations either are not convinced of the benefits of diversity or do not know how to take advantage of it. Diversity will have a greater chance for success if (a) the organizational or workgroup context is supportive of it, (b) the influence of minority members is enhanced, and (c) group tasks require creativity and a variety of perspectives. When these conditions are met, the power and potential of diversity are released.

First, organizational and workgroup cultures that value diversity and cooperation are better suited to capitalize on the potential benefits of diversity (Homan & Greer, 2013). As Ely and Thomas (2001) found, organizations that view diversity as an asset will most likely benefit from it. Jehn and Bezrukova (2004) studied 10,717 members of 1,528 workgroups operating within a Fortune 500 company to evaluate the effects of diversity on performance. In this study, performance was measured by merit-based performance reviews, bonuses, and stock options at both the individual and group levels. Members of functionally diverse groups had higher bonuses in departments that cultivated a people-oriented, cooperative environment. Educationally diverse groups received higher bonuses in environments that emphasized customer service and building customer relationships.

Second, due to the tendency of groups to encourage cohesion and conformity, divergent perspectives are often marginalized. Groups that have more than just nominal representations by minority members are better positioned to succeed.

For example, in mixed-gender groups, women are less likely to contribute when they are the sole female member than when there are other women on the team (Myaskovsky, Unikel, & Dew, 2005). But just how many minority members does it take to empower those members? Kanter's (1977) theory on the proportion of minority to majority members suggests that "skewed" groups, where minority members constitute from between 1% to 15% of the group, are the most problematic for diverse members. Without a significant proportion of minority perspectives, minority members are more likely to be marginalized and subject to stereotyping. Minorities and women suffer disproportionately in their solo status as compared with males or whites. Sekaquaptewa and Thompson (2003) found that white males performed better in their solo status roles than white women, and white women performed better than minority women. On the other hand, groups where minority proportions range from 35% to 65% can lead to hostility and resentment among majority members because they feel that they have become outnumbered (Mannix & Neale, 2005). In reality, they are feeling what it is like to be in the minority. Thus, creating the ideal group composition can be tricky. Knouse and Dansby (1999) found that optimal diversity levels are obtained when the diversity subgroup comprises between 11% to 30% of the total workgroup.

Finally, diversity may be more advantageous for complex tasks that require innovation, creativity, and change, while workgroups that manage existing processes and practices may not benefit as much from a diverse membership (Mannix & Neale, 2005). Yet even in groups that manage existing day-to-day operations, team leaders can utilize the power of diversity to improve task efficiency. Over time, groups can become blind to their own deficiencies and weaknesses. Diverse perspectives can help groups accurately evaluate performance and maintain the highest levels of efficiency and team performance.

LEVERAGING DIFFERENCE TO IMPROVE TEAM PERFORMANCE

Diversity within teams can be a strategic advantage to organizations. But team leaders have to leverage those differences in order to experience the benefits. Noted diversity expert Martin Davidson (2002) suggests that in order to reap the sizable rewards of diversity, teams must first *see* the differences among members; then they must *understand* those differences; and, finally, they must *value* those differences. Only then can diversity be used as a lever to transform teams that have high potential into teams that are high performing.

Seeing Differences

The first step in leveraging difference is to see and acknowledge the differences among team members. As discussed earlier in this chapter, some of those differences are visible and some are not. And even when the differences are visible, some members are not aware of those differences, as seen in the opening parable about the elephant and the mouse. To benefit from diversity, teams must recognize that members are different. Once those differences are acknowledged, they can be leveraged to improve team performance.

In order to see and acknowledge differences among members, teams must adopt a "difference matters" stance. Team leaders can model this attitude and encourage team members to do the same. For example, a team leader might say, "John, how would the marketing department see this problem?" In another example, a team leader might acknowledge the fact that a particular member is from a different country or ethnic background and suggest that the person's unique perspective might benefit the team. Admittedly, conversations like these can be a bit awkward, but they communicate the message that differences are important.

Differences can often be identified by noting points of conflict among members. Conflicts not only reflect different opinions, they can also emerge from different backgrounds, different life experiences, or differences in professional training. Exploring the sources of conflict can identify the specific differences among members that have produced the difference of opinion. A team leader might say, "It seems like you two have very different ideas on this topic. Could those differences be related to your differences in personality, gender, race/ethnicity (if appropriate), or life experiences, etc.?" Questions such as these invite members to step back from the issues at hand and reflect on *why* members see things differently.

And finally, a third way to note differences is to observe silence. When certain members or subgroups within a team are silent, they might be feeling out of place or marginalized. Human beings have a deep need for acceptance and inclusion, so when a member withdraws, he or she might be feeling "different" from others and thus reluctant to participate. A simple question such as "John, I noticed you haven't said anything for a while. How are you feeling about this conversation?" can bring attention to possible feelings of isolation or rejection. It takes courage for members to speak up when they feel like they are seen as a minority or hold a minority position; acknowledging those differences is the first step in understanding those differences.

Understanding Differences

Once differences are seen and acknowledged, they need to be understood. Understanding the differences among members includes understanding member's backgrounds, their worldviews, and their life experiences. Understanding differences requires the time and freedom to explore and inquire about members who are different. In addition, teams need to understand how individual member differences affect the work of the team.

One of the ways to understand differences among members is to be curious. Members who are curious are able to inquire and ask questions of others who seem to be different or who might have a different perspective. It involves the regular practice of asking people to talk about themselves. "Tell me about your background" and "I'd like to hear more about your life experiences" are requests that invite others to tell their stories. A team leader might ask members to describe how they see themselves as both similar and different from other members on the team. Once authentic dialogue is taking place, members have to listen carefully in order to fully understand individual differences and to validate those who are sharing potentially vulnerable information.

Another way of understanding differences is to acquire information about people who come from different ethnic backgrounds, cultural backgrounds, and life experiences. Members can read and do research about what it means to come from a different gender, race, sexual orientation, country, or life experience. In order to be citizens of the world, we must be interested in and knowledgeable about other cultures and lifestyles. We need to be educated and keep an open mind about people who are different from ourselves. Because the world is becoming more multicultural and integrated, we are more likely to interact with those who come from different backgrounds. Communication is greatly enhanced when we have some context and knowledge of different groups of people. While we cannot assume everyone we meet from a certain group will share the typical characteristics of people from that group, it is a starting point that can be verified or refined based upon further conversations.

Valuing Differences

Finally, in order to leverage differences, teams must value those differences (Hentschel, Shemla, Wegge, & Kearney, 2013). Valuing differences among members occurs when teams have a true appreciation for diversity and an appreciation for different perspectives. Valuing differences means that members resist the initial impulse to reject ideas or discount people who are different from them. Instead, they have a posture of openness and appreciation for new ideas and new perspectives because of their potential to improve the performance of the team.

One way to increase the valuing or appreciation of differences is to reduce excessive carefulness in communication. Because members do not wish to offend others, they can be reluctant to acknowledge or explore individual differences. Furthermore, asking for a "woman's perspective" or an "African American" perspective on any given subject can be problematic because it suggests that the person answering the question is speaking for the whole reference group. Instead, team leaders can ask for the perspective of someone who is a woman or someone who is African American. The question can still be awkward, but teams that leverage differences are direct and explore members' perspectives and backgrounds openly without the excessive fear of being perceived as insensitive or inappropriate. If someone does get offended by a direct question, the questioner should be quick to apologize but should also take the opportunity to reinforce the importance of different perspectives, no matter how awkward those conversations can be.

Differences are leveraged when teams persist in the midst of conflict. Conflict often occurs in the storming stage of development, when differences among members are intensified. Different perspectives can cause differences of opinion, which can cause team conflict. Instead of prematurely reverting to a fight-or-flight response, teams that leverage differences are able to stand firm in the midst of conflict and push through the possible discomfort that can be experienced when working within a diverse environment.

Finally, groups that value differences are able to incorporate new perspectives into group discussions and team decisions. Unique perspectives are appreciated, valued, and given thoughtful consideration. In some cases, they are adopted into the processes of the group. In other cases, they are used as a catalyst to uncover unexamined assumptions and blind spots. The most effective teams are able to use difference to sharpen, expand, and then integrate new ideas.

For example, imagine a task force consisting of faculty, students, and college administrators who have been asked by the dean of student life to address the issue of alcohol abuse on campus. Each group of people will have very different ideas about how to define and solve the problem. One can easily imagine how age differences might affect differences of opinion. In the midst of conflicting views, students might realize they have very little power to influence the discussion, and thus only "go through the motions" of participation. If that happens, differences would not be leveraged and an important opportunity for change would have been missed. On the other hand, if students, who represent a minority voice in the creation of campus policies, are valued and empowered, they can offer a perspective on alcohol abuse that is more likely to lead to lasting change on campus.

LEADERSHIP IN ACTION

Globalization is a trend that is rapidly increasing. The best colleges and universities are veritable melting pots that attract scholarly, artistic, and athletic talent from around the world. Many of those students graduate and pursue work for Fortune 500 companies. These international conglomerates leverage the strengths and benefits of a broad range of countries to drive their success. As with any benefit, however, international team management comes with a cost.

In one of his final lectures in a popular course, "Leading and Managing Organizations," a highly respected emeritus professor at the Harvard Graduate School of Education addressed the issue of communication, the power of assumptions, and the unnecessary boundaries leaders unwittingly create for themselves by being unwilling to ask necessary, though potentially embarrassing, questions. He told his students a story about one of the first consulting engagements he had in Japan, where it is customary for the client to host the consultant for a "night on the town." In class, the professor recounted the exquisite meal, exceptional musical entertainment, and luxurious bar to which the group retired after dinner.

As the story goes, he was quite tired from his flight and was ready to retire to his hotel room, when his interpreter told him it was customary to have a post-dinner drink with his hosts before finishing the evening's activities. So, as the professor put it, "I decided to finish my drink as quickly as I could so I could get back to my hotel room and go to bed." Apparently, the businessmen with him *also* finished their drinks quickly and ordered another round of the very expensive Scotch. This seasoned professor and internationally respected organizational expert explained to his students that he stared wearily at a second glass of Scotch and decided to "take one for the team" and tough it out. He hurried through this second glass and, much to his dismay, noticed that the other men around him had finished theirs just as quickly and the servers had brought a *third* glass to everyone.

Just as the professor was raising the third glass to his lips in an effort to get through the end of the night as quickly as possible, his interpreter leaned in, excused the interruption, and asked him very politely how many more drinks he might be planning to have. The Japanese businessmen were struggling to keep up with the professor's drinking and were ready to go home, but because of the customary honoring of a guest, they were unable to say anything. Both groups had been trying to behave respectfully toward their counterpart, but by observing custom without communicating, they had both ended up at a destination neither desired.

The obvious message is that, often, as with the professor and the businessmen, cultures can work past one another, and diverse international teams can bring with them unanticipated challenges, despite the best of intentions. Thus, before an encounter with an unfamiliar cultural group it might be helpful not only to do some research but also to ask team members to describe some of their customs and expectations. Although it might be uncomfortable, leaders can model genuine interest by asking colleagues who come from a different background to describe how that background, whether cultural, racial, ethnic, or functional, influences their work on the team or project.

KEY TERMS

Universalism versus particularism	154	Achievement versus ascription	154
Individualism versus collectivism	154	Attitudes about time	154
Neutral versus emotional	154	Attitudes about the environment	154
Specific versus diffuse	154		

DISCUSSION QUESTIONS

1. Give three examples of visible diversity and three examples of nonvisible diversity.

2. List the various ways people are different from one another. What do people do to fit into the dominant culture, and what do they do to stand out from it?

3. What are the seven differentiating factors that distinguish cultures?

4. What are three benefits of diversity? Three challenges?

5. Describe three cognitive or task-related outcomes of diversity. Why is this so?

6. Describe three affective or relational outcomes of diversity. Why is this so?

7. In order to leverage differences among members, Davidson suggests that teams must first see, then understand, and, finally, value those differences. Describe how a team leader might facilitate this process.

GROUP ACTIVITIES

EXERCISE 8.1 UNCOVERING ASSUMPTIONS

Write down the first two or three characteristics that come to mind when you look at the following categories of people. There are no right or wrong answers. Please do not censor or screen your responses. After you are done, form groups of three to four to discuss your answers.

Characteristics of people in the following occupations:

Teachers: _____

Accountants: _____

Lawyers: _____

Salespeople: _____

Janitors: _____

Secretaries: _____

Nurses: _____

Characteristics of the following types of people:

Extroverts: _____

Open-minded: _____

Depressed: _____

Ambitious: _____

Characteristics of the following groups of people:

Men: _____

Women: _____

Japanese: _____

French: _____

British: _____

Hispanics: _____

Blacks: _____

Whites: _____

Asians: _____

What can you learn from this activity? How do stereotypes hurt or help teams?

EXERCISE 8.2 LEVERAGING DIFFERENCE

You have been appointed by the principal of your local high school to make recommendations about how to improve the school. Test scores and graduation rates have been in decline for five years, and she is desperate to reverse the trend. Form groups of four to five to address this issue but do not actually come up with recommendations for the school. The goal of this activity is become more aware of how diversity could benefit your team on this hypothetical project.

Please do the following:

1. *Seeing*: Describe all the ways the members of your group are different from one another.

2. *Understanding*: Discuss the significance of some of those differences. Share with one another how those differences have affected the way you see yourself, the way you see others, and the way you see the world.

3. *Valuing*: Discuss how member differences could be a benefit to the task of making recommendations to improve the school.

CASE 8.2: THE PRICE OF VALUE

The interdisciplinary task force at James Williams University has been assigned the responsibility of creating a series of integrated programs for a new first-year student dormitory complex that will help students make a successful transition from high school to college. Professors, students, administrators, and student life professionals have been invited to participate on the team. At first, enthusiasm and excitement about the new dorms and the endless possibilities kept the mood high and drove the team's progress. However, when decisions needed to be made about what to include and what to cut from the proposed budget for the program, differences arose:

- Faculty members were adamant about including lectures and discussions about intellectual pursuits. For example, a Renaissance English professor wanted to include formal and structured discussions around poetry and the meaning of life.

- Students, in contrast, wanted autonomy and freedom to define their own living environment. They wanted very few mandatory programs.

- Minority students wanted to emphasize the importance of diversity on campus and to offer programming to educate students on the benefits and challenges of living in integrated communities.

- Administrators were passionate about drafting and implementing alcohol and drug abuse prevention policies to minimize the risk to the university.

- Representatives from student life wanted to hold weekly community meetings to feature core values and social events that would encourage study skills, personal responsibility, and living in community.

Clearly, not all of these things could be featured in full; something had to be sacrificed.

Professor BigWig made the emphatic statement, "Back in my day, we were serious about academic pursuit and didn't need all of this coddling and extracurricular self-actualization. Much of this is rubbish, and we clearly need to focus our attention on giving students enough time for their studies."

Student CoolGuy answered, "Hey, man . . . this is a different world now. With all due respect, people don't come to college to bury their nose in a book. Kids are here to have fun, meet people, and get a good job after they graduate. All of this programming is getting in the way. We just need to let kids do their own thing!"

The minority student interjected, "I disagree. I think the whole purpose of living in this new setting is to learn about people from different cultures, races, and religions. I think it would be a shame if we missed the opportunity to create a global community."

Administrators said, "This is all well and good, but your ideas are going to cost money! We can't afford to hire anyone but resident advisors, who are paid to enforce the rules and maintain order. We can no longer afford to have students drinking and partying in the dorms. We have to stop the epidemic of underage drinking and drug use."

Student life added, "We need to ensure that students have the tools for success in college. We need this to be a cool place to live, and we need it to be a cool place to learn! This will be the only opportunity kids have to learn about living in community, personal responsibility, and life management. Oh! And we need to decorate the hallways. Let's make sure there is money in the budget for that."

- What is the value of the different opinions? If you were the leader of this team, how would you reconcile the differences of opinions? Using content from the chapter, at the end of the day, (a) how would you determine who gets their way, (b) how could you empower minority perspectives, and (c) how could you ensure that every voice gets heard?

Project Management

This chapter will present a number of tools that can aid in the process of effective project management. The first priority is to establish a collaborative vision and set of goals for teams to pursue. Once goals are defined, teams must identify specific tasks that need to be completed in order to reach those goals. This requires members to negotiate their roles and embrace tasks and responsibilities that contribute to the collective purpose of the team. Two project management approaches are presented in this chapter—the DAPEE and FOCUS models. Both models operate in a team environment to systematically use data and data analysis to solve problems. When used diligently, these structured strategies lead to efficient and systematic team collaboration.

CASE 9.1: GOOGLE

A founders' letter from Google, Inc., in 2004 states, "Serving our end users is at the heart of what we do and remains our number one priority" (www.google.com/competition/). That core value is evident in everything Google, Inc., does to meet its users' needs and to keep the company on the frontier of the human/technology interface. In organizations such as Google, well-defined values and a clear vision influence the level of commitment and quality of work that is done at every level of the company. Google was designed to be a collaborative environment embedded in a flat organization (rather than hierarchical). With its single-minded vision, Google has been able to focus on its core business of technology innovation.

One of the best examples of Google's innovation-focused, customer-oriented, solutions-minded, collaborative approach to projects is "20 Percent Time," a program that has been in place since the company's inception. Google employees are essentially given one day each week to work on projects that are novel, experimental, and even outside the primary areas of each employee's expertise. Teams are then formed with people who are passionate about similar concepts, ideas, and objectives regardless of whether they are in the same department or workgroup. While 20% of the week is spent on these projects by design, it is important to recognize that the culture of the company is what drives this value system that has produced technological successes like Gmail and Google Docs. But an innovative culture does not negate the need for structure and planning. Projects must be documented and managed to justify the time employees are investing in them. They must show tangible results. Thus, autonomy is balanced with accountability.

Google's culture also highlights an incredible work ethic, healthy competition, and a passion for problem-solving that permeates the organization. All of these qualities help to form the community's bond and point everyone toward the same goal: to serve the end user. How they do it, though, is the interesting part. According to online resource TechCrunch, Google's corporate engine runs on innovation. Innovation, therefore, is the purpose and the driver of both its project management and 20 Percent Time program.

From the smaller, faster teams brought together by 20 Percent Time to the larger, more traditional teams that work on the higher-profile projects that are driving the business results, Google is pacing the industry in output. That pace, it seems, combined with the innovative core that lies at the heart of the company, is helping Google stay true to its number one priority. In that regard, Google's project management strategy is as it should be at every company: a force that ties every member of the corporate community to the primary organizational mission while defining efficient, timely, valuable, and relevant strategies that produce results.

Case Study Discussion Questions

1. What are your reactions to this case?

2. How do you see Google's 20 Percent Time program fitting within its business model? How can Google justify allowing its employees to spend that much time away from their core functions?

3. What project management fundamentals do you think are most important to the execution of 20 Percent Time?

4. What competitive advantages does Google possess that might make the project management approach to 20 Percent Time impossible at other companies?

The most effective teams and organizations have a clear vision of what they want to accomplish. They know where they are going and have a comprehensive strategy or plan to get there. Project management tools help teams stay on track and make progress, no matter how large or complex the project may be. The starting point of any project, though, is to define exactly what needs to get done. Teams need a clear vision and concrete set of goals before they can formulate a plan that will produce results.

VISION AND PURPOSE

Findings from a group of researchers at Stanford University suggest that successful groups and organizations are purpose-driven and goal-oriented. In 1988, Jim Collins and his colleagues began to identify characteristics associated with visionary, successful organizations and documented their findings in the book *Built to Last* (Collins & Porras, 2002). They began by identifying exemplary and stable organizations through a survey sent out to 700 CEOs of companies on the Fortune 500 and Inc. 500 lists. Each CEO was prompted to nominate up to five companies perceived as "highly visionary." From there, researchers compiled a list of the top 18 exemplary organizations founded before 1950. The longevity of the companies gave them a long-standing track record to analyze. However, the real power of their research stems from the 18 comparable companies that were included in the study. Each truly "great" company was paired with a "good" company from the same industry that fared well over the years but was not able to break into the ranks of greatness. For example, $1 of stock invested in the general stock market from 1926 to 1990 would yield a return of $415. The comparison companies yielded a return of $955, while the visionary companies yielded a return of $6,356.

Collins and his colleagues looked at every facet of both sets of organizations, including their beginnings, strengths, challenges, and evolution. From over 60 thousand pages of data, they identified several fundamental principles that seemed to explain why the "visionary" organizations were significantly outperforming the "good" companies, which were used as a control group in the study. In 17 out of 18 cases, the visionary companies had a sense of mission and an understanding of their core purpose that went well beyond mere revenue production or shareholder equity. For example, the pharmaceutical company Merck defines one of its core values as "improving human life and benefiting humanity." Its mission statement, which is published on the company's website, echoes the sentiment of founder George Merck II that its first priority is its customers, followed by its employees, and then its investors. Importantly, Merck has taken actions that align with its core values, such as developing and donating significant quantities of the medication Mectizan to treat people suffering from "river blindness," a painful disease that affects over a million people in third world countries. These types of decisions that are consistent with the corporate mission and core values are what distinguish a "great" company from a "good" company.

Similar to visionary organizations, the most successful teams are also defined by a clear understanding of where they are going as well as a shared commitment from members to do what it takes to get there (Hackman, 2002; Huszczo, 2004; Kline, 1999; Locke & Latham, 1990, 2002; O'Leary-Kelly, Martocchio, & Frink, 1994; Senge, 1990). Group members must know why the group exists and what they are trying to accomplish. Otherwise, goal ambiguity can produce frustration, apathy, cynicism, and even hostility toward the leader. Because of this, leaders have the challenging task of not only helping their groups define clear and measurable goals, but also inspiring commitment to those goals. Well-defined and manageable goals keep groups on task and focused while strengthening each member's commitment to the group (Arrow, Poole, Henry, Wheelan, & Moreland, 2004; Lee, Sheldon, & Turban, 2003).

While visionary companies are fiercely committed to preserving their mission and core values, they are also still open to stimulating growth and change. They regularly engage in performance assessment and strategic planning in order to pursue progress. Having a clear sense of mission and purpose provides direction and focuses effort, no matter how large the group (Locke & Latham, 2002). In other words, that which works for visionary organizations holds true for small groups and individuals as well. No matter what size the group is, Collins states, "There is absolutely no reason why you can't articulate a core ideology for your own work group, department, or division" (Collins & Porras, 2002, p. 78).

Goals

Specific goals emerge from the mission or purpose of a group. They provide direction for the group but are different from the mission (which is broader) and from the strategies (which are narrower). Goals also provide motivation and can have a powerful effect on team performance (Kleingeld, van Mierlo, & Arends, 2011). According to Michael Dell (1999), CEO and founder of Dell Computers, "Mobilize your people around a common goal. Help them feel a part of something genuine, special, and important, and you inspire real passion and loyalty" (p. 119). Goals that are challenging and meaningful inspire teams to perform at their highest levels (Hackman, 2002; Kelly, Martocchio, & Frink, 1994; Klein, Wesson, Hollenbeck, & Alge, 1999). For example, the mission of a university cafeteria may be as broad as "providing a quality dining experience for faculty and students," but its goals will be more specific. It might strive for an increase in student satisfaction survey ratings by a certain number of percentage points. Specific strategies for achieving that goal might include adapting menus, changing food suppliers, or improving customer service. If team members buy into the goal, they will do anything and everything to improve the quality of their product.

The SMART acronym is a good way to evaluate the quality and clarity of goal statements. In order to be effective, goals must be **specific, measurable, attainable, relevant, and time-bounded.** Goals that are *specific* are clear and unambiguous. For example, a community service organization that has formed a task force or committee to increase membership is working with a goal that is too vague to provide meaningful direction and motivation. "Increasing membership by 30%" is more specific but still lacks criteria against which it can be measured. Goals that are *measurable* are defined in such a way that allows for concrete and objective assessment as to whether or not the goal has been reached. For example, "increase membership by 30% over last year's membership" allows for direct and ongoing evaluation of the goal.

Attainable goals are benchmarks that require a stretch by team members but that are still within the team's reach. Goals that are too ambitious risk not being taken seriously. Meanwhile, insufficiently challenging goals may fail to engage and capture the interest of a team. As a general rule, a sufficiently challenging goal offers a 50/50 chance of success (Hackman, 2002). Goals that are *relevant* are aligned with the capacity and responsibility of the group. For example, a team focused on increasing the membership of a community service organization would not be given a fund-raising goal, since that was not a part of its original charge. Instead, increasing the number of "likes" on the organization's Facebook page is a goal more consistent with its task.

Finally, goals need to be *time-bounded;* they need to be tied to specific deadlines and schedules. In the case of the membership task force, its goal might be to "increase the total number of members on the mailing list by 15% over the previous year by December 31st."

The visionary companies Collins studied did not just have concrete goals and well-defined strategies; they had "big, hairy, audacious goals," which the researchers referred to as BHAGs. Collins and his colleagues were intrigued that ambitious, even outlandish, goals were able to generate immense team spirit and intense, focused effort. BHAGs work best when they are clear, compelling, and engaging to the point of "grabbing people in the gut." For example, under the leadership of legendary CEO Jack Welch, General Electric had the following goal: "To become #1 or #2 in every market we serve and revolutionize this company to have the speed and agility of a small enterprise." This is contrasted with the vague, ambiguous, and more modest goals of Westinghouse, the comparison company, of "Total Quality, Market Leadership, Technology Driven, Global, Focused Growth, and Diversified" as stated in its 1989 annual report (Collins & Porras, 2002, p. 95).

Walmart is an example of how an initially small and seemingly insignificant group of people led by Sam Walton dreamed big and unleashed an international economic force. In 1945, Walton owned a single five-and-dime store, but his goal was to become the "best, most profitable variety store in Arkansas within five years" (Walton & Huey, 1992, p. 22). This was a large goal for a small-scale retailer. But that was typical of the culture Walton created—he set high goals and consistently reached them. By 1977, Walmart was a $1 billion company. In 1990, Walton set a goal of doubling the number of stores the company owned within 10 years. He achieved that goal as well. Sam Walton was a modest man from Arkansas who dreamed big and created one of the most powerful companies in the world (Fishman, 2006).

Big goals should not be viewed as arrogant; nor should they necessarily be considered naive regarding the obstacles and challenges standing in their way. One thing is clear, though: they *are* ambitious. Collins and his team of researchers analyzed the BHAGs of visionary companies and identified the following characteristics:

- A BHAG is clear and requires no additional explanation. It is plainly understandable and calls people to commitment and action.

- A BHAG falls well outside the comfort zone. It requires great effort and even a little luck.

- A BHAG becomes a focal point in the organization. The goal, itself, is more motivating than leaders or charismatic personalities.

- A BHAG is consistent with the organization's core purpose and values.

A BHAG is not limited to the organization as a whole, but can be set for individuals, departments, and teams. For example, Nordstrom, a clothing retailer known for its customer service, sets BHAGs throughout the company down to regional, store, department, and individual levels. Ambitious goal-setting works across organizational levels to mobilize the efforts of individuals and teams. By most measures of success such as year-over-year revenue growth, sustained profitability, human capital turnover rates, and stock price, Nordstrom continues to achieve its goals.

A final example of a famous BHAG is President John F. Kennedy's address to a joint session of Congress on May 25, 1961, where he challenged the United States to put a man on the moon by the end of the decade. The Soviet Union had launched the first satellite, Sputnik, in 1957 and then put the first man, Cosmonaut Yuri Gagarin, into space in 1961. America had lost the first two rounds of important space-related milestones. Thus, the space race became an important symbol of the Cold War between the United States and the

Soviets. Kennedy's address was urgent and compelling. Some thought he was far too optimistic, as the dream far outstripped the technology of the day. However, great resources, energy, and effort went into the space program, and on July 20, 1969, Apollo 11's commander, Neil Armstrong, stepped out of the lunar module onto the moon's surface and proclaimed, "That's one small step for [a] man, one giant leap for mankind."

While competition was clearly the catalyst for innovation and achievement, exploration of outer space is no longer used as an arena for demonstrating technological prowess. In the wake of budget cutbacks and reduced funding, countries have learned to work together to achieve common goals. One such example is the International Space Station, in which five countries joined forces to do research in outer space. In order to maximize resources, competition has given way to collaboration, the topic of the next section.

Collaborative Goal-Setting

Over the last few decades, organizations have been moving away from traditional, top-down authority structures in favor of giving groups more autonomy. Teams that have the freedom to partially define their own goals and to create the strategy that will achieve them tend to have higher levels of commitment among their members (Cohen & Bailey, 1997). Of course, most groups do not have complete autonomy. The executive leadership team of a national sorority might not be able to change the colors of its Greek letters, and a store employee at Starbucks is not going to be able to add new items to the store's menu. But allowing team members to have some input can influence both the quantity and quality of the team's output. Empowering teams by giving them some decision-making latitude does not remove their responsibility or accountability to the organization within which they operate. Groups can be both self-directed and accountable (Bishop & Scott, 2000).

Talented and competent people are more committed when they have some influence over their own goals and strategies (Porter, Hollenbeck, Ilgen, Ellis, West, & Moon, 2003). For example, a team that is responsible for an organization's website development might not respond too favorably to being told by a group of nontechnical executives what the website should look like and how they should go about the task. The group is more likely to be invested in the project if it is given a slightly different charge, such as, "The executive board wants a new website and they suggest that it look like this, but they would like you to present a few alternatives for them to consider." In the first option, the goal of a new website was well defined by a prototype that was given to the project group. In the second, the group was given some structure and direction along with the opportunity to design and create its own solution. In addition to greater levels of commitment, the creative potential of a team expands when more freedom is given with regard to output, direction, and the general spectrum of solutions.

Organizations and workgroups have various ways of encouraging ownership of goals. 3M, one of the 18 visionary companies identified by the Stanford researchers, has a long-standing tradition of encouraging its technical people to spend up to 15% of their time on projects of their choosing. This is one example of the culture at 3M that stimulates innovation and experimentation. In 1980, one of those innovative teams created Post-it notes, a concept originally created by a company employee to help keep scrap paper bookmarks from falling out of his church hymnal.

In another example that took place a number of decades ago, Ford Motor Company was interested in engaging factory workers in the mission of the company, so it designed employee involvement programs that placed workers in key roles on quality improvement teams. The collaboration between management and labor was successful because union workers felt respected and involved in strategic organizational decisions. Philip Caldwell, CEO of Ford at the time, was even made an honorary member of the union upon his retirement, an unprecedented move that demonstrated the quality of their collaboration (Collins & Porras, 2002).

In contrast to companies like 3M and Ford Motor, organizations that fail to empower their employees often perform poorly. Collins and the Stanford research team noticed that there was even an atmosphere of fear and intimidation in the comparison companies. Chase Manhattan Bank was micromanaged by David Rockefeller in the 1960s and 1970s, using a heavy-handed management approach that killed innovation and intrinsic motivation. The computer manufacturer Burroughs Corporation "publicly humiliated managers for failures and mistakes" (Collins & Porras, 2002, p. 166). Even though Burroughs had a technological lead over IBM in the 1960s, senior executives managed the organization with a very rigid, "top-down" philosophy that diminished the opportunity for employees to make decisions and act on their own. Eventually, the company merged with Sperry Corporation to form Unisys and currently plays a relatively small role in the field of technology.

Another one-time technological giant, Texas Instruments (TI), was also very autocratic and did not trust or empower employees. As a result, TI "lost its position as one of the most respected companies in America and suffered significant losses" (Collins & Porras, 2002, p. 166). Allowing talented people the freedom and autonomy to make decisions and take responsibility for their own work has tremendous benefits for teams and organizations. As research and history have shown repeatedly, when team members are empowered and given choices, they tend to be more engaged and committed to the goals of the team, to their teammates, and to the organization as a whole.

PROJECT MANAGEMENT

Workgroups, as opposed to social groups, are designed to accomplish a goal, task, or project. After the mission of the group is understood and some measure of cohesion and reasonable working relationships are in place, a group must devise a strategic plan for accomplishing its mission. It is one thing to know where you are going, but quite another to know how to get there. A well-defined road map or strategy provides the direction and specific task assignments necessary to achieve the goal. As the strategy is formulated and executed, a unique group structure will develop, defining the norms, roles, and culture as described in the previous chapter. This section will present two models of project management that mobilize teams and coordinate the work of members.

DAPEE Model

Project management and problem-solving strategies contain many similar components. First, groups need an accurate understanding of the goal or problem to be solved. Then they can devise a comprehensive plan for achieving the desired results. Next comes an efficient execution of that plan, and, finally, a systematic evaluation of the results. These components describing the basic structure of a task management or problem-solving strategy will be referred to by the acronym DAPEE:

- *Define* the project
- *Analyze* the problem or task
- *Plan* the solution or strategy
- *Execute* the plan
- *Evaluate* the outcome

This model describes how groups can systematically and effectively work toward long-term solutions. Keep in mind that this is not a purely linear model, as real-world problems are often complex, ambiguous, and ill-structured. While the general flow of the project moves from top to bottom, there are often times when a group will need to return to a previous stage.

Figure 9.1 DAPEE Model of Project Management

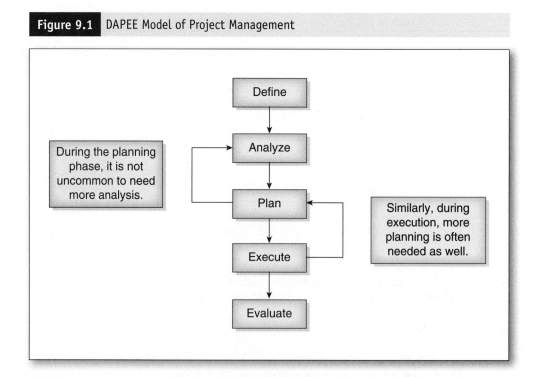

Define the Project or Goal

The first task of a project relates directly to the previous section. Effective teams are guided by SMART goals that are specific, measurable, attainable, relevant, and time-bounded. Groups must know where they are going before they can figure out the best way to get there (Marksberry, Bustle, & Clevinger, 2011). Because this has already been covered at length, let's move to application.

In a class on small-group behavior at Vanderbilt University, students are put into teams of 12 or 13 students to experience firsthand the concepts that are presented in lecture. The following project, which was completed over the course of a semester, demonstrates how students applied the DAPEE model.

Request for Proposal

Vanderbilt University is currently designing a freshman commons on the Peabody College campus. According to a university spokesperson, "The Freshman Commons will be a one-year living/learning environment that includes all the features of a residential college, such as resident faculty and staff, music rooms, study rooms and a dining hall."

The new dining center will be a centerpiece of student life at Peabody. Your task is to construct a proposal for mealtimes, special programs, and general operations that will accomplish the following goals: (a) create a cohesive community for incoming students, (b) ease the transition to college, and (c) facilitate academic development.

Two weeks from today, your group will make a 25-minute PowerPoint presentation that outlines your proposal. Please include graphs or charts of empirical research and collected data that support your recommendations. Also, you will be expected to submit a two-page executive briefing of your proposal.

Presentations will be evaluated by faculty members, graduate assistants, and the director of dining services using the following criteria: (a) persuasiveness of the presentation, (b) effective use of empirical research and collected data, and (c) level of preparation and professionalism.

Typical of many projects and tasks given to groups, an external entity defines the work to be completed, which in this case came from the course instructor. After the assignment was presented to students, they asked a number of questions about what the proposal should include and how it would be evaluated (i.e., "what it would take to get an A"). They sought further clarification of the project until they were reasonably sure that they understood what was being asked of them. Assignments like these leave much room for interpretation and are typical of the ill-structured problems groups face in the workplace.

Motivation and work ethic is a typical challenge that student teams face throughout the semester. As is the case with many class projects, students receive a collective grade on their work, which can be a source of contention. High achievers strive for nothing less than an "A," while other students are quite content with a "B" or "C." Therefore, from the start there is the potential for conflict over personal goals as they relate to the overall group performance. Since member motivation and effort are often related to the relative importance of the grade, project leaders have to find a way to engage their colleagues in order to establish equitable levels of effort.

Creating competition among groups is a common way for leaders to get members invested in the success of a team. However, this has the potential of creating ingroup/out-group bias (overly positive attitudes about one's own group in conjunction with overly negative attitudes about other groups), which can lead to hostility toward other groups. Another way leaders and high achievers ensure success is by doing most of the work themselves. Ironically, this encourages less motivated members to become even more passive and creates resentment on the part of overworked students. These issues are perennial problems within workgroups and often create conflict and tensions.

In the dining center project, the highest-performing teams took the time to clarify their performance goals through open discussion about standards and commitment. Members discussed their expectations and what they were willing and able to contribute to achieve their goals. This kind of open, direct, and mature dialogue allows members to verbalize unspoken assumptions and understand others' perspectives. The process itself helps engage members, build cohesion, and define member expectations and roles.

Analyze the Problem or Task

Problems and projects do not exist in a vacuum. There is always a context, history, and system within which they operate. Organizational learning expert Peter Senge (1990) suggests that today's problems emerge from yesterday's solutions. In other words, current problems are often the unintended results of past attempts to solve other problems. For example, when Nissan Motor Company needed to improve cash flow in the early 1990s, it cut back on product development. While money was saved in the short term, it was losing market share and revenue a decade later due to an outdated product line (Ghosn, 2002).

When problems or projects are not understood in a larger systemic context, solutions have a tendency to generate short-term gains that can turn into long-term liabilities. Before an effective plan of action can be created and executed, teams must thoroughly understand all of the issues related to their project. Unfortunately, members often jump to solution-planning before completely understanding and analyzing the problem.

Comprehensive analysis requires an accurate assessment of the current situation or state of affairs. Senge (1990) describes this creative tension between the current reality and ideal state as a catalyst for innovative problem-solving and planning. An optimal solution that bridges the gap between those extremes is dependent upon a thorough understanding of the starting point or current reality. Thus, the first stage in effective problem-solving is to restrain from brainstorming possible solutions and, instead, have the discipline to collect a broad range and meaningful depth of information about the problem.

While past experiences and personal opinions frequently influence group discussions, teams benefit when they have actual data upon which to design, execute, and evaluate plans. Evidence-based decisions require a substantial amount of data from which to derive effective solutions. A well-formulated action plan is built upon concrete information and critical dialogue (Postmes, Spears, & Cihangir, 2001).

An analytic tool that can help teams understand the dynamics underlying a problem is a force field analysis. It identifies the forces working toward goal attainment as well as those forces working against it (Kayser, 1994; Robson, 2002). First, the group must have a clear understanding of the goal or ideal state. Then, members must define the current reality in relation to that goal. For every goal or ideal state, there are forces and resources that support success and forces that hinder it.

A force field analysis gives a visual representation of the forces working for and against the team. It is helpful to display this graph on a whiteboard or computer projector and then write or type the actual forces on the arrows as members identify them.

The four questions associated with a force field analysis are these:

1. Where are we now (current reality)?

2. Where are we going (goal)?

3. What will help us reach the goal?

4. What is hindering us from making progress and reaching the goal?

Once the supporting and hindering forces have been identified, the group can decide which of the forces to focus on. In theory, if supporting forces are strengthened and hindering forces are removed, the current reality will move closer toward the goal. Some of the hindering forces are hard realities and cannot be changed; others are not significant enough to address. With the help of a skilled facilitator, the team can decide how to strengthen or remove various forces.

Figure 9.2   Force Field Analysis

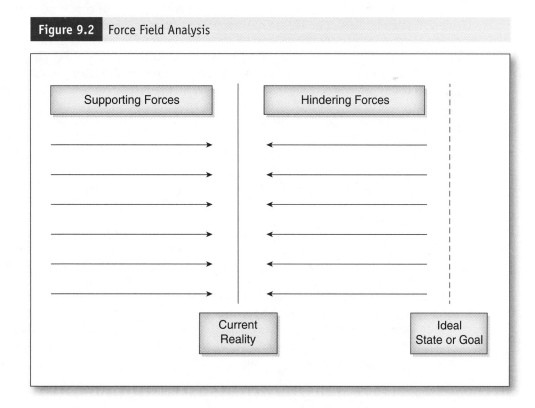

For example, a thorough analysis of the present dining situation helped students understand whether or not the three goals in the request for proposal were currently being met and to what degree. Teams needed to understand how the goals (creating a cohesive community for incoming students, facilitating the transition to college, and promoting academic development) were defined, measured, and implemented in the lives of college students. In addition, students acquired information about the concept of "residential colleges" within which the new dining center was to be embedded. Before teams could proceed with a specific proposal, they needed to collect and analyze a significant amount of data. Furthermore, projects like this, which attempt to change the campus culture, will have political forces working for and against them. Thus, a strong proposal would need to address the political issues related to the project. Furthermore, since other universities have dealt with the same issues, the most thorough proposals included examples of best practices in their analysis. Once students thoroughly understood the project and obstacles, they were ready to create a proposal and plan the presentation.

Plan the Solution or Strategy

A thorough understanding of both the existing reality and the ideal state has the potential to unleash the power of creative problem-solving. During the planning stage, high-performing teams allow a sufficient amount of time to brainstorm possible ideas or solutions to the problem while withholding judgment as those ideas are being generated. Then once all the ideas are out on the table, they can be systematically critiqued and/or combined (Kramer, Fleming, & Mannis, 2001). Contrary to popular belief, a good brainstorming session is first measured by the quantity of ideas generated versus the quality of those ideas. Evaluating the quality of various options comes next. Team members should be encouraged to participate without self-screening or censuring their thoughts, as the most creative ideas are often withheld out of fear of what others might think. In addition, it is helpful for teams to appoint a recorder or scribe to keep track of all the ideas that are generated so that none are lost.

Ideas can be presented and discussed in any number of formats. In some groups, members shout out ideas spontaneously. In other groups, the leader solicits ideas from each member in a systematic way in order to give everyone an opportunity to contribute. Another useful method requires members to write one idea per index card or Post-it note for as many ideas as they can generate. Cards are then collected or posted and a master list is created (Kayser, 1994). Once a comprehensive list of possible options has been generated, critical discussion can commence.

Teams must evaluate the ideas that have been generated with critical dialogue and discussion. For larger lists, ideas can be grouped together and combined, but with shorter lists (less than 15 items), ideas can be examined sequentially (Kayser, 1994). Members might ask for clarification, give opinions, or evaluate the quality and/or viability of each of the options. At this point, some ideas may need more analysis to determine their relative worth in solving the problem or advancing the project. Another meeting might be needed to allow time for members to do additional research and report their findings. When the group has sufficiently discussed the various ideas and has enough supporting evidence to make an informed decision, it is ready to choose the best course of action.

While some problems require a single solution, it is more common for groups to use a combination of ideas. Furthermore, there are a number of ways groups determine the specific components of their project plan. Decisions can be made by consensus, group vote, or by leader proclamation. Alternate approaches to group decision making will be discussed in a later chapter. Returning to our dining center example, some teams settled on an idea before thoroughly brainstorming all of their options. In those cases, only a few ideas were shared before an influential group member endorsed a certain idea. Then, other members validated the idea, momentum built, and the group would begin dividing up the tasks and assigning responsibilities. Unless someone slowed down the process, teams would often make premature and short-sighted decisions.

After teams have discussed various options and made a decision, it is time to make a plan. A **work plan** identifies, defines, and assigns the tasks that need to be completed by group members or subgroups. Since certain tasks are dependent on the completion of other tasks, due dates and completion schedules are formulated. After the tasks are defined, sequenced, and scheduled, group members either volunteer or are assigned to those tasks. Having the right people assigned to the right tasks is an important step in successfully completing the project. Issues of availability, motivation, and competence will influence these assignments. One particularly difficult issue is when a team member volunteers for an important assignment for which he or she is not particularly qualified. Team leaders can either guide task assignments with well-placed suggestions or they can simply ask the team if the tasks are assigned to the right people. If there is trust and good communication in the group, the wisdom of the collective will prevail. Otherwise, the leader may need to intervene and make an "executive" decision.

In our example, students identified the key work processes of the project and the specific tasks that needed to be completed. Some groups drew the work plan out on the classroom whiteboard; others simply verbalized it and relied on loose commitments. Of course, the more detailed and thorough the work plan, the better the outcome, in general. After the tasks were identified, students volunteered to be on one or more of the task groups based upon interest, ability, and experience. In the sample work plan below, the sequencing of tasks moves from left to right, with only the first key process (student interviews) described in detail. The information gathered from student interviews, including analyzed data in the form of charts and tables and an edited video clip, was needed by the research team to complete its task. The research group would then give its information to the group assigned to create PowerPoint slides and the like.

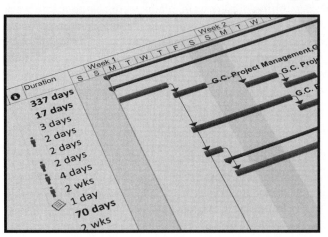

Table 9.1	Work Breakdown Structure		
Major Task	**Subtasks**	**Person Responsible**	**Due Date**
STUDENT INTERVIEWS			
	Design interviews	John	9/14
	Create questions	Bob	9/14
	Select participants	Sue	9/16
	Acquire video equipment	Ben	9/17
	Conduct interviews	Mary	9/22
	Analyze data	John	9/25
RESEARCH			
PRESENTATION SCRIPT			
EXECUTIVE SUMMARY			
POWERPOINT SLIDES			

Working backward from the date of the presentation, teams were able to create work schedules that included due dates for each individual task. Interdependencies were accounted for as members identified what they needed from one another in order to complete their own task. Those who participate in the planning process typically feel more committed to the solution and to its implementation. Their involvement in the process also enhances their understanding of what needs to be done and thus facilitates quality implementation.

Execute the Plan

The best decision, solution, or plan is only as good as its implementation, and successful implementation is anything but a guarantee. Organizations spend hundreds of millions of dollars every year hiring consultants to develop strategies and make recommendations that never get fully implemented. In fact, research by Becker, Huselid, and Ulrich (2001) suggests that the "ability to execute strategy" is the top nonfinancial variable that analysts consider in determining a company's stock value. Once work tasks have been assigned and deadlines have been established, the group is ready to execute its plan. Some tasks will be done by solitary members; others will be done in subgroups. Tasks are often underestimated in terms of difficulty and time required, and as a result, members can become frustrated when their work is dependent on the work of others. The most effective groups closely monitor this process and manage the interdependencies of tasks and subgroups.

During the execution phase, a well-defined communication structure that reports on both the progress and the inevitable problems is invaluable. Status meetings allow members to update the team on their own tasks and, in turn, hear how the project is developing in other areas. Typically, individuals and task groups report (a) the progress they've made on specific tasks, (b) any problems or obstacles they may have encountered, and (c) whether or not they are still on schedule. The answers to these questions will determine whether resources need to be reallocated to meet deadlines, whether deadlines need to be adjusted, or whether more planning or analysis is needed. Team members may be tempted to minimize their difficulties and report their progress in overly positive terms in order to appear competent and save face. The reporting of problems should not be a source of failure or embarrassment, or they will likely go underground only to resurface later (and often at the most inopportune times). When problems are openly acknowledged and discussed proactively, they can be effectively resolved through the collective wisdom of the group (Ranieri, 2004).

During the execution phase of the project, issues related to the quality of team members' contributions and their work ethic are common. Members of cohesive groups feel loyalty toward their colleagues and are motivated to do their part for the team. But this is not always the case. As discussed in Chapter 2, social loafing occurs when certain members rely upon the efforts of others and minimize their own contribution. Social loafing not only diminishes group morale but also has a negative impact on group performance (Mulvey & Klein, 1998). In addition, certain members might not have the same standards of excellence as their team-mates and don't complete their tasks to the highest standards. The most effective teams monitor their progress on a collective and individual level and confront members who are not fulfilling their responsibilities (Lencioni, 2002, 2005). Indeed, mutual accountability is one of the hallmarks of high-performance teams (Katzenbach & Smith, 2005).

Regarding the dining center project, the concept of mutual accountability was fairly difficult for students to embrace. After creating a plan, students volunteered for various tasks and committed to target dates. High-performing teams had regular status meetings and e-mail updates. Unfortunately, some groups neglected to set up adequate reporting structures to keep everyone on task and aware of the group's progress. When individuals or subgroups failed to meet deadlines, they left other members impatiently waiting for the information they needed to complete their own tasks. When these bottlenecks occurred, tempers would often flare.

For example, the PowerPoint subgroup was dependent on the student interview and research subgroups for the content on their slides. Obviously, the presentation group was not able to write the presentation script until it knew what content was covered in the PowerPoint slides. Each missed deadline created a larger backlog. Inevitably, a few members were stuck at the 11th hour throwing the last-minute details together for a number of the teams. This created frustration and resentment, both of which could have been avoided with better communication and regular status updates.

Evaluate the Outcome

The final step in the DAPEE model is evaluation. After defining project goals, analyzing relevant data, and creating and executing work plans, the group is ready to evaluate the results. As previously stated, a well-defined project goal or problem statement will have clear and measurable criteria from which to evaluate success. Therefore, the evaluation phase compares the project outcomes to the initial criteria for success. It is also helpful to evaluate the relative strengths and weaknesses of the team and how they might have improved its results.

In the case of the dining center project, criteria for evaluation were given to students when they received the assignment. After the projects were completed, students received multiple evaluation sheets from instructors and teaching assistants with feedback on their presentations and a grade for the project. The criteria for evaluation, though specified in the assignment, were still somewhat subjective. Evaluators tried to provide as much concrete evidence as possible to support their judgments. For example, they might have observed that charts and graphs in the PowerPoint presentation were not clearly labeled or that the method of data sampling was not clearly communicated by the speakers. While some students were dissatisfied with their grade, they still learned much from the feedback.

Students were also asked to assess their own team's preparation and presentation of the project. This helped members identify the strengths and weaknesses of the team. Here is a sample of some of those questions:

- What part of the project are you most proud of?

- How did the group go about making decisions?

- What part of the preparation process created unfinished business (i.e., tension that hasn't been resolved)? What needs to happen about that issue?

- Who were the unsung heroes for this presentation?

- Who seemed to work the hardest?

- Who were the most influential members in the process?

- If you were giving awards, which team members would win the following categories? (You can have more than one per person per category.)
  - The most encouraging of others?
  - The most creative?
  - The most fun to work with?
  - The most reliable?
  - The most helpful standard setters?
  - The best presenters of information?
  - The best technical experts?

- What could have been done to improve the presentation?

During a debriefing session, both the external feedback and self-assessments were shared and discussed. As Argyris (1994) suggests, most workers have sophisticated defense mechanisms that prevent them from learning meaningful lessons. A competent facilitator can help individuals move past their tendency to blame others, take responsibility for their own shortcomings, and hold themselves and others accountable to standards of excellence (Cannon & Witherspoon, 2005).

FOCUS Model

The FOCUS model is another commonly used framework that helps teams systematically solve problems and manage projects. Unlike the DAPEE model, which includes the implementation of proposed solutions, the FOCUS model only makes recommendations. For that reason, it is commonly used by management consulting teams to make recommendations to clients. Thus, the FOCUS acronym represents an effective step-by-step process for identifying and solving problems within organizations. Similar to the DAPEE model, it emphasizes the importance of data collection and analysis in solving problems:

- *Frame* the problem, project, or task
- *Organize* the team
- *Collect* data
- *Understand* the data
- *Solve* the problem

Essentially, FOCUS is a strong and helpful approach to developing and proposing a solution to an identified problem or task. If the project requires execution, implementation, or follow-through, the FOCUS model would require an implementation strategy under a new project charter designed to overcome the challenges inherent in realizing and institutionalizing the proposed solutions identified by the team.

Frame the Problem

The first step in the FOCUS model is to frame the problem by getting together as a team in order to understand the task at hand. What is the goal? What is the challenge? What are the potential barriers to success? What are the constraints to consider? Gap analyses (the current state versus the ideal state), needs assessments, and requests for proposal (RFPs) are good tools to use during this primary stage, because they facilitate the team's understanding of what needs to be done in order to successfully complete the project. They can also help clarify the obstacles that stand in the way of success. Project charters also help lend scope and scale to the problem, project, or task; essentially, they are a clear charge to the team.

To effectively frame the problem, a team typically engages in an initial discussion to gain a clear understanding between the "client" and the team. What does the client want? What does the client need? Are those the same or different? If they're different, what will your team have to do in order to effectively educate and empower the client? The key to the first step in solving the problem is *inquiry*. The fundamental step of successful project management is to begin by getting a comprehensive understanding of the task at hand. Once the team has established its purpose and understands its task, the leader can begin to organize the assets on the team.

Organize the Team

In organizing the team, the top priorities are maximizing the team's resources and creating an efficient team structure. A project team is similar to a finely tuned sports team comprised of experts or specialists at various positions or tasks. Thus, tasks should be assigned according to skill and experience. This assumes that the team has been formed to ensure that there is a diversity of skill and specialization.

Maximizing the team's human resources is productive for the team in three specific ways. First, it leverages the natural talents and inclinations of the team members, raising morale and improving the quality of the product. Second, it shortens the timeline between assignment and production because there is no additional learning curve for each individual in his or her task. And finally, it facilitates team chemistry by fortifying trust and interdependence among the team members. Together, these three points drive value and quality of product while improving team efficiency and general rapport.

The second step in organizing the team is creating an efficient structure from which to operate. This includes discussing ground rules and norms that set clear expectations for member behavior. As we described in the previous chapter, leaders should thoughtfully plan the launch in a way that builds a solid infrastructure and increases cohesion. The team also needs to decide when, where, and how often it will meet. It is very helpful if agendas are prepared before those meetings and that minutes are kept in order to ensure efficiency. The "organize" step is often overlooked and undervalued. However, prioritizing this step leads to a higher-quality product and a more consistent performance.

Collect Data

Once the team has assigned responsibilities and created an operational structure, it is ready to collect (and clarify) the data. In this step, team members work to gain as much insight as possible into the issues and forces relevant to the task. While it is easy to respond with short-sighted opinions and premature judgments, the best teams are disciplined and wait to see the data. With the increasingly abundant access to information through technology, this step has become shorter and more efficient. Groups can take advantage of web searches, published research, and volumes of online interviews, forums, and first-person accessibility. One very real challenge that exists in the collect step is duration: How much time and effort should be allocated for this step? Because there is often a wealth of information available in today's world, teams can get lost in a never-ending search for more data.

In addition to problems related to quantity, not all data are of equal quality. High-performing groups attempt to acquire the freshest, most robust information available. However, a common mistake many groups make is that, because information is so readily accessible, they don't spend the necessary time making sure that the data they collect are the most relevant, up-to-date, and reliable pieces of information available. Once team members are sure they have gathered the best information, they are then ready to analyze it.

Understand the Data

Having gathered the data, the team is now positioned to organize and analyze the information. "Understanding the data" is a process that relies upon concrete evidence and empirical data to gain clarity about a problem and point the team toward the best solution. The amount of information can be overwhelming, and many teams have become immobilized in the morass of numbers, charts, and graphs. Furthermore, there is rarely a situation in which all the data point to the same conclusion, so it only follows that the team must engage in a fair amount of critical dialogue, inquiry, and consensus-building. What

happens to the team's motivation and direction in the face of conflicting or divergent data findings? Does this create crisis or encourage innovation? The answers are dependent upon the ability of the leader to guide the team through ambiguity.

Leaders must remain vigilant in requiring their team members to rely upon hard data and to report the data as data, rather than infusing their reports with normative, value-laden, or emotional language. Leaders can ask themselves and their team the following questions:

- Are we taking an objective stance on the information we retrieved?

- If so, what do the data suggest?

- If not, what are we missing?

- Do we need to delve deeper into any specific area?

- If we move beyond the next logical step, where might we find ourselves?

- Are there any pitfalls to account for, given the data at our disposal?

- Repercussions and popularity aside, what is the real conclusion here?

Honest answers to these questions will naturally lead to the final step of the FOCUS model: arriving at a solution to the problem, task, or assignment.

Solve the Problem

If executed properly, the FOCUS model should deliver solutions that are both self-evident and evidence based. However, the conclusion obviously cannot present itself to the client group. And this is what makes the final step so complex. How does a group propose a foreign or novel solution to an otherwise skeptical client? American journalist and social critic H. L. Mencken once said, "For every problem, there is a solution that is simple, compelling, and wrong." Team leaders must be aware of the challenges related to preparing and presenting their solution to a client—whether that client is a professor, a paying customer, a manager, or the executive board of a company.

As is obvious from the preceding four steps, the FOCUS model builds on itself through the course of the project. The quality of the solution is dependent upon each preceding step, which creates a systematic approach that increases the chances for an excellent outcome. Given the right amount of time, teams can actually walk backward through the model to find the point at which the process disintegrated, fix it, and then progress once again to the best possible solution. But how does a team know it has reached the best possible solution?

Strong and inclusive leadership, slavish dedication to research and data gathering, as well as robust analysis, creative thinking, and member commitment are all fundamental contributors to the best possible solutions. Before submitting the final solution, the team will have ensured that it maximized benefit to the client group, that it offered the greatest progress for the lowest cost, and that it aligned with the identity, purpose, mission, and vision of the client group. Here again, if the solution yielded from the FOCUS model process is unacceptable to the client, the team can easily backtrack and analyze its steps to determine where it went awry. In that sense, it is the agility of the model that makes it so useful.

LEADERSHIP IN ACTION

College graduates are often surprised by how much of their professional lives involve working and performing in teams. Many of our former students have reported that the majority of their work during the first two years in the workplace is performed in a team environment. Because of this, it is important to become comfortable with at least one model of project management before entering an internship or full-time job. Project management is essentially a structure that affords groups and individuals the discipline required for timely and consistent performance across tasks and conditions.

In one student's e-mail, he specifically mentioned that the most productive teams had a set of well-defined, shared goals (i.e., "What do we want to accomplish?"), specific task assignments ("Who will do what and by when?"), predetermined meeting frequency ("Where, when, and how often will we meet?"), official protocols ("How do we make the best decisions? What are our ground rules? What happens if we violate a protocol?"), and formal leadership structures ("Who is doing what? Who is in charge of what?"). He was pleased that the material we had discussed at length in class was reinforced by his employer. Not surprisingly, the business world continues to prove that team success requires a comprehensive and well-defined project plan.

Effective project management can help navigate the ambiguity that is often present in complex team projects and can reduce the propensity toward inefficient team operation. Models such as DAPEE or FOCUS clearly define individual assignments and timelines for delivery of products, and include a built-in system of accountability. Deliberate planning and structured problem-solving ultimately lead to a foundation of safety, trust, confidence, and consistency that allows teams to manage projects effectively. In order to carry this out, leaders need a clear, consistent, and candid communication style so members understand their roles and responsibilities to the project.

Granted, projects are often constrained by resources such as time, money, and human capital. Many readers will believe that there is just not enough time to go through these steps as a group plans the project. However, as experience has proven and history reveals, the groups that actually take this time to plan and intentionally manage their project, thereby establishing the groundwork for their engagement together, are the ones that will ultimately succeed (Kirkman & Rosen, 1999). As a project leader in action, the key takeaway is to stay committed to a structured process of planning and managing the project even when members resist. Teams will often jump to solutions prematurely without really understanding the task or problem and without finding evidence to guide the discovery of the best solution. In addition, members are quick to haphazardly assign responsibilities without any accountability structure or consideration of finding the best person for each task. Without a well-defined and systematic approach, managing any project will be unnecessarily frustrating and potentially exhausting.

KEY TERMS

Specific   170
Measurable   170
Attainable   170
Relevant   170

Time-bounded   170
Ingroup/outgroup bias   176
Force field analysis   176
Work plan   179

DISCUSSION QUESTIONS

1. What challenges might a leader face if members do not share a clear understanding of the mission or purpose of the team?

2. Define SMART and BHAG goals and discuss their similarities and differences.

3. What are the benefits and drawbacks of giving teams more autonomy and freedom when defining goals?

4. Describe social loafing and identify specific things that a team leader can do to prevent it.

5. Explain the importance of self-assessment and feedback when working in a group.

6. Compare and contrast the DAPEE model of project management with the FOCUS model of project management.

7. The FOCUS model of project management highlights the importance of organizing the team. What are some of the specific things that need to be done to ensure an organized effort?

GROUP ACTIVITIES

EXERCISE 9.1 CREATING A VIRAL VIDEO

After forming groups of five to seven students, you are to create a two- to four-minute-long "viral video" that demonstrates the disasters that can happen on teams. Use the DAPEE model as a framework for carrying out this project:

1. *Define:* How would you define this task? Describe the characteristics of a successful viral video.

2. *Analyze:* What are the typical problems that occur in teams? What kinds of situations would resonate most with viewers?

3. *Plan:* Create a plan to make your video. Create an outline of the script, assign roles, decide where you will film it, and determine what equipment you will need.

4. *Execute:* Record the video and do any editing that you might have the capability to do.

5. *Evaluate:* Play the video for the class and get feedback from others about the quality of your product.

EXERCISE 9.2 THE MARSHMALLOW CHALLENGE

Break into groups of four to design and build a freestanding structure using as much or as little of the following materials: 20 sticks of spaghetti, three feet of kite string, three feet of masking tape, and one marshmallow. The entire marshmallow has to sit on top of your structure to be successful. You have 18 minutes to accomplish this task. The goal is to build the tallest freestanding structure from the top surface of the table to the top of the marshmallow.

When you have completed the activity, go to www.marshmallowchallenge.com for a debriefing.

CASE 9.2: SOAP AND SPARE TIME

You are trying to figure out a way to make some extra spending money at school. One day, it dawns on you that there might be an opportunity to get paid to do laundry for your fellow students. With your parents coming in a few days for Parents' Weekend, you were so embarrassed by your roommate's dirty clothes strewn all over his side of the room that you offered to do his laundry for him. He was more than happy to take you up on your offer and even was willing to pay you $5 per load to take that responsibility off his plate. You made a little money, he got clean laundry, and both of you pulled Parents' Weekend off without a hitch.

Word got out that you did laundry for your neighbor, and before you knew it, you had three e-mails from other students wanting you to do the same thing for them. After two afternoons of work you did 14 loads of laundry and made $70. You started to think this might be a good way to earn some extra cash for the semester.

- *Using what you know about project management from this chapter—and adapting the DAPEE model in particular—create a business plan for your student laundry company that will allow you to maintain focus on your studies while maximizing your income.*

CHAPTER 10

Performance Evaluation

The best teams have such a strong commitment to success that they are constantly evaluating their performance and learning from their mistakes. In most successful organizations, there is a similar urgency to continually improve and refine internal processes. This requires evaluation, learning, intervention, and follow-through. This chapter presents tools for performance evaluation and strategies for continuous improvement. It begins by describing two types of assessments—task and interpersonal—before exploring the typical dysfunctions of teams. Then it discusses how teams can learn from their experiences, change, and improve their performance.

CASE 10.1: SOUTHWEST AIRLINES

From its beginning, Southwest Airlines faced one challenge after another. Although the Texas Aeronautics Commission approved Southwest's request to fly on February 20, 1968, competitors used legal and political pressure to keep Southwest planes out of the air for three years. Not one to be intimidated, CEO Herb Kelleher fought all the way to the Texas and United States Supreme Courts for the right to be in business (Jackson & Schuler, 2002). In 1971, Southwest began flying four Boeing 737 planes among a select number of cities within the state of Texas. Due to early financial problems, one of those planes had to be sold. The airline industry is a challenging business, and companies have only a limited amount of time to become profitable. Since the Airline Deregulation Act of 1978, many carriers have gone bankrupt due to fierce competition and lower fares.

Southwest positioned itself in the market as a low-cost, no-frills carrier with a strong commitment to customer satisfaction. The mission of Southwest is to deliver exemplary customer service with a "sense of warmth, friendliness, individual pride, and Company Spirit." In order to keep costs down and customer satisfaction high, Southwest had to turn planes around with the utmost efficiency and service (Gittell, 2003). With only three planes, company officials needed to keep them filled and flying as much as possible. According to the industry average, planes take 55 minutes from landing to takeoff (Jackson & Schuler, 2002). Crews use this time to unload and load luggage, to clean out and restock the planes, and to fuel and prepare them for the next flight. Southwest wanted to cut this turnaround time to 10 minutes. This would be a formidable challenge.

The airline industry has traditionally held one of the highest concentrations of union membership and representation among U.S. corporations (Gittell, 2003). There is a long history of management-labor problems that has led to an adversarial and, at times, contentious relationship between the two. Not only did labor distrust management, different functional roles within Southwest distrusted one another. For example, flight attendants were suspicious of pilots, who were perceived as condescending toward gate agents, who in turn got frustrated with mechanics. So one can imagine that baggage handlers and flight crews would not have been overly enthusiastic about the prospect of 10-minute turnarounds; workers were being asked to work harder with no increase in pay. In order to be successful, Southwest had to create a culture of mutual respect and collaboration, the likes of which had never before been seen in the airline industry. Everyone had to pitch in to get the planes back in the air, even if it was not in their job description.

Over time, they were able to turn planes around 50% faster than the industry average. According to Gittell (2003), the primary reason for Southwest's success can be summed up in one word: relationships. *More specifically, the company places high value on the relationships between and among its managers, employees, unions, and suppliers. Somehow, Southwest has created a rich, relational environment characterized by a shared vision, shared identity, and mutual respect. In the first half of the 1990s, Southwest was number 1 in on-time arrivals, luggage handling, and customer service for five years running, an accomplishment that is unrivaled in the airline industry. Southwest evaluated performance and set the standard for success with concrete measures such as average turnaround times and customer satisfaction ratings. Not only did the company benefit from a concentrated commitment to performance standards, its customers did as well.*

Case Study Discussion Questions

1. How do you get different people from different departments who do not trust one another to work together as a united organization?

2. What are some common reasons why people are suspicious of others and engage in turf battles?

3. What are some of the unique characteristics of Southwest that sets it apart from other airlines?

4. How did Southwest measure performance?

In order to become a high-performing team, workgroups must evaluate themselves regularly and monitor various benchmarks that measure team performance. Ongoing data collection, analysis, and application are necessary for a team (or organization) of any size to get a sense of relative performance. Depending upon the metrics or "key performance indicators" of the team or organization, data collection methods will vary. For example, baseball teams are notorious for their collection, analysis, and application of situational performance data. A pitcher's tendencies and pitch-selection patterns can be identified over time, which can help batters anticipate the next pitch in a range of circumstances. Conversely, pitchers can get their coaches' help in determining the weaknesses of opposing batters by analyzing film data and batting performance in a variety of situations.

A great example of the power of data analysis is the now-famous story of the 2002 Oakland A's, the Major League Baseball club featured in Michael Lewis's 2003 book, *Moneyball: The Art of Winning an Unfair Game* (also a 2011 feature film starring Brad Pitt).

Led by Billy Beane, the A's used objective, empirical evidence of players' performance to assemble a winning team that could compete with the superstar players and enormous payrolls of larger-market teams. Backed into a financial corner, the A's organization turned to a statistical analysis method known as "sabermetrics" (based on the acronym SABR, for "The Society for American Baseball Research") in order to determine that players with a high on-base percentage were more valuable yet cheaper to acquire than players with strengths in other, more popular metrics like batting average or runs scored. Essentially, Beane's approach to recruiting was driven by a major financial constraint. He was operating with a third of the payroll of the New York Yankees, so he had to find undervalued players who could win games. A detailed analysis of player statistics helped him find those players, and the Oakland A's were able to build their championship team with players who were overlooked by other clubs.

The key to using data effectively is first to identify factors that represent a connection to positive outcomes or team success. Then this information can be collected and analyzed to determine how well a team is doing in relation to its goals. When evaluating team performance, there are two areas that need to be examined: task assessment (e.g., assignments, deliverables, goal achievement, and timelines) and interpersonal assessments (cohesion, interpersonal skills, and member satisfaction). The most successful teams regularly evaluate their own performance and utilize the results to foster continuous improvement.

TASK ASSESSMENT

Outcome-based assessments require and presuppose the establishment of team goals. The ultimate goal or mission of a team is often defined by the organization or institution within which it operates. In one particular college course, students are assigned to teams and spend an entire semester working on a consulting project that involves identifying and solving a real problem on campus. At the end of the semester, they have to present their recommendation and submit a report to support their findings. In this example, every team has the same two tasks (a presentation and a report) that can be evaluated according to the same objective criteria. Most teams have similar performance goals related to grade achievement; they want to earn an "A" on the project. But this loose definition of success will rarely produce the results students want. As discussed in Chapter 9, on project management, successful teams find ways to define, plan, and monitor progress toward their stated goals. When specific goals are defined concretely, it is much easier to set out a project time line with milestones in order to chart progress and gauge relative success. This, then, facilitates an opportunity for members to have honest and open dialogue because of objective standards that allow constructive discussion based on whether or not individual members and the team as a whole have measured up to their own standards of success.

Team performance is strongly related to the way in which work is distributed among its members. In order to avoid problems of work inequity, groups should discuss how they will approach the workload before they make task assignments. If a given member is unable to commit fully to the team throughout the project, there are likely ways that he or she can add value on more concentrated tasks. Perhaps this individual can take on the responsibility of presenting the final product, or be a part of another task that doesn't require as much time but is still of value to the team. There may very well be members on the team who are motivated to step forward and own certain parts of the project that are of particular interest to them. Regardless of how the workload is divided up, expected member contributions must be made explicit in order to establish a reference point for tracking individual contributions relative to the responsibilities, tasks, and goals of the team.

INTERPERSONAL ASSESSMENT

Group Cohesion

Hollywood feature films in which leaders brilliantly galvanize their group or team through shared hardship and inspire commitment to a common goal are plentiful. Films like *Braveheart* (depicting William Wallace's leadership of the Scottish resistance to King Edward's rule), *We Are Marshall* (about the Marshall University football program's recovery from a tragic plane crash that killed nearly every member of the team), *Miracle* (about the 1980 U.S. men's hockey team's quest to defeat the indomitable Russian team), or *Remember the Titans* (about a football team from a newly integrated high school that fights to overcome adversity, personal challenges, and social prejudice) all emphasize the importance of group cohesion. Cohesion can be deduced by observing the ways members interact with one another before, during, and after meetings. Teams that have high levels of group cohesion are not only committed to the mission of the group; they are committed to one another. Rollie Massimino, the legendary coach of the 1985 Villanova men's basketball team that defeated the highly favored Georgetown Hoyas to win the NCAA national championship, said that good players play for themselves but great players play for each other. Members of highly cohesive teams are quick to take personal responsibility for team failures but give credit to the team for successes.

Another way to measure group cohesion is by conducting team surveys. Members can fill out an online or paper-and-pencil survey that measures team constructs such as commitment, camaraderie, and cohesion. The following survey is an example of the kind of questions that can be asked to measure the cohesion of a group. Average scores below 3.0 on any question could signal a potential problem.

When interpreting the results of these types of surveys, leaders must consider the group's stage of development. Groups will generally begin their project at a moderate level of cohesion, dip during the storming and norming phases, and then increase as the group begins to see improved coordination, trust, and progress.

Another example of group cohesiveness can be found in the military's approach to training and onboarding. Basic training is a crucible through which all new recruits must pass. New members are stripped down as individuals and built back up as a unit. Individual goals are broken by drill instructors and replaced by shared goals that value team success. Their code of conduct is defined by the expectations of their military branch, their drill instructors, and the culture that permeates their units. Regardless of one's stance on military action, without group cohesiveness to this degree, the confusion, ambiguity, and intensity

Table 10.1	Group Attitude Questionnaire				
	Strongly Disagree	Disagree	Neutral	Agree	Strongly Agree
I enjoy working with this group	1	2	3	4	5
People in this group seem to like one another	1	2	3	4	5
Everyone does an equal share of the work	1	2	3	4	5
Everyone is free to express their ideas	1	2	3	4	5
People are respectful of others	1	2	3	4	5
This group works well together	1	2	3	4	5
I feel appreciated in this group	1	2	3	4	5
People are committed to this group	1	2	3	4	5
This group understands its goals and purpose	1	2	3	4	5
Relationships are an important part of this group	1	2	3	4	5

of battle would pose an insurmountable threat. Again, this facet of interpersonal assessment is important to the group's ability to withstand hardship, overcome obstacles, and succeed as a team. Thus, drill sergeants and other military leaders are constantly monitoring the level of cohesion in their troops.

Interpersonal Skills

Chapter 3, on interpersonal dynamics, suggested that typical interpersonal problems emerge when members have extreme amounts of assertiveness (being either dominant or submissive), sociability (being either overly friendly or cold and aloof), or interpersonal sensitivity (being either overly sensitive or insensitive). Team leaders or group observers can measure these three variables by watching the interaction among members (Haynie, 2012). In addition, members can reflect on their own strengths and weaknesses and ask teammates for feedback about their interpersonal performance. Kim Vella, chief people officer at Tractor Supply Company, encourages the use of "start, stop, and continue." She regularly asks team members what they would like her to start doing that she is not already doing, what they would like her to stop doing that is not very helpful, and what they would like her to continue doing. This way, not only does she get rich feedback about her own performance, but she also models a commitment to continuous improvement to her colleagues and direct reports.

Accurate feedback can significantly impact personal and interpersonal development. Multirater surveys or 360 degree assessments typically include a self-assessment and an assessment from peers, coworkers, or teammates. They can also include an assessment from a boss or supervisor, direct reports, or customers. These multiple viewpoints give individuals a more complete view of their strengths and potential weaknesses. The feedback can be very useful because it raises self-awareness, identifies areas that need to be strengthened and developed, and begins a process of personal growth and learning.

Groups benefit when members are actively engaged in team discussions. Thus, a group observer might simply count the number of comments each member makes during a team meeting. That information can help determine if certain members are talking too much or too little, which can signal potential communication problems. Nonverbal behavior and seating arrangements can also be used to identify members who are at the interpersonal extremes. Dominant members like to be in the middle of the action and tend to speak loudly, while detached members prefer to stay on the fringes and are tentative when they speak. In either case, members may need training in either active listening or assertiveness in order to achieve more balanced communication. The following list identifies some of the important interpersonal dynamics to look for in groups:

- There is balanced participation from all members.

- Members feel free to express themselves.

- Members "suspend" their assumptions and stay open to new ideas.

- Members work hard to understand other perspectives.

- Dialogue is always respectful yet spirited at times.

Formal measures of emotional intelligence are also available to assess the interpersonal skills of members. The following website contains a wealth of information on emotional intelligence including assessment tools and training materials: www.eiconsortium.org.

Member Satisfaction

One of the criteria for successful groups is the level of satisfaction among its members. Teams can be tremendously successful, but if the members were dissatisfied with the experience the success was limited. Levine (1973) studied 64 three-person teams of college students who engaged in role-playing exercises and measured two specific variables: (1) the *amount* of control possessed by all members, and (2) *how* this control was distributed. He found that the total amount of control members had over decision making and the degree to which that control was equally shared among the members had a positive influence on the team performance and on member satisfaction. Put another way, Levine's results showed that group members tend to be more satisfied in groups in which they have some influence and control.

Conversely, in groups in which the power to make and influence decisions and take action is limited to only a few members, with others being dismissed and marginalized, the average satisfaction score decreases (Levine, 1973).

FIVE DYSFUNCTIONS OF A TEAM

Lencioni (2002, 2005) has identified five specific challenges or team dysfunctions that commonly prevent groups from realizing their potential. One of the most detrimental problems he has observed in teams is the **absence of trust**. Without trust, groups are reluctant to confront pressing issues; as a result, team members develop a **fear of conflict**. A reluctance to speak up and challenge the status quo then produces a **lack of commitment** to the group. And since a lack of commitment means that members are not giving their best effort, this leads to an **avoidance of accountability**. People do not want to be held accountable; thus, they do not hold their fellow members accountable to the goals of the group. Finally, without mutual commitment and accountability, group members will often put their own agendas before that of the group and display **inattention to results.** Each of these dysfunctions is described below, along with practical suggestions to improve them.

Absence of Trust

Researchers have long recognized the importance of trust in group and organizational performance (Costa & Taillieu, 2001; Duarte & Snyder, 2001; Kanawattanachai & Yoo, 2002). Lencioni (2002) suggests that trust requires vulnerability and the willingness to share weaknesses and admit mistakes. An open, honest environment tends to lead to more of the same. Trust is developed when members believe that their teammates are competent, diligent, and committed to the team. In contrast, an absence of trust creates a tense environment where members hold back and are reluctant to pursue collective goals or engage in genuine communication. In the opening case study, members of different groups within Southwest Airlines such as the pilots, flight attendants, and mechanics did not trust one another. In general, members of each group did not believe the other groups were committed to the overall success of the organization. Some may have also believed that members of other groups got many more benefits than they deserved. Once perceptions such as these are established, they are hard to reverse and can quickly spiral out of control.

Lencioni (2002, 2005) makes a number of practical suggestions for building trust in teams. Groups can engage in a personal histories exercise, where members share personal information about themselves. It is difficult to think poorly of others when members see one another as authentic human beings with similar life experiences. Since it can be hard to for members

Figure 10.1 The Five Dysfunctions of a Team

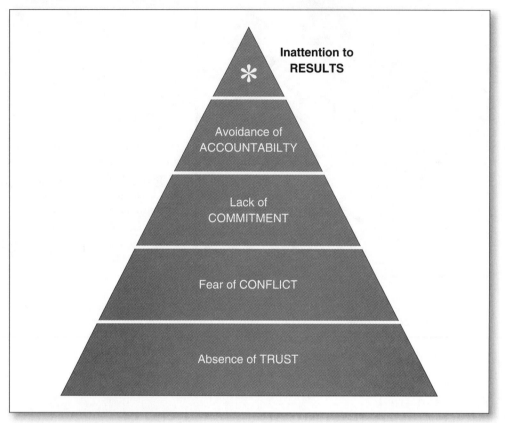

Inattention to
RESULTS

Avoidance of
ACCOUNTABILTY

Lack of
COMMITMENT

Fear of CONFLICT

Absence of TRUST

SOURCE: Adapted from Amabile (1985, 1990).

to trust people they do not know, this activity can go a long way in establishing a shared identity and building bridges among them (Mannix & Neale, 2005). Other ways to learn about colleagues include personality profiles such as the DISC, Myers-Briggs Temperament Indicator (MBTI), or Learning Styles Inventory. These profiles give members an opportunity to understand one another better and to value individual differences. In the team effectiveness exercise, members identify the most important contribution they think each of their teammates brings to the group. This allows members to recognize one another's strengths and generates goodwill among them. It also creates an environment where members feel valued and appreciated. Finally, team leaders can be influential in building trust as they model vulnerability and initiate the willingness to critique their own mistakes and shortcomings. This establishes group norms that value honesty, learning, and respectful feedback.

Fear of Conflict

For some people, conflict can be uncomfortable even when it is healthy and productive (Lencioni, 2005). In the midst of a heated debate, conflict often provokes a "fight-or-flight" response, which is detrimental to group functioning. As a result, groups can default to an artificial harmony to avoid conflict. Ironically, highly cohesive groups avoid conflict and, instead, encourage conformity. Conflicts that do erupt are often attempts to win arguments and convince the group of a certain way of doing things. When it turns personal and bitter, it can sabotage the work of the team and is often the most distasteful part of group life. In contrast, healthy conflict exists when members vigorously debate and challenge one another without resorting to personal attacks that create an atmosphere of hostility, fear, and guardedness.

On one end of the conflict spectrum is avoidance of conflict and an overemphasis on cohesion and conformity. On the other end of the spectrum is conflict that is personal and hostile. Even the most effective groups will have difficulty finding the right balance. For example, Lencioni (2005) suggests a forum for group members to discuss their own comfort level and experiences with conflict. Tools such as the Thomas-Kilmann Conflict Mode Instrument allow members to identify and describe their style of conflict. Discussing various conflict styles allows groups to create norms that define and value productive conflict. Another strategy is to assign the role of "miner of conflict" to a group member who will identify and call attention to potential conflicts that are not being addressed in group discussions. Finally, group leaders can model healthy conflict management skills by not avoiding issues and encouraging group members to engage in vigorous discussion by respectfully challenging one another's ideas (Eisenhardt, Kahwajy, & Bourgeois, 1997).

Lack of Commitment

Commitment in teams begins with a shared vision. Effective teams have clearly defined goals and a commitment from all members to achieve those goals (Porter, 2005). A lack of commitment on the part of any member weakens the whole group. When members do not feel like they can be open and speak their minds, they will tend to slide toward either marginal commitment or even passive-aggressive resistance. Lencioni (2005) has consistently found that members will buy into group decisions, even when their ideas are not adopted, as long as their ideas have been heard. The Intel Corporation describes this as the ability of team members to "disagree and commit."

A lack of commitment can occur at the group level when teams are indecisive and reluctant to make a decision or choose a course of action. While consensus is an admirable goal in group decision making, it is not always possible or even advisable. To assess and address issues related to commitment, the leader can ask for a "commitment clarification" at the end of meetings so members can summarize what was decided and review individual commitments (with deadlines) for each of the members. This simple practice removes uncertainty and reinforces responsibility. In addition, a regular assessment of group goals and progress toward those goals helps keep the group motivated and focused. Leaders can help engender commitment by clarifying the decisions of the group, pushing for action on open issues, and adhering to agreed-upon schedules and deadlines.

Avoidance of Accountability

Lencioni (2002, 2005) has noticed that many group members have a hard time holding one another accountable to performance standards. They assume that is the leader's job. But groups reach a higher level of effectiveness when members hold one another accountable. Members of high-performing teams work hard because they do not want to let their team-mates down. Thus, positive peer pressure can be an effective tool for maintaining high standards of performance and accountability.

A helpful way to encourage members to hold one another accountable is to publish the group's goals and work plan for all to see. If everyone is clear about the tasks of the group and each member's role, then there is a standard against which individual performance can be measured. Members can give regular progress or status reports to update the group. If a member is not performing, the leader could ask the group what needs to be done. This empowers the group to take responsibility for its own maintenance and to address the underperforming member collectively. Similarly, the leader should be willing to be held accountable to the group and model gracious acceptance of constructive feedback. Another way to increase the likelihood of peer accountability is to use team performance incentives. If the team, as opposed to the individual, is rewarded for performance, members will be more inclined to hold one another to higher standards.

Inattention to Results

Effective groups have clearly defined goals and regularly evaluate their progress toward those goals. Measurable goals and regular assessment provides continuous feedback that helps groups stay focused and on task. Over time, though, members can lose sight of team goals and become more concerned with their own personal success. Individual egos, personal agendas, career development goals, money, and loyalties to other groups can deter them from focusing on the success of the workgroup.

To overcome these tendencies, Lencioni (2002, 2005) encourages the use of a scoreboard or dashboard that gauges the performance of the group. Various quantitative metrics can be charted such as revenue, expenses, new accounts, or deadlines in a graphically appealing fashion. In addition, those results can be made available to the larger organization in the same way that box scores document the performance of baseball players and teams the day after a ballgame. Public accountability ensures that members will pay more attention to their own performance. Finally, reward systems that are tied to team performance reinforce the importance of collective success.

TEAM LEARNING

Evaluating team performance and measuring progress allows teams to learn from their experiences, identify problems, and make mid-course corrections (Wiedow & Konradt, 2011). A playful definition of "insanity" is doing the same thing over and over again and expecting different results. In general, if a team wants different results, members have to learn from their mistakes, make changes, and do something different. When established as part of a team's culture, the following three learning practices can drive performance to new heights and help teams reach their potential: (a) timely identification of mistakes, (b) effective and ongoing analysis, and (c) deliberate experimentation.

Timely Identification of Mistakes

Timely review, identification, and response to mistakes require openness and a willingness to look critically at individual and group performance (Cannon & Edmondson, 2005). In order to improve group performance and facilitate learning, teams need "blameless reporting systems"—the shared understanding that identifying mistakes is different from placing blame. Mistakes should be seen as learning opportunities and not opportunities to punish someone. This requires psychological safety in which members are secure in their role; they know that a mistake will not have severe, negative repercussions. Team leaders need to reinforce the importance of identifying and learning from mistakes instead of covering them up and saving face (Garvin, Edmondson, & Gino, 2008).

Many units in the military perform an "after action review" to identify problems and mistakes. For example, the U.S. Army's 160th Special Forces Unit, based in Fort Campbell, KY, debriefs all of its training activities and military operations as an opportunity to hone skills, improve coordination, and execute more efficiently. These debriefings are task-oriented, data-driven sessions that add a great deal of value and precision to this highly trained, expertly assembled, interdependent group of military specialists. In this case, identifying mistakes and learning from them can literally save lives.

Effective and Ongoing Analysis

In order to learn from their mistakes, groups must be able to effectively analyze their performance, whether in a corporate office, on a sports field, on the battlefield, or in a college classroom. In every industry there are "benchmarks" or exemplars of best practice. Until recently, Toyota was the common standard against which companies in the auto industry measured themselves. Its relentless commitment to *kaizen,* a philosophy of continuous improvement, in its production lines drove down incidents of flawed assembly. For a long time in professional baseball, the New York Yankees were the standard bearer. In consulting, McKinsey & Co. leads the way; in banking, Goldman-Sachs; and in higher education, Harvard University. These are the benchmarks against which organizations and institutions can measure their performance.

Comparative assessment is an example of how groups can approach objective, externally implied self-assessment. In order to make benchmarks useful, however, groups and teams need regular debriefings and evaluations. As with the 160th Special Forces unit described above, "after action reviews" are regularly conducted in the high-stakes, high-stress environment of emergency medicine. Health care, in general, uses debriefings and evaluations quite effectively, holding review boards and requiring meticulous record-keeping in order to establish and refine best practice as well as guard against malpractice. As with "after action reviews," morning meetings for care teams and medical review boards for physicians involve specific, critical evaluation of successes and failures in an effort to minimize variability and improve quality of care. Such formal review processes are also standard in the airline industry with FAA investigations into plane crashes and emergency landings. Without a dedication to critical review and ongoing evaluation, team performance stagnates, mistakes proliferate, and progress stalls.

Deliberate Experimentation

Once mistakes and shortcomings have been identified and analyzed, it is time to make changes. But changing structures, roles, or operating procedures can be met with resistance. Fostering innovation, creativity, and thinking outside of the box requires a posture of deliberate experimentation and a willingness to take risks. While change can be uncomfortable, it is necessary. With a rapidly changing marketplace, groups need to be flexible and adaptive. The most innovative groups fail early and fail often, providing an ongoing opportunity to learn and improve. Knowing what does not work can be just as important as knowing what does work. Whether on a group or organizational level, strong leadership is needed to drive change and stay the course in the face of resistance and less than impressive early results.

CHANGE AGENTS

Change is an unavoidable part of organizational life, regardless of the industry or setting. Jack Welch, former CEO of General Electric, once famously stated, "When your company is not changing as fast as its environment, it is already beginning to die." The same applies to teams and workgroups. If a team, group, or organization finds itself falling behind the change curve, something drastic must be done to revitalize it and turn things around. A change agent is someone who can bring a fresh perspective, a strong vision, and the willingness and drive to see change through. Steve Jobs was one such catalyst. In fact, it is not easy to encapsulate the extent to which his leadership style was suited to initiating and sustaining innovation.

From his early days with Apple Computer, Jobs consistently demonstrated his transcendental capacity for entrepreneurial drive and for building successful companies. Jobs was a visionary, a driver, and a high-profile change agent. After his return to Apple in 1997, he proved himself to be a major turnaround expert. What made Jobs a powerful and effective change agent also made him a contentious figure. He was not only demanding but had a huge ego. He pushed his teams to be the best they could be but also had the reputation of being a dictator and was known as an "enfant terrible" (Berlas, 1999).

That description is rich with imagery that paints a picture of Jobs as an uncompromising, driven, aggressive, magnetic figure. Such a strong personality with singular vision was bound to be divisive.

Turnaround experts often have a mercurial approach that involves the highest highs and the lowest lows, demanding the absolute extremes of performance from everyone involved. But this is understandable, given the scale of effort required to create change in an organization whose momentum is headed in the wrong direction. This involves changes of habits, processes, protocols, and standards. Change in any form is difficult; change on an organizational level approaches the impossible. Real turnaround experts—from Steve Jobs to Lee Iacocca to Theo Epstein—do not seem to allow public or common perception of them affect the way they work.

For a workgroup or team to turn around its performance, there needs to be a strong voice that can compel the members of the group to follow a new path, a leader who can keep the team on the new bearing regardless of obstacles or resistance, and a personality magnetic enough to make people want to do the extra work required to create sustainable change. Sometimes that person comes from within and sometimes that person comes from the outside in the form of a team coach (Ben-Hur, Kinley, & Jonsen, 2012). The following areas are typical problems that teams experience and are good places to start initiating change.

Improve project coordination

- Start with clear roles, expectations, and deadlines for specific tasks
- Have regular status updates
- See if there are any problems
- See if the project is still on schedule
- Make adjustments as needed

Improve brainstorming and decision making

- The facilitator introduces the problem. Members silently write down their ideas for 10 to 15 minutes.
- Members share their ideas one at a time (i.e., round robin). The ideas are displayed for all to see.
- The group discusses each idea.
- Members anonymously rank their top five ideas, giving a score of 5 to their top choice, 4 to the second choice, and so on. The group's top choice will have the highest total.

Reduce social loafing

- Increase visibility of individual contributions
- Promote involvement
- Reward team members
- Strengthen cohesion
- Increase personal responsibility
- Use team contracts
- Provide feedback

Conduct regular training workshops on various topics such as these:

- Conflict resolution
- Collaborative problem-solving
- Communication
- Goal-setting and performance management
- Planning and task coordination

MANAGING PARADOX

For teams to make the leap from average to excellent, a number of subtle paradoxes must be managed (Hill, 1994). Many of the difficulties teams face have to do with managing the fine balance between competing priorities. The Carleton Ultimate Frisbee team, for example, managed paradox by embracing individual differences *and* collective identity and goals. After finishing second at the national championships in 2000, the team met and reached the conclusion that it needed to move from a system that utilized "all-star" players as often as possible, to a "role-player" model that relied on specialized skills that each player brought to the team.

By focusing on teamwork and commitment, the team was able to **optimize individual and collective performance,** dominating the national tournament and winning the 2001 National Championship final, 15–11, over the University of Colorado. The Carleton team continued to nurture this focus on balancing individual contribution and collective excellence; as a result,

it won another national championship in 2009 and again in 2011. What makes this level of national success even more impressive is that Carleton's team hails from a school of fewer than 2,000 students and competes against teams from the largest universities in the nation.

The next paradox to be managed is the tension between fostering **support and confrontation**. Teams need to support and encourage one another, but they also need to be able to confront one another and to engage in authentic conversations about what is working and what is not working on the team. Effective leaders need to create a culture of trust that empowers members to ask questions, make suggestions, give candid feedback, and challenge processes. This pushes everyone to strive for the highest standards of performance.

Attention must also be paid to striking a balance between **process and product**. Effective teams need to focus not only on operating procedures but also on performance outcomes. The challenge that exists is a perceptual one: many groups and teams can view process evaluation as a distraction from performance. Yet discussing the interpersonal dynamics within a group can have long-term benefits. Improving the processes within a team will often improve its outcomes.

The fourth component, finding a balance between **authority and autonomy**, is an elusive balance. Autocratic leadership—the sort we tend to see from turnaround experts—is the easiest way to lead. Give a command, have people take action, gather the results; lather, rinse, repeat. Distributing leadership power and influence requires greater coordination and interdependence. Military Special Forces units such as the Navy SEALs strike this balance particularly well. In training, the members of these elite, Special Forces units are pushed to the end of their physical, psychological, and emotional capacity as they are honed for battle conditions and extenuating circumstances. Each individual is given specialized training in order to complement other members of the team. They are able to embrace the authority structure while being empowered to act with autonomy with regard to their own specialization.

Finally, it is important for teams and groups to attend to the triangle of relationships between the individual and the manager, the manager and the team, and the individual and the team. Relationships commonly compete with one another, so the challenge that exists is one of finite resources and leadership bandwidth. Cliques and social preference can obstruct progress, especially on heterogeneous teams where differences can create a barrier to mutual trust and understanding. However, striking the relationship balance can help to create the necessary environment conducive to psychological safety, trust, and interdependence that can harness the potential of diversity.

LEADERSHIP IN ACTION

John Kotter's theory of change management is widely accepted as *the* approach to carrying out successful and ongoing change initiatives in organizations of all sizes, from small teams to sprawling Fortune 500 conglomerates. Below are Kotter's eight steps of change management as they appear in *Leading Change* (1996), the author's authoritative work on the topic. By applying this rigorous and deliberate approach to executing change initiatives, what was once an unwieldy process becomes manageable, measurable, and sustainable:

1. Create a sense of urgency

2. Form a powerful coalition

3. Create a vision for change

4. Communicate that vision throughout the organization

5. Remove obstacles and empower others to act on the vision

6. Create short-term wins

7. Build on the change

8. Institutionalize the new approaches

First and foremost, Kotter encourages leaders to "create a sense of urgency," because he recognizes that it takes a meaningful amount of motivation to overcome the resistance of the status quo. Because groups and organizations resist change, leaders need to "light a fire" under their teams and organizations. Billy Beane successfully got his organization to focus on the pressing fact that they were outgunned and outfunded in terms of the players on their team. To field a winning team, they had to change their talent identification and acquisition model.

Once a sense of urgency has been established, leaders need to assemble a coalition of the most influential members of the organization and work with that group to create a shared vision. Kotter explained this clearly when he said, "Leadership defines what the future should look like, aligns people with that vision, and inspires them to make it happen despite the obstacles" (*Leading Change*, p. 25). Then that vision can be communicated and executed within teams. Obstacles to change and old ways of doing things need to be replaced by new and improved processes created from the bottom up.

Hopefully, teams and organizations will begin to see some positive results, which should be communicated and celebrated. Celebrating short-term wins is a great way to keep energy levels high and to keep people invested in the shared vision of the team. Turning the corner from implementing change to institutionalizing it requires the ability to see progress and to measure it objectively. This will reinforce the feasibility of the changes and create opportunities for people to embrace new habits and ideas.

Change management is strongly linked to performance management and is part of the work that leaders regularly perform. Teams must continually improve and refine internal processes in order to perform at their best. This requires evaluation, learning, intervention, and follow-through. The most effective teams continually evaluate their performance, learn from their mistakes, and make improvements. If leaders are not vigilantly pushing for continuous improvement, teams will become complacent. Kotter's eight steps of change management can help teams move from high potential to high performance.

KEY TERMS

Absence of trust   195
Fear of conflict   195
Lack of commitment   195
Avoidance of
   accountability   195
Inattention to results   195

Optimize individual and collective
   performance   202
Support and confrontation   202
Process and product   202
Authority and autonomy   202
Triangle of relationships   203

DISCUSSION QUESTIONS

1. What is the key to using data effectively to help team performance?

2. What is the difference between task assessment and interpersonal assessment? What specific things can be done to assess a team in each area?

3. What are the five dysfunctions of a team, as identified by Lencioni? Provide a description and example for each.

4. How can each of these dysfunctions be fixed? Be specific.

5. What are the three types of team learning? Explain each.

6. What are change agents, and what do they do?

7. What are the paradoxes teams must manage? How can these paradoxes be managed?

GROUP ACTIVITIES

EXERCISE 10.1 EVALUATING TEAM PERFORMANCE

Most classes that use this text will do team projects at some point in the course. Get into those project teams and answer the following questions. (If you don't have a regular project team for this class, get into groups of four to five and describe previous team experiences.)

1. What are the strengths of your project team?

2. What are the weaknesses of your team?

3. What specific things can you do to improve the team's performance?

4. What can you implement at your next meeting?

EXERCISE 10.2 ASSIGNING PARTICIPATION GRADES

Many college courses assign participation grades to evaluate the performance of students. Form groups of four to five students, and based upon the behavior you've observed in this course, assign a participation grade to each member of your group. Use the following rubric to guide your evaluation. Feel free to use plusses and minuses to fine-tune the letter grades.

A. *Analytical:* Frequently raises insightful questions, initiates discussions, integrates material from reading and lectures into discussions.

B. *Descriptive:* Describes events and issues, asks questions, contributes opinions, completes exercises.

C. *Minimal:* Participates when asked to do so.

D. *Marginal:* Frequently inattentive or works on other assignments.

After grades have been assigned to each member, discuss how you experienced the process.

CASE 10.2: REINFORCING WAX WINGS

The Daedalus Foundation is a nonprofit organization that reaches out to at-risk teenagers and offers programs to help them succeed in school. The foundation's executive director, Tanya, often feels torn between doing everything she can to save kids who have been fighting drug and alcohol addictions, abusive family environments, and other major challenges, and ensuring the financial viability of Daedalus by focusing on fund-raising and expanding relationships with donors. Tanya, herself, is a recovering drug addict who came from a wealthy family in Gross Pointe. She found herself at rock bottom as a teenager after her parents kicked her out of the house, and she spiraled deeper into her addiction on the streets of Detroit. She knows that, without a helping hand from a program like Daedalus, she'd either be dead or in prison.

In spite of her passion, in team meetings, Tanya often seems scattered and is too frequently interrupted by phone calls and people knocking on her door. She is a true servant to her cause and gives everything she has to everyone, all day. Occasionally, her service can become a problem, though, because she cannot dedicate the kind of focus or attention necessary to plan fund-raising events, execute disciplinary interventions with some of the struggling young people, or even carry out necessary interviews for interns, volunteers, and potential hires.

Ramón, Tanya's head of operations, is a former gang member whom Daedalus helped by getting him back into school. He, too, is dedicated to the cause on a deeply personal level, but doubts that Tanya is the right person to lead the organization. He thinks she is too soft, preferring the "tough love" model of the executive director who led the foundation during Ramón's youth. He doesn't think that Tanya really understands the needs of the students due to the fact that she grew up in a very wealthy environment on "The Pointe." As a result, Ramón and Tanya are often short with each other and dismissive of the other's ideas in meetings.

Stacie, who leads donor relations, has only been with Daedalus for six months. She is just over two years out of college but is passionate about the cause. She often feels that the conflict between Tanya and Ramón is unproductive but can't bring herself to address it. She often feels too young, too new, and too unfamiliar with the lives of the young people Daedalus serves to have the right to speak up. Still, she is convinced that she could get more money behind the cause if her team could work together more productively.

Devon is the director of programming and has been there since the beginning. He has instant rapport with the kids and does not lack credibility on any front. Devon is a driver, doling out tough love and holding the kids accountable to their commitments. To him, Daedalus will never reach its full potential if Tanya doesn't get her act together and start delivering results. He doesn't think that program participants are turning around their lives quickly enough; therefore, he no longer feels that Daedalus is making a meaningful enough impact. His distaste is obvious, as he spends meetings alternating between reclining in his seat with his arms crossed and pounding the table with a big, life-worn fist. He's given his life to this cause and believes that if only everyone else were as committed as he, it would be a different organization.

Will is the student intern. He often comes late to meetings and occasionally can't be found around the office. While he feels sorry for the kids that Daedalus serves, he feels he can't really relate to them because they "come from such different places," as he says. Given that he has so many other commitments at college, he is unable to fully engage the tasks that he's been assigned. He always gets the job done, but with much room for improvement. A handsome and charismatic young man, he is often able to escape much of the wrath of his colleagues with wit and charm—but that is wearing thin.

- *You are the leader of a group of student consultants brought in to advise the Daedalus Foundation on how to manage and improve its performance. Using content from this chapter, how would you assess the strengths and weaknesses of the Daedalus leadership team, what dysfunctions can you diagnose in the organization, and what action plan would you recommend to improve the team's performance?*

Appendix: Virtual Teams

On September 4, 2011, author and columnist Thomas Friedman was a guest on NBC's *Meet the Press* to promote his new book. His previous book, *The World Is Flat: A Brief History of the Twenty-first Century,* describes the impact of technology on civilization. Surprisingly, the book, which was written in 2004, did not even mention technological innovations such as Facebook, Twitter, and Skype; they either were not yet invented or were not yet mainstream. Friedman, himself, was surprised at the rapid advance of technology:

> When I said the world is flat, Facebook didn't exist. Or for most people it didn't exist. Twitter was a sound. The Cloud was in the sky. 4G was a parking place. LinkedIn was a prison. Applications were something you sent to college. And, for most people, Skype was a typo. That all happened in the last seven years. And what it has done is taken the world from connected to hyper-connected. And that's been a huge opportunity and a huge challenge. (NBC News, 2011)

Virtual teams, like the technological tools mentioned by Friedman, have tremendous potential. They offer organizations the ability to assemble the best and brightest members for particular projects regardless of geographic restrictions. However, virtual teams also have specific challenges that have to be addressed and managed. Designing and launching a virtual team requires planning and forethought.

BUILDING EFFECTIVE VIRTUAL TEAMS

Hertel, Geister, and Konradt (2005) have created a model of team effectiveness that considers the unique needs of virtual groups at various stages of development. They have identified five key areas, each with its own unique tasks and challenges that need to be addressed. Effective leaders are aware of these potential snags and provide appropriate structuring and guidance to ensure success. Beginning with a belief in the importance of preparation, effective leaders know that the launch of a virtual team is an important event. And because there is typically a lack of direct supervision in virtual teams, leaders design creative ways to manage team performance. In addition, they facilitate development through training and give appropriate guidance when it is time to disband.

Preparation

The implementation of a virtual team requires planning to ensure that the conditions for success are met and that an adequate virtual structure is created. First, the purpose of the group has to be clearly defined, and leaders must evaluate whether or not a virtual team is the best strategy to accomplish that purpose. The type of tasks that are best suited for virtual teams are (a) information or service-based tasks such as research and development (R&D), project management, or sales; (b) tasks that are easily separated into subtasks that can be distributed across different locations and easily coordinated; and (c) tasks that have clear metrics that allow members to evaluate progress and the success of the team (Hertel, Geister, & Konradt, 2005).

Then, based upon the purpose and specific tasks that need to be accomplished, the right personnel have to be identified and enlisted. In selecting members for a virtual team, leaders should consider whether or not potential members have the following competencies:

- *Task-related competencies:* Knowledge, skills, abilities, and experience related to the mission of the group, commitment to the task, and conscientiousness.

- *Team-related competencies:* Cooperativeness, communication skills, benevolence, integrity, and the general ability to trust and work with others.

- *Virtual competencies:* Technological competence and comfort, self-management skills, and the ability to work in diverse and abstract environments.

Selecting the right members is crucial for a successful team. Although there may be a multitude of talented and competent people to consider, many will not make good choices because they lack the technological capabilities necessary in a virtual environment. Potential members must be both comfortable and competent with technology.

Once the project has been defined and members selected, leaders must decide upon a technology platform, and the importance of this task cannot be emphasized enough. With advances in technology, there are plenty of options to consider. To begin, leaders can survey team members on the strengths and weaknesses of the systems they may have used in the past. This invites input from members and increases the chances for buy-in. Ultimately, leaders will need to invest a significant amount of time researching various options and looking at the costs and benefits of each. Once a virtual communication medium has been decided upon, members will need the necessary hardware (computers, cameras, Internet access, etc.) and software (e-mail, online chat, knowledge-based systems, groupware, etc.) before the first official meeting. The training and support plan might include face-to-face workshops, online tutorials, published lists of frequently asked questions (FAQs), online help sessions, or a help center staffed by technology support personnel.

Launch

A concise and well-designed launch can build cohesion and create momentum for a new team (Blackburn, Furst, & Rosen, 2003). Because initial meetings set a pattern for future interactions, the launch is an important event in the life of a group. Researchers have

| Figure A.1 | Managing a Virtual Team |

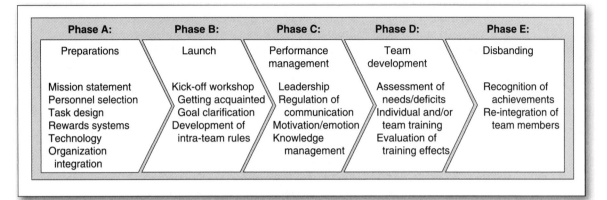

Phase A:	Phase B:	Phase C:	Phase D:	Phase E:
Preparations	Launch	Performance management	Team development	Disbanding
Mission statement Personnel selection Task design Rewards systems Technology Organization integration	Kick-off workshop Getting acquainted Goal clarification Development of intra-team rules	Leadership Regulation of communication Motivation/emotion Knowledge management	Assessment of needs/deficits Individual and/or team training Evaluation of training effects	Recognition of achievements Re-integration of team members

consistently found that virtual teams benefit greatly from an initial face-to-face "kick-off" meeting or workshop (Hertel, Geister, & Konradt, 2005). Getting members together to jump-start the team can save time and preempt unnecessary confusion. An initial face-to-face meeting helps members get acquainted with one another and begins to build trust and commitment to shared goals (Warkentin & Beranek, 1999). In addition, members can receive training and define norms and protocols about how they will communicate and work together. These group dynamics will eventually emerge in a virtual environment, but an initial meeting can serve as a catalyst for development and hasten productivity.

If group members are not able to meet face to face, team leaders will have to be more creative in launching a team. Ideally, members should have information about one another and about the purpose of the group before the first meeting. Written biographies with pictures will help members "envision" their teammates and begin to build trust. To avoid any technical problems, the communication medium should be tested before the first official meeting, and members should be trained if necessary. A successful launch should create an atmosphere of trust, a clear understanding of the group's purpose, and anticipation for success.

Performance Management

One of the primary roles of any team leader is to monitor progress and motivate members toward task completion. Both of these leadership functions tend to be more difficult in an abstract, virtual context, where it is harder to assess both task progress and member commitment. Leaders have less direct control and influence over the functioning of group members. In a study of 13 virtual teams operating in Europe, Mexico, and the United States, Kayworth and Leidner (2001) found that the most effective team leaders were mentors who demonstrated a high degree of concern for others. These team leaders were able to assert their authority without being overbearing. In addition, they were effective at providing regular, detailed, and prompt communication about the status of the project.

The task/project management strategy described in Chapter 9, on project management (DAPEE or FOCUS), applies to virtual teams as well. After the project is defined and analyzed, the team creates a plan to achieve the desired results. A detailed work plan defines assignments and schedules for completion. During the execution of a plan, one or more people will need to monitor the progress of individual members and the group as a whole. Some team tasks can be divided, performed separately by group members, and then combined into a finished product. In this case, leaders monitor the progress of individual members and then oversee the integration of each member's contribution. But as tasks become more complex and member roles and responsibilities become increasingly interdependent, monitoring becomes more difficult (Bell & Kozlowski, 2002). Complex tasks require greater levels of synchronous collaboration, communication, and information-sharing with the whole team. Progress indicators and feedback should be frequent, concrete, and timely on both the individual and group levels (Hertel, Geister, & Konradt, 2005).

Without formal hierarchies or traditional structures, leaders tend to function more as coaches or trainers than as traditional managers or supervisors. Among other things, virtual leaders monitor the relational dimension of the team, including the motivation and commitment of members, the level of trust and cohesion in the group, and the satisfaction of group members. If interpersonal or communication problems have developed and are not addressed by the group, the leader may need to act as a catalyst to bring issues to the group's attention. Instead of saying, "We need to be prompt about deadlines," virtual leaders may need to be more subtle and ask members how they feel about the pattern of missed deadlines in the group.

Because members are not in the same physical space, it may be difficult to develop and maintain motivation (Hertel, Geister, & Konradt, 2005). Leaders and members can increase the individual and collective motivation within the team by becoming aware of a number of issues (Hertel, Konradt, & Orlikowski, 2004). First, motivation is related to how members evaluate the team's goals. If members understand the goals and see their importance, they will be more motivated to work toward achieving them. Second, members are more motivated to perform when they believe their contribution to the team is needed. Leaders should regularly remind the team that it cannot reach its potential unless every member is contributing. Third, members work hard when they believe they have the necessary skills to fulfill their responsibilities. Positive feedback from others can help reinforce adequate levels of self-efficacy. Finally, members work hard when they believe others are also working hard. Therefore, if members know what others are doing, they will be more motivated to accomplish their own assigned tasks.

Team Development

An initial investment in training and development can minimize some of the problems inherent in virtual communication. Specifically, training has been shown to increase levels of cohesiveness and team satisfaction (Warkentin & Beranek, 1999). In addition, periodic assessment of both the relational and performance dimensions of virtual teams provides leaders and members with data that can help improve performance. For example, an assessment of 10 virtual procurement teams operating within a large organization found three major areas for improvement: (a) clarification of the team goals, (b) effective use of communication media, and (c) development of group communication norms (Hertel, Geister, & Konradt, 2005). Three months after participating in a two-day training workshop, members not only reported improvement in each of these areas but in overall team effectiveness as well. The most effective leaders are aware of the needs and deficits of their teams and proactively plan individual and team interventions to address those issues.

Teams experience personnel changes as existing members leave and new members are added. When new members join an existing team, they need to be oriented to the goals, strategies, structures, rules, and roles of the group (Bell & Kozlowski, 2002). Team development includes the assimilation and training of new members into the existing structure. Simultaneously, the existing structure may need to adapt and redefine itself as resources are lost or gained.

Disbanding

As projects come to an end and groups are about to disband, team members have the opportunity to reflect upon the successes and failures of the group. The last meeting can include an evaluation of the strengths and weaknesses of the team, an assessment of individual contributions, and a celebration of successes. This encourages members to learn from their experiences and to take those lessons with them into their next team experience. For example, leaders might ask each member to describe the biggest "takeaways" from their experience, as well as what they wish they would have done differently in the group.

Finally, group members need to bring closure to their experience and say goodbye to one another. They may also choose to resolve any interpersonal issues that may have developed over the course of the project. If the group was successful, there may be sadness and promises to stay in touch. Being a part of a high-performance team can be an extremely satisfying and rewarding experience, and relationships may continue long after the termination of the project. Successful teams not only contribute to the mission of the organization, they also meet the interpersonal and existential needs of individual members.

Glossary

Absence of trust The foundational problem that occurs within teams when members do not trust one another.

Accommodating conflict style The style of conflict that defers to others and allows them to have their way.

Achievement versus ascription The way various cultures define status and success.

Adjourning stage of development The final stage of group development, in which the group is ending and members are about to say goodbye to one another.

Advocacy The ability to articulate one's ideas effectively and persuasively.

Amiable social style The interpersonal style that values relationships and being friendly toward others.

Analytic social style The social style that describes a person who is task-oriented and reserved.

Attainable Goals that are reasonable and within the reach of a team.

Attitudes about the environment The degree to which members of a culture try to control the natural environment or honor and cooperate with it.

Attitudes about time The attitudes various cultures have about deadlines and schedules.

Authority and autonomy The challenge to be both a strong leader with a clear vision and a leader who empowers the team to manage itself.

Avoidance of accountability The condition within teams in which members resist being held responsible for their personal contribution to the team.

Avoiding conflict style The style of conflict that is reluctant to engage in interpersonal conflict.

Coaching style of leadership The style of leadership that gives both clear directions and a lot of support and encouragement.

Collaborating conflict style The style of conflict in which members work together to achieve the desires of all involved.

Competing conflict style The style of conflict that focuses on getting one's way.

Compromising conflict style The style of conflict in which everybody gives up some of their desires in order to arrive at a solution.

Confirmation bias The tendency of individuals to look for evidence to confirm what they have already decided.

Confirmation bias The tendency of teams to look for evidence to confirm what they have already decided.

Delegating style of leadership The style of leadership that gives members the freedom to do their work with a minimal amount of interaction from the leader.

Descriptive norms The ways in which members interact with and relate to one another.

Diffuse status characteristics Highly valued member traits that are not related to the purpose or task of a team.

Directing style of leadership The style of leadership that takes charge and gives clear instructions to team members.

Driver social style The interpersonal style that is focused on achieving results and being assertive with others.

Efficiency A characteristic of teams that use their resources wisely.

Elaboration The ability to develop and implement creative ideas.

Escalation of commitment The tendency of groups to become more committed to a decision after it has been made, even if that decision has proven to be a bad one.

Ethical standards of behavior A commitment to the highest standards of ethics and moral principles that guide group decisions and behavior.

Expressive social style The interpersonal style that is outgoing and enthusiastic.

Fear of conflict The condition within teams when members are not willing to challenge one another and deal with unresolved issues or unspoken conflict.

Flexibility The ability to generate different types of ideas.

Fluency The ability to generate a large number of creative ideas.

Force field analysis A tool that is used to identify the forces that are working for and against a team.

Forming stage of development The stage of group development in which members are just beginning to work together.

Fundamental attribution error The tendency to assume that people's behavior is related to their personality without giving consideration to the social context or situation they are in.

Group polarization The tendency of members to become more extreme in their beliefs when there are differing viewpoints on a team.

Groupthink The condition within groups in which a dominant idea or member has too much influence over the direction of the group.

Groupthink The condition within groups in which a dominant idea or member has too much influence over the direction of the group.

Ideal size The challenge of team designers to have the optimal number of members on a team, avoiding the tendency of having too many or too few members.

Inattention to results The team dysfunction in which team members are not focused on achieving any tangible or concrete goals.

Individual roles Member roles and behaviors that are counterproductive to the success of the team.

Individualism versus collectivism The degree to which members of a culture give priority to the individual or to the community.

Influence tactics The specific ways that leaders influence and motivate team members.

Information processing The process by which individuals perceive and interpret incoming information.

Ingroup/outgroup bias The tendency of team members to overvalue their own group and undervalue other groups.

Ingroup/outgroup bias The tendency of team members to overvalue their own group and undervalue other groups.

Injunctive norms Expectations about how members should behave in the team.

Inquiry The ability to draw out the ideas of others through probing questions and active listening.

Intellectual competence Characteristic of members who are perceived as being smart and knowledgeable.

Interpersonal competence Characteristic of members who are perceived as having strong interpersonal skills.

Interpersonal conflict A common problem in groups in which members do not get along with one another.

Interpersonal skills Skills related to the ability of members to work together effectively.

Lack of commitment The problematic situation when one or more members is not committed to the goals and objectives of the team.

Lack of commitment A common problem that happens in groups when not all of the members are 100% committed to the team.

Losses in productivity The inevitable loss of efficiency in groups due to the challenge of coordinating the work of multiple team members.

Measurable Goals that can be objectively measured to determine progress or achievement.

Member satisfaction A characteristic of successful teams in which members enjoy working together.

Neutral versus emotional Cultural norms regarding the amount of emotion that is demonstrated in workplace conversations.

Norming stage of group development The stage of group development in which groups figure out a more effective way to work together.

Ongoing self-evaluation The practice of continually evaluating team performance and discovering more effective ways to work together.

Optimize individual and collective performance The challenge for leaders to develop both individual members and the team as a whole.

Originality The ability to generate ideas that are unlike anything that already exists.

Overconfidence The tendency of teams to think more highly of their ideas and decisions than they ought.

Participative safety The dynamic within a team in which members feel safe to communicate their ideas and perspectives.

Performing stage of development The time in the life of a group in which members are working collaboratively at peak performance.

Personal character Personal traits such as honesty, integrity, and dependability.

Pooled interdependence When members work on tasks individually and then add their contributions in the end.

Poor communication The common experience of groups in which members communicate poorly and/or misunderstand one another.

Poor leadership A typical problem that happens when groups lack clear goals and members do not know what they are supposed to do.

Predictability One of the benefits of working in well-designed teams in which everyone knows their roles and knows how the team operates.

Premature decisions The tendency of groups to consider only a few options before making a decision.

Process and product The challenge of leaders both to focus on the process of how the group is working as well as pay attention to the output or products of the team.

Reciprocal interdependence When each member works in conjunction with others at the same time to accomplish a task.

Relationship roles Member roles that increase cohesion and strong interpersonal bonds.

Relevant Goals that are aligned with the primary purpose and mission of a team.

Schemas The internal cognitive framework of beliefs, values, and goals that influence the way individuals perceive and interpret new information.

Self-enhancement The desire to be seen as a competent and valuable member of the team.

Self-managed work teams Teams that have some degree of autonomy and members collectively share the responsibility of leadership.

Sequential interdependence When members build upon the work they receive from other members.

Shared information bias The tendency of groups only to discuss information that everybody already knows.

Shared vision The characteristic of groups in which members are committed to a clear set of goals and objectives.

Situational leadership The theory of leadership that emphasizes the need for leaders to adapt their leadership style to the needs of the team.

Social loafing A common problem within teams in which members do less than their fair share of the work.

SOLER The acronym that describes effective listening skills including facing the person squarely, maintaining an open posture, leaning in slightly, maintaining appropriate eye contact, and having a relaxed posture.

Specific status characteristics Highly valued member traits that are directly related to the purpose or task of a team.

Specific versus diffuse The degree to which people share personal information in their business relationships.

Specific Goals that are well defined, concrete, and detailed.

Storming stage of development The stage of group development in which members start to challenge one another and challenge the leadership.

Support and confrontation The challenge of leaders both to be supportive and hold members accountable for results.

Support for innovation The context of groups that allows for unique and novel ideas to be shared.

Supporting style of leadership The style of leadership that gives members freedom and autonomy while at the same time being supportive and encouraging to members.

Systems thinking The ability of individuals to understand problems within a larger social or organizational framework.

Task orientation The characteristic of groups that are focused, efficient, and get work done.

Task roles Roles that members play to help the team reach its goals and objectives.

Task-related knowledge and skills Knowledge and skills related to the task and objectives of the group.

Time-bounded Goals that have a specific deadline and end date.

Triangle of relationships The challenge of leaders to be aware of how they relate to the team as a whole, how they relate to individual members, and how individual members relate to one another.

Universalism versus particularism The degree to which members of a culture believe the rules apply to everyone or if they can be negotiated on a case-by-case basis.

Work plan A detailed strategy that outlines the major tasks, deadlines, and specific responsibilities of each team member.

References

AACU. (2010). *Raising the bar: Employers' views on college learning in the wake of the economic downturn*. Retrieved from http://www.aacu.org/leap/documents/2009_EmployerSurvey.pdf

AACU. (2007). *College learning for the new global century: A report from the national leadership council for liberal education and America's promise*. Retrieved from http://www.aacu.org/leap/documents/GlobalCentury_final.pdf

Aberson, C. L., Healy, M., & Romero, V. (2000). Ingroup bias and self-esteem: A meta-analysis. *Journal of Personality and Social Psychology Review, 4,* 157–173.

Adorno, T. W., Frankel-Brunswick, E., Levinson, D., & Sanford, R. (1950). *The authoritarian personality.* New York, NY: HarperCollins.

Agazarian, Y., & Gantt, S. (2005). The systems perspective. In S. A. Weelan (Ed.), *The handbook of group research and practice* (pp. 187–200). Thousand Oaks, CA: Sage Publications.

Allen, B. C., Sargent, L. D., & Bradley, L. M. (2003). Differential effects of task and reward interdependence on perceived helping behavior, effort, and group performance. *Small Group Research, 34,* 716–740.

Amabile, T. M. (1985). Motivation and creativity: Effects of motivational orientation on creative writers. *Journal of Personality and Social Psychology, 48,* 393–399.

Amabile, T. M. (1990). Within you, without you: The social psychology of creativity and beyond. In M. A. Runco & R. S. Albert (Eds.), *Theories of creativity* (pp. 61–91). Newbury Park, CA: Sage.

Amabile, T. M., Conti, R., Coon, H., Lazenby, J., & Herron, M. (1996). Assessing the work environment for creativity. *Academy of Management Journal, 39,* 1154–1184.

Anderson, N. R., & West, M. A. (1998). Measuring climate for work group innovation: Development and validation of the team climate inventory. *Journal of Organizational Behavior, 19,* 235–258.

Ante, S. E. (2001, August 27). Simultaneous software: Tools from a new generation of companies make it easier for employees and business partners to work together. *Business Week,* 46–47.

Arana, J. M., Chambel, M. J., Curral, L., & Tabernero, C. (2009). The role of task-oriented versus relationship-oriented leadership on normative contract and group performance. *Social Behavior and Personality: An International Journal, 37,* 1391–1404.

Argote, L. (1999). *Organizational learning: Creating, retaining, and transferring knowledge.* Boston, MA: Kluwer Academic Publishers.

Argyris, C. (1994). Good communication that blocks learning. *Harvard Business Review, 72,* 77–85.

Arrow, H., Poole, M. S., Henry, K. B., Wheelan, S., & Moreland, R. (2004). Time, change, and development: The temporal perspective on groups. *Small Group Research, 35,* 105–173.

Asch, S. E. (1956). Studies on independence and conformity: A minority of one against a unanimous majority. *Psychological Monographs, 70,* 1–70.

Ashforth, B. E., & Mael, F. A. (1998). The power of resistance: Sustaining valued identities. In R. M. Kramer & M. A. Neale (Eds.), *Power and influence in organizations* (pp. 89–119). Thousand Oaks, CA: Sage.

Aubè, C., & Rousseau, V. (2005). Team goal commitment and team effectiveness: The role of task interdependence and supportive behaviors. *Group Dynamics: Theory, Research, and Practice, 9,* 189–204.

Aubert, B. A., & Kelsey, B. L. (2003). Further understanding of trust and performance in virtual teams. *Small Group Research, 34,* 575–618.

Baer, J. (1993). *Creativity and divergent thinking: A task-specific approach.* Hillsdale, NJ: Lawrence Erlbaum Associates.

Baker, D. (2010). Enhanced group decision making: An exercise to reduce shared information bias. *Journal of Management Education, 34,* 249–279.

Baker, D. F. (2010). Enhancing group decision making: An exercise to reduce shared information bias. *Journal of Management Education, 34,* 249–279.

Ballard, C. (2010, March 15). The metaphysical significance, staggering ubiquity, and sheer joy of high fives. *Sports Illustrated, 112,* 36–41.

Baltes, B. B., Dickson, M. W., Sherman, M. P., Bauer, C. C., & LaGanke, J. S. (2002). Computer-mediated communication and group decision making: A meta-analysis. *Organizational Behavior and Human Decision Processes, 87,* 156–179.

Bandura, A. (1977). *Social learning theory.* New York, NY: General Learning Press.

Baney, J. (2004). *Guide to interpersonal communication.* Upper Saddle River, NJ: Pearson.

Baran, B. E., Shanock, L. R., Rogelberg, S. G., & Scott, C. W. (2012). Leading group meetings: Supervisors' actions, employee behaviors, and upward perceptions. *Small Group Research, 43,* 330–355.

Barbuto, J. E. (1997). A critique of the Myers-Briggs Type Indicator and its operationalization of Carl Jung's psychological types. *Psychological Reports, 80,* 611–625.

Barker, L. L., Wahlers, K. J., & Watson, K. W. (2001). *Groups in process: An introduction to small group communication* (6th ed.). Boston, MA: Allyn and Bacon.

Barsade, S. G. (2002). The ripple effect: Emotional contagion and its influence on group behavior. *Administrative Science Quarterly, 47,* 644–675.

Bass, B. M. (1998). *Transformational Leadership.* Mahwah, NJ: Lawrence Erlbaum.

Bazerman, M. (2006). *Judgment in managerial decision making* (6th ed.). New York: John Wiley & Sons.

Beck, J. S. (1995). *Cognitive therapy: Basics and beyond.* New York, NY: Guilford Press.

Becker, R. E., Huselid, M. A., & Ulrich D. (2001). *The HR scorecard: Linking people, strategy, and performance.* Boston, MA: Harvard Business School Press.

Behfar, K. J., Mannix, E. A., Peterson, R. S., & Trochim, W. M. (2011). Conflict in small groups: The meaning and consequences of process conflict. *Small Group Research, 42,* 127–176.

Bell, B. S., & Kozlowski, S. W. J. (2002). A typology of virtual teams: Implications for effective leadership. *Group and Organizational Management, 27,* 14–49.

Ben-Hur, S., Kinley, N., & Jonsen, K. (2012). Coaching executive teams to reach better decisions. *Journal of Management Development, 31,* 711–723.

Benne, K. D., & Sheats, P. (1948). Functional roles of group members. *Journal of Social Issues, 4,* 41–49.

Bergman, J. Z., Rentsch, J. R., Small, E. E., Davenport, S. W., & Bergman, S. M. (2012). The shared leadership process in decision-making teams. *Journal of Social Psychology, 152,* 17–42.

Birtchnell, J. (1993). *How humans relate: A new interpersonal theory.* Westport, CT: Praeger.

Bishop, J. W., & Scott, K. D. (2000). An examination of organizational and team commitment in a self-directed team environment. *Journal of Applied Psychology, 85,* 438–450.

Blackburn, R. S., Furst, S. A., & Rosen, B. (2003). Building a winning virtual team: KSAs, selection, training, and evaluation. In C. Gibson, and S. Cohen (Eds.), *Virtual teams that work: Creating the conditions for virtual team effectiveness* (pp. 95–120). San Francisco, CA: Jossey-Bass.

Blake, R. R., & Mouton, J.S. (1961). *Group dynamics: Key to decision making.* Houston, TX: Gulf Publishing Co.

Blanchard, K., Zigarmi, P., & Zigarmi, D. (1999). *Leadership and the one minute manager: Increasing effectiveness through situational leadership.* New York, NY: William Morrow.

Bolman, L. G., & Deal, T. E. (2003). *Reframing organizations: Artistry, choice, and leadership* (3rd ed.). San Francisco, CA: Jossey-Bass.

Bolton, R., & Bolton, D. G. (1996). *People styles at work: Making bad relationships good and good relationships better.* New York, NY: AMACON.

Bond, R., & Smith, P. B. (1996). Culture and conformity: A meta-analysis of studies using Asch's (1952b, 1956) line judgment task. *Psychological Bulletin, 119,* 111–137.

Boos, M., Schauenburg, B., Strack, M., & Belz, M. (2013). Social validation of shared and nonvalidation of unshared information in group discussions. *Small Group Research, 44,* 257–271.

Boyatzis, R. E., & McKee, A. (2005). *Resonant leadership: Renewing yourself and connecting with others through mindfulness, hope, and compassion.* Boston, MA: Harvard Business Review Press.

Boyatzis, R. E., Smith, M. L., & Blaize, N. (2006). Developing sustainable leaders through coaching and compassion. *Academy of Management Learning & Education, 5,* 8–24.

Bradley, B. H., Postlethwaite, B. E., Klotz, A. C., Hamdani, M. R., & Brown, K. G. (2012). Reaping the benefits of task conflict in teams: The critical role of team psychological safety climate. *Journal of Applied Psychology, 97,* 151–158.

Bray, S. R., & Brawley, L. R. (2002). Role efficacy, role clarity, and role performance effectiveness. *Small Group Research, 33,* 233–253.

Brief, A. P., & Weiss, H. M. (2002). Organizational behavior: Affect in the workplace. *Annual Review of Psychology, 53,* 279–307.

Brock, D., Abu-Rish, E., Chiu, C., Hammer, D., Wilson, S., Vorvick, L., Blondon, K., Schaad, D., Liner, D., & Zierler, B. (2013). Interprofessional education in team communication: Working together to improve patient safety. *BMJ Quality and Safety: The International Journal of Healthcare Improvement,* 414–423.

Bronfenbrenner, U. (2005). *Making human beings human: Bioecological perspectives on human development.* Thousand Oaks, CA: Sage Publications.

Brown, T. M., & Miller, C. E. (2000). Communication networks in task-performing groups: Effects of task complexity, time pressure, and interpersonal dominance. *Small Group Research, 31,* 131–157.

Bruins, J. (1999). Social power and influence tactics: A theoretical introduction. *Journal of Social Issues, 55,* 7–14.

Buckman, R. H. (2004). *Building a knowledge-driven organization.* New York: McGraw-Hill.

Burrows, P. (2006, September 25). Who is Jonathan Ive? *Business Week.* Retrieved from http://www .businessweek.com/magazine/content/06_39/b4002414.htm?campaign_id = macslash

Camacho, L. M., & Paulus, P. B. (1995). The role of social anxiousness in group brainstorming. *Journal of Personality and Social Psychology, 68,* 1071–1080.

Cannon, M. D., & Edmondson, A. C. (2005). Failing to learn and learning to fail (intelligently): How great organizations put failure to work to innovate and improve. *Long Range Planning, 38,* 299–319.

Cannon, M. D., & Witherspoon, R. (2005). Actionable feedback: Unlocking the power of learning and performance improvement. *Academy of Management Executive, 19,* 120–134.

Carton, A. M., & Cummings, J. N. (2012). A theory of subgroups in work teams. *The Academy of Management Review, 37,* 441–470.

Chang, A., & Bordia, P. (2001). A multidimensional approach to the group cohesion-group performance relationship. *Small Group Research, 32,* 379–405.

Chang, A., Bordia, P., & Duck, J. (2003). Punctuated equilibrium and linear progression: Toward a new understanding of group development. *Academy of Management Journal, 46,* 106–117.

Chang, J. W., Sy, T., & Choi, J. N. (2012). Team emotional intelligence and performance: Interactive dynamics between leaders and members. *Small Group Research, 43,* 75–104.

Chen, G., Sharma, P. N., Edinger, S. K., Shapiro, D. L., & Farh, J. (2011). Motivating and demotivating forces in teams: Cross-level influences of empowering leadership and relationship conflict. *Journal of Applied Psychology, 96,* 541–557.

Cherniss, C., & Goleman, D. (2001). *The emotionally intelligent workplace: How to select for, measure, and improve emotional intelligence in individuals, groups, and organizations.* San Francisco, CA: Jossey-Bass.

Christensen, P. N., Rothgerber, H., Wood, W., & Matz, D. C. (2004). Social norms and identity relevance: A motivational approach to normative behavior. *Personality and Social Psychology Bulletin, 30,* 1295–1309.

Christie, A. M., & Barling, J. (2010). Beyond status: Relating status inequality to performance and health in teams. *Journal of Applied Psychology, 95,* 920–934.

Cialdini, R. B., & Goldstein, N. J. (2004). Social influence: Compliance and conformity. *Annual Review of Psychology, 55,* 591–621.

Cohen, S. G., & Bailey, D. E. (1997). What makes teams work: Group effectiveness research from the shop floor to the executive suite. *Journal of Management, 23,* 239–290.

Collins, J. (2001). *From good to great: Why some companies make the leap . . . and others don't.* New York, NY: HarperCollins.

Collins, J., & Porras, J. I. (2002). *Built to last: Successful habits of visionary companies.* New York, NY: HarperCollins.

Conger, J. A. (1998). The necessary art of persuasion. *Harvard Business Review, 76,* 88–95.

Costa, A. C., Roe, R. A., & Taillieu, T. (2001). Trust within teams: The relation with performance effectiveness. *European Journal of Work and Organizational Psychology, 10,* 225–244.

Cox, T. H., & Blake, S. (1991). Managing cultural diversity: Implications for organizational competitiveness. *Academy of Management Executive, 5,* 45–56.

Crotty, S. K., & Brett, J. M. (2012). Fusing creativity: Cultural metacognition and teamwork in multicultural teams. *Negotiation and Conflict Management Research,* 210–234.

Csikszentmihalyi, M. (1988). Society, culture, and person: A systems view of creativity. In R. J. Sternberg (Ed.), *The nature of creativity: Contemporary psychological perspectives* (pp. 325–339). New York, NY: Cambridge University Press.

Csikszentmihalyi, M. (1990). The domain of creativity. In M. A. Runco & R. S. Albert (Eds.), *Theories of creativity* (pp. 190–212). Newbury Park, CA: Sage.

Csikszentmihalyi, M. (1996). *Creativity: Flow and the psychology of discovery and invention.* New York, NY: HaperCollins.

Dacey, J. S., & Lennon, K. H. (1998). *Understanding creativity: The interplay of biological psychological and social factors.* San Francisco, CA: Jossey-Bass.

Davenport, T. H. (2005). *Thinking for a living: How to get better performance and results from knowledge workers.* Boston, MA.: Harvard Business School Press.

Davidson, M. (2002). *Leveraging difference for organizational excellence: Managing diversity differently* (*Darden* case, UVA-OB-0767). Charlottesville, VA: University of Virginia Darden School Foundation.

Davis, D. D. (2004). The Tao of leadership in virtual teams. *Organizational Dynamics, 33,* 47–62.

De Dreu, C. K. W. (2002). Team innovation and team effectiveness: The importance of minority dissent and reflexivity. *European Journal of Work and Organizational Psychology, 11,* 285–298.

De Dreu, C. K. W., & Weingart, L. R. (2003). Task versus relationship conflict, team performance, and team member satisfaction: A meta-analysis. *Journal of Applied Psychology, 88,* 741–749.

De Dreu, C. K. W., & West, M. A. (2001). Minority dissent and team innovation: The importance of participation in decision making. *Journal of Applied Psychology, 86,* 1191–1201.

Dell, M. (1999). *Direct from Dell: Strategies that revolutionized an industry.* New York, NY: HarperBusiness.

DeRue, D. S., Barnes, C. M., & Morgeson, F. P. (2010). Understanding the motivational contingencies of team leadership. *Small Group Research, 41,* 621–651.

Devine, D. J. (2002). A review and integration of classification systems relevant to teams in organizations. *Group Dynamics: Theory, Research, and Practice, 6,* 291–310.

Devine, D. J., Clayton, L. D., Dunford, B. B., Seying, R., & Pryce, J. (2001). Jury decision making: 45 years of empirical research on deliberating groups. *Psychology Public Policy and Law, 7,* 622–727.

Dewey, J. (1910). *How we think.* Boston, MA: D. C. Heath & Co.

Diehl, M., & Stroebe, W. (1987). Productivity loss in brainstorming groups: Toward the solutions of a riddle. *Journal of Personality and Social Psychology, 53,* 497–509.

Dindia, K., & Canary, D. J. (Eds.). (2006). *Sex differences and similarities in communication* (2nd ed.). Mahwah, NJ: Lawrence Erlbaum Associates.

Dion, K. L. (2000). Group cohesion: From "field of forces" to multidimensional construct. *Group Dynamics: Theory, Research, and Practice, 4,* 7–26.

Doney, P. M., Cannon, J. P., & Mullen, M. R. (1998). Understanding the influence of national culture in the development of trust. *Academy of Management Review, 23,* 601–620.

Driskell, J. E., Radtke, P. H., & Salas, E. (2003). Virtual teams: Effects of technological mediation on team performance. *Group Dynamics: Theory, Research, and Practice, 7,* 297–323.

Druskat, V. U., & Wolff, S. B. (2001). Building the emotional intelligence of groups. *Harvard Business Review, 79,* 81–90.

Duarte, D. L., & Snyder, N. T. (2001). *Mastering virtual teams: Strategies, tools, and techniques that succeed* (2nd ed.). San Francisco, CA: Jossey-Bass.

Dugosh, K. L., & Paulus, P. B. (2005). Cognitive and social comparison processes in brainstorming. *Journal of Experimental Social Psychology, 41,* 313–320.

Edwards, R. C. (1979). *Contested terrain: The transformation of the workplace in the twentieth century.* New York, NY: Basic Books.

Eisenhardt, K. M., Kahwajy, J. L., & Bourgeois III, L. J. (1997). How management teams can have a good fight. *Harvard Business Review, 75,* 77–85.

Ely, R. J., & Thomas, D. A. (2001). Cultural diversity at work: The effects of diversity perspectives on work group processes and outcomes. *Administrative Science Quarterly, 46,* 229–273.

Evans, C. R., & Dion, K. L. (2012). Group cohesion and performance: A meta-analysis. *Small Group Research, 43,* 690–701.

Falbe, C. M., & Yukl, G. (1992). Consequences for managers of using single influence tactics and combinations of tactics. *Academy of Management Journal, 35,* 638–652.

Feldman, D. C. (1984). The development and enforcement of group norms. *Academy of Management Review, 9,* 47–53.

Fisher, K. (2000). *Leading self-directed work teams: A guide to developing new team leadership skills* (rev. ed.). New York: McGraw-Hill.

Fisher, R., Ury, W., & Patton, B. (1991). *Getting to yes: Negotiating agreement without giving in* (2nd ed.). Boston, MA: Houghton Mifflin.

Fishman, C. (2006). *The Wal-Mart effect: How the world's most powerful company really works–and how it's transforming the American economy.* New York, NY: Penguin Press.

Foels, R., Driskell, J. E., Mullen, B., & Salas, E. (2000). The effects of democratic leadership on group member satisfaction: An integration. *Small Group Research, 31,* 676–701.

Forsyth, D. R. (2006). *Group dynamics* (4th ed.). Belmont, CA: Thompson Wadsworth.

Forsyth, D. R. (2010). *Group dynamics* (5th ed.). Belmont, CA: Wadsworth, Cengage Learning.

French, J. R. P., Jr., & Raven, B. (1959). The bases of social power. In D. Cartwright (Ed.), *Studies in social power* (pp. 150–167). Ann Arbor, MI: Institute for Social Research.

Friedman, M. I., & Lackey, G. H., Jr. (1991). *The psychology of human control: A general theory of purposeful behavior.* New York, NY: Praeger.

Friedman, T. L. (2006). *The world is flat: A brief history of the twenty-first century* (1st rev. and expanded ed.). New York, NY: Farrar, Straus and Giroux.

Gammage, K. L., Carron, A. V., & Estabrooks, P. A. (2001). Team cohesion and individual productivity: The influence of the norm for productivity and the identifiability of individual effort. *Small Group Research, 32,* 3–18.

Gamson, W. A. (1961). A theory of coalition formation. *American Sociological Review, 26,* 373–382.

Gardner, H. (1988). Creative lives and creative works: A synthetic scientific approach. In R. J. Sternberg (Ed.), *The nature of creativity: Contemporary psychological perspectives* (pp. 298–321). New York, NY: Cambridge University Press.

Gardner, H. (1993). *Creating minds: An anatomy of creativity seen through the lives of Freud, Einstein, Picasso, Stravinsky, Eliot, Graham, and Gandhi.* New York, NY: Basic Books.

Garvin, D. A., Edmondson, A. C., & Gino, F. (2008). Is yours a learning organization? *Harvard Business Review, 86,* 109–116.

George, J. M. (1992). Extrinsic and intrinsic origins of perceived social loafing in organizations. *Academy of Management Journal, 35,* 191–203.

Gersick, C. J. G. (1988). Time and transition in work teams: Toward a new model of group development. *Academy of Management Journal, 31,* 9–41.

Gersick, C. J. G. (1989). Marking time: Predictable transitions in task groups. *Academy of Management Journal, 32,* 274–309.

Ghosh, R., Shuck, B., & Petrosko, J. (2012). Emotional intelligence and organizational learning in work teams. *Journal of Management Development, 31,* 603–619.

Ghosn, C. (2002). Saving the business without losing the company. *Harvard Business Review, 80,* 37–45.

Ghuman, U. (2011). Building a model of group emotional intelligence. *Team Performance Management, 17,* 418–439.

Gibson, C. B., & Manuel, J. A. (2003). Building trust: Effective multicultural communication processes in virtual teams. In C. B. Gibson & S. G. Cohen (Eds.), *Virtual teams that work: Creating conditions for virtual team effectiveness* (pp. 59–86). San Francisco, CA: Jossey-Bass.

Gill, D. L. (1984). Individual and group performance in sport. In J. M. Silva & R. S. Weinberg (Eds.), *Psychological foundations of sport* (pp. 315–328). Champaign, IL: Human Kinetics.

Gillespie, D., Rosamond, S., & Thomas, E. (2006). Grouped out? Undergraduates' default strategies for participating in multiple small groups. *Journal of General Education, 55,* 81–102.

Gittell, J. H. (2003). *The Southwest Airlines way: Using the power of relationships to achieve high performance.* New York, NY: McGraw-Hill.

Gladwell, M. (2002). *The tipping point: How little things can make a big difference.* New York, NY: Little, Brown, and Company.

Gladwell, M. (2005). *Blink: The power of thinking without thinking.* New York, NY: Little, Brown, and Company.

Gold, M. (Ed.). (1999). *The complete social scientist: A Kurt Lewin reader.* Washington, DC: American Psychological Association.

Goldenberg, O., Larson, J. R., Jr., & Wiley, J. (2013). Goal instructions, response format, and idea generation in groups. *Small Group Research, 44,* 227–256.

Goleman, D. (1995). *Emotional intelligence.* New York, NY: Bantam Books.

Goleman, D. (2006). *Social intelligence: The new science of human relationships.* New York, NY: Bantam Books.

Goleman, D., Boyatzis, R., & McKee, A. (2001). Primal leadership: The hidden driver of great performance. *Harvard Business Review,* 1–11. December.

Goleman, D., Boyatzis, R. E., & McKee, A. (2004). *Primal leadership: Learning to lead with emotional intelligence.* Boston, MA: Harvard Business School Press.

Gratton, L. (2007). *Hot spots: Why some teams, workplaces, and organizations buzz with energy—and others don't.* San Francisco, CA: Berrett-Koehler Publishers.

Gratton, L., & Erickson, T. J. (2007). Eight ways to build collaborative teams. *Harvard Business Review, 85,* 101–109.

Greer, L. L., Saygi, O., Aaldering, H., & de Dreu, C. K. W. (2012). Conflict in medical teams: Opportunity or danger? *Medical Education, 46,* 935–942.

Griffith, B. A. (2004). The structure and development of internal working models: An integrated framework for understanding clients and promoting wellness. *Journal of Humanistic Counseling, Education, and Development, 43,* 163–177.

Griffith, B. A., & Frieden, G. (2000). Facilitating reflective thinking in counselor education. *Counselor Education and Supervision, 40,* 82–93.

Griffith, B. A., & Graham, C. C. (2004). Meeting needs and making meaning: The pursuit of goals. *Journal of Individual Psychology, 60,* 25–41.

Gude, R., Moum, R., Kaldestad, E., & Friis, S. (2000). Inventory of interpersonal problems: A three-dimensional balanced and scalable 48-item version. *Journal of Personality Assessment, 74,* 296–310.

Guilford, J. P. (1967). *The nature of human intelligence.* New York, NY: McGraw-Hill.

Guillen, M. F. (1994). *Models of management: Work, authority, and organization in a comparative perspective.* Chicago, IL: University of Chicago.

Gully, S. M., Devine, D. J., & Whitney, D. J. (2012). A meta-analysis of cohesion and performance: Effects of level of analysis and task interdependence. *Small Group Research, 43,* 702.

Haas, H., & Nüesch, S. (2012). Are multinational teams more successful? *The International Journal of Human Resource Management, 23,* 3105–3113.

Haasen, A., & Shea, G. F. (2003). *New corporate cultures that motivate.* Westport, CT: Praeger.

Hackman, J. R. (1986). The psychology of self-management in organizations. In M. S. Pallack & R. O. Perloff (Eds.), *Psychology and work: Productivity, change, and employment* (pp. 89–136). Washington, DC: American Psychological Association.

Hackman, J. R. (1999). Thinking differently about context. In R. Wageman (Ed.), *Research on managing groups and teams* (Vol. 2): *Teams in context* (pp. 233–247). Stamford, CT: JAI Press.

Hackman, J. R. (2009). Why teams don't work. Interview by Diane Coutu. *Harvard Business Review, 87,* 98–105, 130.

Hackman, J. R. (2002). *Leading teams: Setting the stage for great performances.* Boston, MA: Harvard Business School Press.

Halfhill, T., Sundstrom, E., Lahner, J., Calderone, W., & Nielsen, T. M. (2005). Group personality composition and group effectiveness: An integrative review of empirical research. *Small Group Research, 36,* 83–105.

Hamel, G., & Skarzynski, P. (2002). Innovation: The new route to new wealth. In F. Hesselbein & R. Johnston (Eds.), *On creativity, innovation, and renewal: A leader to leader guide.* San Francisco, CA: Jossey-Bass.

Hamper, B. (1986). *Rivethead—tales from the assembly Line.* New York, NY: The Warner Book Group.

Haney, C., & Zimbardo, P. (1998). The past and future of U.S. prison policy: Twenty-five years after the Stanford Prison Experiment. *American Psychologist, 53,* 709–727.

Hannah, S. T., Walumbwa, F. O., & Fry, L. W. (2011). Leadership in action teams: Team leader and members' authenticity, authenticity strength, and team outcomes. *Personnel Psychology, 64,* 771–802.

Hannan, M. T. (1988). Organizational population dynamics and social change. *European Sociological Review, 4,* 95–109.

Harkins, S. G., & Petty, R. E. (1982). Effects of task difficulty and task uniqueness on social loafing. *Journal of Personality and Social Psychology, 43,* 1214–1229.

Haynie, J. J. (2012). Core-self evaluations and team performance: The role of team-member exchange. *Small Group Research, 43,* 315–329.

Hays-Thomas, R. (2004). Why now? The contemporary focus on managing diversity. In M. S. Stockdale & F. J. Crosby (Eds.), *The psychology and management of workplace diversity* (pp. 3–30). Malden, MA: Blackwell Publishing.

Hazan, C., & Shaver, P. (1987). Romantic love conceptualized as an attachment process. *Journal of Personality and Social Psychology, 52,* 511–524.

Helms, J. E. (1993). *Black and white racial identity: Theory, research, and practice.* Westport, CT: Praeger.

Henderson, W. D. (1985). *Cohesion: The human element in combat.* Washington, DC: National Defense University Press.

Hentschel, T., Shemla, M., Wegge, J., & Kearney, E. (2013). Perceived diversity and team functioning: The role of diversity beliefs and affect. *Small Group Research, 44,* 33–61.

Hersey, P. (1985). *The situational leader* (4th ed.). New York, NY: Warner Books.

Hertel, G. (2011). Synergetic effects in working teams. *Journal of Managerial Psychology, 26,* 176–184.

Hertel, G., Geister, S., & Konradt, U. (2005). Managing virtual teams: A review of current empirical research. *Human Resource Management Review, 15,* 69–95.

Hertel, G., Konradt, U., & Orlikowski, B. (2004). Managing distance by interdependence: Goal setting, task interdependence, and team-based rewards in virtual teams. *European Journal of Work and Organizational Psychology, 13,* 1–28.

Hesselbein, F., & Johnston, R. (Eds.). (2002). *On creativity, innovation, and renewal: A leader to leader guide.* San Francisco, CA: Jossey-Bass.

Hill, L. A. (1994). *Managing your team* (case no. 9-494-081). Boston, MA: Harvard Business Publishing.

Hinds, P. J., & Weisband, S. P. (2003). Knowledge sharing and shared understanding in virtual teams. In C. B. Gibson & S. G. Cohen (Eds.), *Virtual teams that work: Creating conditions for virtual team effectiveness* (pp. 21–36). San Francisco, CA: Jossey-Bass.

Hirokawa, R. Y., DeGooyer, D., & Valde, K. (2000). Using narratives to study task group effectiveness. *Small Group Research, 31,* 573–591.

Hoegl, M., & Gemuenden, H. G. (1998). Teamwork quality and the success of innovative projects: A theoretical concept and empirical evidence. *Organizational Science, 12,* 435–449.

Hoegl, M., & Parboteeah, K. P. (2003). Goal setting and team performance in innovative projects: On the moderating role of teamwork quality. *Small Group Research, 34,* 3–19.

Hoffman, B. (1972). *Albert Einstein: Creator and rebel.* New York, NY: Viking.

Hogarth, R. (1987). *Judgment and choice: The psychology of decision.* Chichester, England: Wiley.

Hogg, M. A. (2005). The social identity perspective. In S. A. Weelan (Ed.), *The handbook of group research and practice* (pp. 133–157). Thousand Oaks, CA: Sage Publications.

Hogg, M. A., & Reid, S. A. (2006). Social identity, self-categorization, and the communication of group norms. *Communication Theory, 16,* 7–30.

Hollenbeck, J. R., DeRue, D. S., & Guzzo, R. (2004). Bridging the gap between I/O research and HR practice: Improving team composition, team training, and team task design. *Human Resource Management, 43,* 353–366.

Holtzman, Y., & Anderberg, J. (2011). Diversify your teams and collaborate: Because great minds don't think alike. *Journal of Management Development, 30,* 75–92.

Holzner, S. (2006). *How Dell does it: Using speed and innovation to achieve extraordinary results.* New York, NY: McGraw-Hill.

Homan, A. C., & Greer, L. L. (2013). Considering diversity: The positive effects of considerate leadership in diverse teams. *Group Processes & Intergroup Relations, 16,* 105–125.

Honeywell-Johnson, J. A., & Dickinson, A. M. (1999). Small group incentives: A review of the literature. *Journal of Organizational Behavior Management, 19,* 89–120.

Horne, C. (2001). The enforcement of norms: Group cohesion and meta-norms. *Social Psychology Quarterly, 64,* 253–266.

Howard, J. A., Blumstein, P., & Schwartz, P. (1986). Sex, power, and influence tactics in intimate relationships. *Journal of Personality and Social Psychology, 51,* 102–109.

Huang, S., & Cummings, J. N. (2011). When critical knowledge is most critical: Centralization in knowledge-intensive teams. *Small Group Research, 42,* 669–699.

Hüffmeier, J., & Hertel, G. (2011). Many cheers make light the work: How social support triggers process gains in teams. *Journal of Managerial Psychology, 26,* 185–204.

Huszczo, G. E. (2004). *Tools for team leadership: Delivering the X-factor in team eXcellence.* Palo Alto, CA: Davies-Black Publishing.

Hüttermann, H., & Boerner, S. (2011). Fostering innovation in functionally diverse teams: The two faces of transformational leadership. *European Journal of Work and Organizational Psychology, 20,* 833–854.

Ibarra, H., & Hansen, M. T. (2011). Are you a collaborative leader? *Harvard Business Review, 89,* 68–74.

Ilgen, D. R., Hollenbeck, J. R., Johnson, M., & Jundt, D. (2005). Teams in organizations: From input-process-output models to IMOI models. *Annual Review of Psychology, 56,* 517–543.

Industry Report. (1999, October). *Training, 36(10),* 37–81.

Islam, G., & Zyphur, M. J. (2005). Power, voice, and hierarchy: Exploring the antecedents of speaking up in groups. *Group Dynamics: Theory, Research, and Practice, 9,* 93–103.

Ive, J. (2007). Design Museum British Council. Retrieved from http://www.designmuseum.org/design/jonathan-ive

Jackson, S. E. (1992). Team composition in organizational settings: Issues in managing an increasingly diverse work force. In S. Worchel, W. Wood, & J. A. Simpson (Eds.), *Group process and productivity* (pp. 138–173). Newbury Park, CA: Sage.

Jackson, S. E., Joshi, A., & Erhard, N. L. (2003). Recent research on team and organizational diversity: SWOT analysis and implications. *Journal of Management, 29,* 801–830.

Jackson, S. E., & Ruderman, M. N. (1995). Introduction: Perspectives for understanding diverse work teams. In S. E. Jackson & M. N. Ruderman (Eds.), *Diversity in work teams: Research paradigms for a changing workplace* (pp. 1–13). Washington, DC: American Psychological Association.

Jackson, S. E., & Schuler, R.S. (2002). *Managing human resources through strategic partnership* (8th ed.). Belmont, CA: South-Western College Publishing.

Janis, I. L. (1982). *Groupthink* (2nd ed.). Boston, MA: Houghton Mifflin.

Janis, I. L. (1972). *Victims of groupthink: A psychological study of foreign-policy decisions and fiascoes.* Boston, MA: Houghton Mifflin.

Janss, R., Rispens, S., Segers, M., & Jehn, K. A. (2012). What is happening under the surface? Power, conflict and the performance of medical teams. *Medical Education, 46,* 838–849.

Jayne, M. E. A., & Dipboye, R. L. (2004), Leveraging diversity to improve business performance: Research findings and recommendations for organizations. *Human Resource Management, 43,* 409–424.

Jehn, K. A., & Bezrukova, K. (2004). A field study of group diversity, workgroup context, and performance. *Journal of Organizational Behavior, 25,* 703–729.

Johnson, D. W. (2003). Social interdependence: The interrelationships among theory, research, and practice. *American Psychologist, 58,* 931–945.

Johnson, D. W., & Johnson, F. P. (2006). *Joining together: Group theory and group skills.* Boston, MA: Allyn and Bacon.

Kahney, L. (2005). *The cult of iPod.* San Francisco, CA: No Starch Press.

Kalliath, T., & Laiken, M. (2006). Use of teams in management education. *Journal of Management Education, 30,* 747–750.

Kanawattanachai, P., & Yoo, Y. (2002). Dynamic nature of trust in virtual teams. *Journal of Strategic Information Systems, 18,* 7–40.

Kanter, R. (1977). *Men and women of the organization.* New York, NY: Basic Books.

Kao, J. J. (1996). *Jamming: The art and discipline of business creativity.* New York, NY: HarperCollins.

Karau, S. J., & Williams, K. D. (1993). Social loafing: A meta-analytic review and theoretical integration. *Journal of Personality and Social Psychology, 65,* 706–681 .

Karau, S. J., & Williams, K. D. (1997). The effects of group cohesiveness on social loafing and social compensation. *Group Dynamics: Theory, Research, and Practice, 1,* 156–168.

Karen, A. J., Northcraft, B., & Neale, M. A. (1999). Why differences make a difference: A field study of diversity, conflict, and performance in work groups. *Adv ministrative Science Quarterly, 44,* 741–763.

Katz-Navon, T. Y., & Erez, M. (2005). When collective- and self-efficacy affect team performance: The role of task interdependence. *Small Group Research, 36(4),* 437–465.

Katzenbach, J. R., & Smith, D. K. (1973). *The wisdom of teams: Creating the high-performance organization.* Boston, MA: Harvard Business School Press.

Katzenbach, J. R., & Smith, D. K. (2005). The discipline of teams. *Harvard Business Review, July–August,* 1–11.

Kauffeld, S., & Lehmann-Willenbrock, N. (2012). Meetings matter: Effects of team meetings on team and organizational success. *Small Group Research, 43,* 130–158.

Kayser, T. A. (1994). *Building team power: How to unleash the collaborative genius of work teams.* New York, NY: Irwin Professional Publishing.

Kayworth, T. R., & Leidner, D. E. (2001) Leadership effectiveness in global virtual teams. *Journal of Management Information Systems, 18,* 7–40.

Kegan, R. (1994). *In over our heads: The mental demands of modern life.* Cambridge, MA: Harvard University Press.

Kelley, T., & Littman, J. (2001). *The art of innovation: Lessons in creativity from IDEO, America's leading design firm.* New York, NY: Currency Books.

Kelly, A., Martocchio, J., & Frink, D. D. (1994). A review of the influence of group goals on group performance. *Academy of Management Journal, 37,* 1285–1301.

Keltner, D., Gruenfeld, D. H., & Anderson, C. (2003). Power, approach, and inhibition. *Psychological Review, 110,* 265–284.

Kerr, N. L., & Tindale, R. S. (2004). Group performance and decision making. *Annual Review of Psychology, 55,* 623–655.

Kerr, N. L., & Tindale, R. S. (2004). Small group decision making and performance. *Annual Review of Psychology, 55,* 623–656.

Kessel, M., Kratzer, J., & Schultz, C. (2012). Psychological safety, knowledge sharing, and creative performance in healthcare teams. *Creativity and Innovation Management, 21,* 147–157.

Kilmann, R. H., & Thomas, K. W. (1977). Developing a forced-choice measure of conflict-handling behavior: The "Mode" instrument. *Educational and Psychological Measurement, 37,* 309–325.

King, P. M., & Kitchener, K. S. (1994). *Developing reflective judgment: Understanding and promoting growth and critical thinking in adolescents and adults.* San Franscisco, CA: Jossey-Bass.

Kinnick, D. N., & Parton, S. R. (2005). Workplace communication: What the apprentice teaches about communication skills. *Business Communication Quarterly, 68,* 429–456.

Kipnis, D. (1976). *The powerholders.* Chicago, IL: University of Chicago Press.

Kirkman, B., & Rosen, B. (1999). Beyond self-management: Antecedents and consequences of team empowerment. *Academy of Management Journal, 24,* 58–74.

Klein, H. J., Wesson, M. J., Hollenbeck, J. R., & Alge, B. J. (1999). Goal commitment and the goal-setting process: Conceptual clarification and empirical synthesis. *Journal of Applied Psychology, 84,* 885–896.

Kleingeld, A., van Mierlo, H., & Arends, L. (2011). The effect of goal setting on group performance: A meta-analysis. *Journal of Applied Psychology, 96,* 1289–1304.

Kline, T. (1999). *Remaking teams: The revolutionary research-based guide that puts theory in practice.* San Francisco, CA: Jossey-Bass/Pfeiffer.

Kline, T. J. B., & McGrath, J. (1998). Development and validation of five criteria for evaluating team performance. *Organizational Development Journal, 16,* 19–27.

Knouse, S. B., & Dansby, M. R. (1999). Percentage of work-group diversity and work-group effectiveness. *Journal of Psychology, 133,* 486–494.

Kotter, J. P. (1985). *Power and influence.* New York, NY: Free Press.

Kotter, J. P. (1988). *The leadership factor.* New York, NY: Free Press.

Kotter, J. P. (1996). *Leading change.* Boston, MA: Harvard Business School Press.

Kotter, J. P. (1998). Winning at change. *Leader to Leader, 10,* 27–33.

Kouzes, J. M., & Posner, B. Z. (2007). *The leadership challenge* (4th ed.). San Francisco, CA: Jossey-Bass.

Kozlowski, S. W. J., & Bell, B. S. (2003). Work groups and teams in organizations. In W. Borman, D. Ilgen, & R. Klimoski (Eds.), *Comprehensive handbook of psychology, Vol. 12: Industrial and organizational psychology* (pp. 333–375). New York, NY: Wiley.

Krackhardt, D. (1990). Assessing the political landscape: Structure, cognition, and power in organizations. *Administrative Science Quarterly, 35,* 342–369.

Kramer, R. M. (1999). Trust and distrust in organizations: Emerging perspectives, enduring questions. *Annual Review of Psychology, 50,* 569–598.

Kramer, R. M., & Neale, M. A. (Eds.). *Power and influence in organizations.* Thousand Oaks, CA: Sage.

Kramer, T. J., Fleming, G. P., & Mannis, S. M. (2001). Improving face-to-face brainstorming through modeling and facilitation. *Small Group Research, 32,* 533–557.

Krause, D. E., & Kearney, E. (2006). The use of power bases in different contexts. *Power and influence in organizations* (59–86). Thousand Oaks, CA: Sage.

Kravitz, D. A., & Martin, B. (1986). Ringelmann rediscovered: The original article. *Journal of Personality and Social Psychology, 50,* 936–941.

Kristof-Brown, A. L., & Stevens, C. K. (2001). Goal congruence in project teams: Does the fit between members' personal mastery and performance goals matter? *Journal of Applied Psychology, 86,* 1083–1095.

Krolokke, C., & Sorensen, A. S. (2006). *Gender communication theories and analyses: From silence to performance.* Thousand Oaks, CA: Sage.

Kruglanski, A. W., & Webster, D. M. (1991). Group members' reactions to opinion deviates and conformists at varying degrees of proximity to decision deadline and of environmental noise. *Journal of Personality and Social Psychology, 61,* 212–225.

Lafond, D., Jobidon, M., Aubé, C., & Tremblay, S. (2011). Evidence of structure-specific teamwork requirements and implications for team design. *Small Group Research, 42,* 507–535.

Laughlin, P. R., Hatch, E. C., Silver, J. S., & Boh, L. (2006). Groups perform better than the best individuals on letters-to-numbers problems: Effects of group size. *Journal of Personality and Social Psychology, 90,* 644–651.

Lee, F. K., Sheldon, K. M., & Turban, D. B. (2003). Personality and the goal-striving process: The influence of achievement goal patterns, goal level, and mental focus on performance and enjoyment. *Journal of Applied Psychology, 88,* 256–265.

Lemme, B. (2006). *Development in adulthood* (4th ed.). Boston, MA: Allyn and Bacon.

Lencioni, P. (2002). *The five dysfunctions of a team: A leadership fable.* San Franscisco, CA: Jossey-Bass.

Lencioni, P. (2004). *Death by meeting.* San Francisco, CA: Jossey-Bass.

Lencioni, P. (2005). *Overcoming the five dysfunctions of a team: A field guide for leaders, managers, and facilitators.* San Francisco, CA: Jossey-Bass.

Levenson & Cohen (2003). Meeting the performance challenge: Calculating return on investment for virtual teams. In C. Gibson & and S. Cohen (Eds.), *Virtual teams that work: Creating the conditions for virtual team effectiveness* (pp. 145–174). San Francisco, CA: Jossey-Bass.

Levine, E. L. (1973). Problems with organizational control in microcosm: Group performance and group member satisfaction as a function of differences in control structure. *Journal of Applied Psychology, 58,* 186–196.

Lewis, M. (2003). *Moneyball: The art of winning an unfair game.* New York: W. W. Norton.

Lingard, L., Espin, S., Whyte, S., Regehr, G., Baker, G. R., Reznick, R., Bohnen, J., Orser, B., Doran, D., & Grober, E. (2004). Communication failures in the operating room: An observational classification of recurrent types and effects. *Quality and Safety in Healthcare, 13,* 330–334.

Liswood, L. A. (2010). *The loudest duck: Moving beyond diversity while embracing differences to achieve success at work.* Hoboken, NJ: Wiley.

Liu, D., Zhang, S., Wang, L., & Lee, T. W. (2011). The effects of autonomy and empowerment on employee turnover: Test of a multilevel model in teams. *Journal of Applied Psychology, 96,* 1305–1316.

Locke, E. A., & Latham, G. P. (1990). *A theory of goal setting and task performance.* Englewood Cliffs, NJ: Prentice Hall.

Locke, E. A., & Latham, G. P. (2002). Building a practically useful theory of goal setting and task motivation: A 35-year odyssey. *American Psychologist, 57,* 705–717.

Mann, R. D. (1959). A review of the relationships between personality and performance in small groups. *Psychological Bulletin, 56,* 241–270.

Mannix, E., & Neale, M. A. (2005). What differences make a difference? The promise and reality of diverse teams in organizations. *Psychological Science in the Public Interest, 6,* 31–55.

Marksberry, P., Bustle, J., & Clevinger, J. (2011). Problem solving for managers: A mathematical investigation of Toyota's 8-step process. *Journal of Manufacturing Technology, 22,* 837–852.

Marques, J. M., Abrams, D., Paez, D., & Hogg, M. A. (2001). Social categorization, social identification, and rejection of deviant group members. In M. A. Hogg & R. S. Tindale (Eds.), *Blackwell handbook of social psychology: Group processes* (pp. 400–424). Malden, MA: Blackwell.

Martin, J. (2002). *Organizational culture: Mapping the terrain.* Thousand Oaks, CA: Sage.

Martin, R., & Hewstone, M. (2001). Conformity and independence in groups: Majorities and minorities. In M. A. Hogg & R. S. Tindale (Eds.), *Blackwell handbook of social psychology: Group processes* (pp. 207–234). Malden, MA: Blackwell.

Martins, L. L., Gilson, L. L., & Maynard, M. T. (2004). Virtual teams: What do we know and where do we go from here? *Journal of Management, 30,* 805–835.

Martins, L. L., Schilpzand, M. C., Kirkman, B. L., Ivanaj, S., & Ivanaj, V. (2013). A contingency view of the effects of cognitive diversity on team performance: The moderating roles of team psychological safety and relationship conflict. *Small Group Research, 44,* 96–126.

Mauzy, J., & Harriman, R. (2003). *Creativity, Inc.: Building an inventive organization.* Boston, MA: Harvard Business School Press.

Mayer, R. C., Davis, J. H., & Schoorman, F. D. (1995). An integrative model of organizational trust. *Academy of Management Review, 20,* 709–734.

McClellan, D. C. (1975). *Power: The inner experience.* New York, NY: Irvington.

McCrae, R. R., & Costa, P. T. (1987). Validation of the five-factor model of personality across instruments and observers. *Journal of Personality and Social Psychology, 52,* 81–90.

McIntyre, H. H., & Foti, R. J. (2013). The impact of shared leadership on teamwork mental models and performance in self-directed teams. *Group Processes & Intergroup Relations, 16,* 46–57.

McKay, M., Davis, M., & Fanning, P. (1995). *Messages: The communication skills book* (2nd ed.). Oakland, CA: New Harbinger Publications.

McKee, A., Boyatzis, R. E., & Johnston, F. (2008). *Becoming a resonant leader: Develop your emotional intelligence, renew your relationships, sustain your effectiveness.* Boston, MA: Harvard Business School Press.

Mehrabian, A. (1981). *Silent messages: Implicit communication of emotions and attitudes* (2nd ed.). Belmont, CA: Wadsworth Publishing.

Merrill, D. W., & Reid, R. H. (1981). *Personal styles and effective performance.* Boca Raton, FL: CRC Press.

Meyer, C. (1994). How the right measures help teams excel. *Harvard Business Review, 72,* 95–103.

Michaels, E., Handfield-Jones, H., & Axelrod, B. (2001). *The war for talent.* Boston, MA: Harvard Business School.

Milgram, S. (1974). *Obedience to authority.* New York, NY: Harper & Row.

Miller, D. L. (2001). Reexamining teamwork KSAs and team performance. *Small Group Behavior, 32,* 745–766.

Milliken, F. J., & Martins, L. L. (1996). Searching for common threads: Understanding the multiple effects of diversity in organizational groups. *The Academy of Management Review, 21,* 402–433.

Mockros, C. A., & Csikszentmihalyi, M. (1999). The social construction of creative lives. In A. Montuori & R. E. Purser (Eds.), *Social creativity* (Vol. 1). Cresskill, NJ: Hampton Press.

Moen, P., Elder, G. H., Jr., & Lüscher, K. (Eds.). (1995). *Examining lives in context: Perspectives on the ecology of human development.* Washington, DC: American Psychological Association.

Molleman, E., Nuata, A., & Jehn, K. A. (2004). Person-job fit applied to teamwork: A multilevel approach. *Small Group Research, 35,* 515–539.

Morrill, C. (1995). *The executive way.* Chicago, IL: University of Chicago Press.

Moser, K., Wolff, H. G., & Kraft, A. (2013). The de-escalation of commitment: Predecisional accountability and cognitive processes. *Journal of Applied Social Psychology, 43,* 363–376.

Mueller, J. S. (2012). Why individuals in larger teams perform worse. *Organizational Behavior and Human Decision Processes, 117,* 111–124.

Mullen, B., Johnson, C., & Salas, E. (1991). Productivity loss in brainstorming groups: A meta-analytic integration. *Basic and Applied Social Psychology, 12*(1): 3–23.

Mulvey, P. W., & Klein, H. J. (1998). The impact of perceived loafing and collective efficacy on group goal processes and group performance. *Organizational Behavior and Human Decision Processes, 74,* 62–87.

Myaskovsky, L., Unikel, E., & Dew, M. A. (2005). Effects of gender diversity on performance and interpersonal behavior in small work groups. *Behavioral Science, 52,* 645–657.

Nemeth, C. J. (1986). Differential contributions of majority and minority influence. *Psychological Review, 93,* 23–32.

Nemeth, C. J. (1992). Minority dissent as a stimulant to group performance. In S. Worchel, W. Wood, & J. A. Simpson (Eds.), *Group process and productivity* (pp. 95–111). Newbury Park, CA: Sage.

Nemeth, C. J. (1995). Dissent as driving cognition, attitudes, and judgments. *Social Cognition, 13,* 273–291.

Neuman, G. A., & Wright, J. (1999). Team effectiveness: Beyond skills and cognitive ability. *Journal of Applied Psychology, 84,* 376–389.

Nickerson, R. S. (1998). Confirmation bias: A ubiquitous phenomenon in many guises. *Review of General Psychology, 2,* 175–220.

Nijstad, B. A., Stroebe, W., & Lodewijkx, H. F. M. (2003). Production blocking and idea generation: Does blocking interfere with cognitive processes? *Journal of Experimental Social Psychology, 39,* 531–548.

Nijstad, B. A., Stroebe, W., & Lodewijkx, H. F. M. (2006). The illusion of group productivity: A reduction of failures explanation. *European Journal of Social Psychology, 36,* 31–48.

Oh, S. (2012). Leadership emergence in autonomous work teams: Who is more willing to lead? *Social Behavior and Personality, 40,* 1451–1464.

O'Leary, M. B., Mortensen, M., & Woolley, A. W. (2011). Multiple team membership: A theoretical model of its effects on productivity and learning for individuals and teams. *Academy of Management Review, 36*(3), 461–478.

O'Leary-Kelly, A. M., Martocchio, J. J., & Frink, D. D. (1994). A review of the influence of group goals on group performance. *Academy of Management Journal, 37,* 1285–1301.

O'Neill, T. A., & Allen, N. J. (2012). Team meeting attitudes: Conceptualization and investigation of a new construct. *Small Group Research, 43,* 186–210.

O'Reilly, C. A., Caldwell, D. F., & Barnett, W. P. (1989). Work group demography, social integration, and turnover. *Administrative Science Quarterly, 34,* 21–37.

Osborn, A. F. (1953). *Applied imagination.* New York, NY: Scribner.

Page, S. E. (2007). *The difference: How the power of diversity creates better groups, firms, schools, and societies.* Princeton, NJ: Princeton University Press.

Parayitam, S., & Dooley, R. S. (2011). Is too much cognitive conflict in strategic decision-making teams too bad? *International Journal of Conflict Management, 22,* 342–357.

Parker, G. M. (1994). *Cross-functional teams: Working with allies, enemies, and other strangers.* San Francisco, CA: Jossey-Bass.

Paulus, P. B., Nakui, T., Putman, V. L., & Brown, V. R. (2006). Effects of task instructions and brief breaks on brainstorming. *Group Dynamics: Theory, Research, and Practice, 10,* 206–219.

Paulus, P. B., & Yang, H. C. (2000). Idea generation in groups: A basis for creativity in organizations. *Organizational Behavior and Human Decision Processes, 82,* 76–87.

Pescosolido, A. T., & Saavedra, R. (2012). Cohesion and sports teams: A review. *Small Group Research, 43,* 744–758.

Pfeffer, J. (1992). *Managing with power: Politics and influence in organizations.* Boston, MA: Harvard Business School Press.

Pfeiffer, J. W. & Jones, J. E. (Eds.). (1974). *Structured experiences for human relations training, Vol. I–IV.* San Diego, CA: University Associates Publishers and Consultants.

Pink, D. H. (2009). *Drive: The surprising truth about what motivates us.* New York, NY: Riverhead books.

Pirola-Merlo, A. (2010). Agile innovation: The role of team climate in rapid research and development. *Journal of Occupational and Organizational Psychology, 83,* 1075–1084.

Polzer, J. T. (2003). Leading teams. *Harvard Business Review, 44,* 78–94.

Poole, M. S., & Dobosh, M. (2010). Exploring conflict management processes in jury deliberations through interaction analysis. *Small Group Research, 41,* 408–426.

Porter, C. O. L. H. (2005). Goal orientation: Effects on backing up behavior, performance, efficacy, and commitment in teams. *Journal of Applied Psychology, 90,* 811–818.

Porter, C. O. L. H., Gogus, C. I., & Yu, R. C. (2011). The influence of early efficacy beliefs on teams' reactions to failing to reach performance goals. *Applied Psychology: An International Review, 60,* 645–669.

Porter, C. O. L. H., Hollenbeck, J. R., Ilgen, J. R., Ellis, A. P. J., West, B. J., & Moon, H. (2003). Backing up behaviors in teams: The role of personality and legitimacy of need. *Journal of Applied Psychology, 88,* 391–403.

Postmes, T., Spears, R., & Cihangir, S. (2001). Quality of decision making and group norms. *Journal of Personality and Social Psychology, 80,* 918–930.

Postmes, T., Spears, R., Lee, A. T., & Novak, R. J. (2005). Individuality and social influence in groups: Inductive and deductive routes to group identity. *Journal of Personality and Social Psychology, 89,* 747–763.

Powell, A., Piccoli, G., & Ives, B. (2004). Virtual teams: A review of current literature and directions for future research. *The DATABASE for Advances in Information Systems, 35,* 6–36.

Proudfoot, J., Jayasinghe, U. W., Holton, C., Grimm, J., Bubner, T., Amoroso, C., Beilby, J., & Harris, M. (2007). Team climate for innovation: What difference does it make in general practice? *International Journal for Quality in Health Care, 19,* 164–169.

Purvanova, R. K. (2013). The role of feeling known for team member outcomes in project teams. *Small Group Research, 44,* 298–331.

Putnam, R. (2000). *Bowling alone: The collapse and revival of American community.* New York, NY: Simon & Schuster.

Qin, Z., Johnson, D. W., & Johnson, R. T. (1995). Cooperative versus competitive efforts and problem solving. *Review of Educational Literature, 65,* 129–143.

Ranieri, K. L. (2004). Toward group problem solving guidelines for 21st century teams. *Performance Improvement Quarterly, 17,* 86–105.

Rholes, W. S., & Simpson, J. A. (Eds.). (2004). *Adult attachment: Theory, research, and clinical implications.* New York, NY: Guilford Press.

Ridgeway, C. L. (2001). Social status and group structure. In M. A. Hogg & R. S. Tindale (Eds.), *Blackwell handbook of social psychology: Group processes* (pp. 352–375). Malden, MA: Blackwell.

Rimal, R. N., & Real, K. (2005). How behaviors are influenced by perceived norms: A test of the theory of normative social behavior. *Communication Research, 32,* 389–414.

Robson, M. (2002). *Problem-solving in groups* (3rd ed.). Hampshire, England: Gower Publishing.

Rom, E., & Mikulincer, M. (2003). Attachment theory and group processes: The association between attachment style and group-related representations, goals, memories, and functioning. *Journal of Personality and Social Psychology, 84,* 1220–1235.

Rosenfeld, P. (1990). Self-esteem and impression management explanations for self-serving biases. *Journal of Social Psychology, 130,* 495–500.

Rousseau, V., Aubé, C., & Savoie, A. (2006). Teamwork behaviors: A review and an integration of frameworks. *Small Group Research, 37,* 540–570.

Rowe, A. J. (2004). *Creative intelligence: Discovering the innovative potential in ourselves and others.* Upper Saddle River, NJ: Pearson/Prentice Hall.

Roy, M. H. (2001). Small group communication and performance: Do cognitive flexibility and context matter? *Management Decision, 39,* 323–330.

Russell, B. (1938). *Power: A new social analysis.* New York, NY: W. W. Norton.

Savitsky, K., Van Boven, L., Epley, N., & Wight, W. M. (2005). The unpacking effect inallocations of responsibility for group tasks. *Journal of Experimental Social Psychology, 41,* 447–457.

Sawyer, R. K. (2003). *Group creativity: Music, theater, collaboration.* Mahwah, NJ: Lawrence Erlbaum.

Schachter, S. (1961). Deviation, rejection, and communication. *Journal of Abnormal and Social Psychology, 46,* 190–207.

Schilpzand, M. C., Herold, D. M., & Shalley, C. E. (2011). Members' openness to experience and teams' creative performance. *Small Group Research, 42,* 55–76.

Schon, D. A. (1983). *The reflective practitioner.* New York, NY: Basic Books.

Schon, D. A. (1987). *Educating the reflective practitioner.* San Francisco, CA: Jossey-Bass.

Schriesheim, C. A., & Neider, L. L. (2006). *Power and influence in organizations.* Greenwich, CT: Information Age Publishing.

Schultz, H., & Yang, D. J. (1997). *Pour your heart into it: How Starbucks built a company one cup at a time.* New York, NY: Hyperion.

Schutz, W. C. (1958). *FIRO: A three-dimensional theory of interpersonal behavior.* New York, NY: Rinehart.

Scott, C. W., Shanock, L. R., & Rogelberg, S. G. (2012). Meetings at work: Advancing the theory and practice of meetings. *Small Group Research, 43,* 127–129.

Seifert, C. F., Yukl, G., & McDonald, R. A. (2003). Effects of multisource feedback and a feedback facilitator on the influence behavior of managers toward subordinates. *Journal of Applied Psychology, 88,* 561–569.

Seijts, G. H., & Latham, G. P. (2000). The effects of goal setting and group size on performance in a social dilemma. *Canadian Journal of Behavioural Science, 32,* 104–116.

Sekaquaptewa, D., & Thompson, M. (2003). Solo status, stereotype threat, and performance expectancies: Their effects on women's performance. *Journal of Experimental Social Psychology, 39,* 68–74.

Sell, J., Lovaglia, M. J., Mannix, E. A., Samuelson, C. D., & Wilson, R. K. (2004). Investigating conflict, power, and status within and among groups. *Small Group Research, 35,* 44–72.

Senate Intelligence Committee. (2004). *Report on the U.S. Intelligence Community's Prewar Intelligence Assessments on Iraq.* Retrieved from http://intelligence.senate.gov/108301.pdf

Senge, P. M. (1990). *The fifth discipline: The art and practice of the learning organization.* New York, NY: Doubleday.

Shannon, W. T. (1996). *The power struggle: How it enhances or destroys our lives.* New York, NY: Plenum Press.

Simons, T., Pelled, L. H., & Smith, K. A. (1999). Making use of difference: Diversity, debate, and discussion in top management teams. *The Academy of Management Review, 42,* 662–673.

Sivasubramaniam, N., Murry, W. D., Avolio, B. J., & Jung, D. I. (2002). A longitudinal model of the effects of team leadership and group potency on group performance. *Group & Organization Management, 27,* 66–96.

Smith, E. R., Murphy, J., & Coats, S. (1999). Attachment to groups: Theory and measurement. *Journal of Personality and Social Psychology, 77,* 94–110.

Smith-Lovin, L., & Brody, C. (1989). Interruptions in group discussions: The effects of gender and group composition. *American Sociological Review, 54,* 424–435.

Stevens, M. J., & Campion, M. A. (1994). The knowledge, skill, and ability requirements for teamwork: Implications for human resource management. *Journal of Management, 20,* 503–530.

Stevens, M. J., & Campion, M. A. (1999). Staffing work teams: Development and validation of a selection test for teamwork settings. *Journal of Management, 25,* 207–228.

Stiles, W. B., Lyall, L. M., Knight, D. P., Ickes, W., Waung, M., Hall, C. L., & Primeau, B. E. (1997). Gender differences in verbal presumptuousness and attentiveness. *Personality and Social Psychology Bulletin, 23,* 759–772.

Stogdill, R. M. (1948). Personal factors associated with leadership: A survey of the literature. *Journal of Psychology, 25,* 35–71.

Straus, S. G. (1999). Testing a typology of tasks: An empirical validation of McGrath's (1984) group task circumplex. *Small Group Research, 30,* 166–187.

Sundstrom, E., McIntyre, M., Halfhill, T., & Richards, H. (2000). Work groups: From Hawthorne studies to work teams of the 1990s and beyond. *Group Dynamics: Theory, Research, and Practice, 4,* 44–67.

Suroweicki, J. (2004). *The wisdom of crowds: Why the many are smarter than the few and how collective wisdom shapes business, economies, societies, and nations.* New York, NY: Double Day.

Terry, D. J., & Hogg, M. A. (Eds.). (2000). *Attitudes, behavior, and social context: The role of norms and group membership.* Mahwah, NJ: Erlbaum Associates.

Thomke, S., & Nimgade, A. (2002). Bank of America (*Harvard Business School* case, 9-603-022).

Thompson, L. L. (2004). *Making the team: A guide for managers* (2nd ed.). Upper Saddle River, NJ: Pearson Prentice Hall.

Thompson, L. L. (2008). *Making the team: A guide for managers* (3rd ed.). Upper Saddle River, NJ: Prentice Hall.

Thoms, P., Pinto, J. K., Parente, D. H., & Druskat, V. U. (2002). Adaptation to self-managing work teams. *Small Group Research, 33,* 3–31.

Torrance, E. P. (1988). The nature of creativity as manifest in its testing. In R. J. Sternberg, *The nature of creativity: Contemporary psychological perspectives* (pp. 43–75). New York: Cambridge University Press.

Trompenaars, F., & Hampden-Turner, C. (1998). *Riding the waves of culture: Understanding cultural diversity in global business* (2nd ed.). New York, NY: McGraw Hill.

Tuckman, B. (1965). Developmental sequence in small groups. *Psychological Bulletin, 63,* 384–399.

Urban, M. S., & Witt, L. A. (1990). Self-serving bias in group member attributions of success and failure. *Journal of Social Psychology, 130,* 417–418.

Valley, K. L., & Thompson, T. A. (1998). Sticky ties and bad attitudes: Relational and individual bases of resistance to change in organizational structure. In R. M. Kramer & M. A. Neale (Eds.), *Power and influence in organizations* (pp. 39–66). Thousand Oaks, CA: Sage.

Van Gundy, A. B. (1984). *Managing group creativity: A modular approach to problem solving.* New York, NY: American Management Associations.

Van Knippenberg, D., De Dreu, C. K. W., & Homan, A. C. (2004). Work group diversity and group performance: An integrative model and research agenda. *Journal of Applied Psychology, 89,* 1008–1022.

Van Mierlo, H., & Kleingeld, A. (2010). Goals, strategies, and group performance: Some limits of goal setting in groups. *Small Group Research, 41,* 524–555.

Wageman, R. (1995). Interdependence and group effectiveness. *Administrative Science Quarterly, 40,* 145–180.

Wageman, R., & Baker, G. (1997). Incentives and cooperation: The joint effects of task and reward interdependence on group performance. *Journal of Organizational Behavior, 18,* 139–158.

Wageman, R., Gardner, H., & Mortensen, M. (2012). The changing ecology of teams: New directions for teams research. *Journal of Organizational Behavior, 33,* 301–315.

Wageman, R., & Mannix, E. A. (1998). Uses and misuses of power in task-performing teams. In R. M. Kramer & M. A. Neale (Eds.), *Power and influence in organizations* (pp. 261–285). Thousand Oaks, CA: Sage.

Wagner, J. A., III. (1995). Studies of individualism-collectivism: Effects on cooperation in groups. *Academy of Management Journal, 38,* 152–172.

Walsh, J. P., & Maloney, N. G. (2007). Collaboration structure, communication media, and problems in scientific work teams. *Journal of Computer-Mediated Communication, 12,* 712–732.

Walton, S., & Huey, J. (1992). *Sam Walton: Made in America.* New York, NY: Doubleday.

Warkentin, M., & Beranek, P. M. (1999). Training to improve virtual team communication. *Information Systems Journal, 9,* 271–289.

Watson, W. E., Johnson, L., & Zgourides, G. D. (2002). The influence of ethnic diversity on leadership, group process, and performance: An examination of learning teams. *International Journal of Intercultural Relations, 26,* 1–16.

Weingart, L. R., & Todorova, G. (2010). Jury tensions: Applying communication theories and methods to study group dynamics. *Small Group Research, 41,* 495–502.

Wheelan, S. A. (1999). *Creating effective teams: A guide for members and leaders.* Thousand Oaks, CA: Sage Publications.

Wheelan, S. A. (2004). *Group Processes: A developmental perspective* (2nd ed.). Boston, MA: Allyn and Bacon.

Wheelan, S. A. (2005). The developmental perspective. In S. A. Weelan (Ed.), *The handbook of group research and practice* (pp. 119–132). Thousand Oaks, CA: Sage Publications.

Wheelan, S. A., Davidson, B., & Tilin, F. (2003). Group development across time: Reality or illusion? *Small Group Research, 34,* 223–245.

Wheelan, S. A., Verdi, A., & McKeage, R. (1994). *The group development observation system: Origins and applications.* Provincetown, MA: GDQ Associates.

Whitt, E. J., Edison, M. I., Pascarella, E. J., Terenzini, P. T., & Amuray, N. (2001). Influences on students' openness to diversity and challenge in the second and third years of college. *The Journal of Higher Education, 72,* 172–204.

Wicks, T. G., & Parish, T. S. (1990). Enhancing communication through the use of control theory applied to social styles. *College Student Journal, 23,* 294–295.

Widmeyer, W. N. (1990). Group composition in sport. *International Journal of Sport Psychology, 21,* 264–285.

Wiedow, A., & Konradt, U. (2011). Two-dimensional structure of team process improvement: Team reflection and team adaptation. *Small Group Research, 42,* 32–54.

Wittenbaum, G. M., & Bowman, J. M. (2005). Member status and information exchange in decision-making groups. In M. C. Thomas-Hunt, *Status and Groups* (pp. 143–168). Oxford, UK: Elsevier.

Wood, W. (1987). A meta-analytic review of sex differences in group performance. *Psychological Bulletin, 102,* 53–71.

Woodman, R. W., Sawyer, J. E., & Griffin, R. W. (1993). Toward a theory of organizational creativity. *Academy of Management Review, 18,* 293–321.

Yukl, G., Chavez, C., & Seifert, C. F. (2005). Assessing the construct validity and utility of two new influence tactics. *Journal of Organizational Behavior, 26,* 705–725.

Yukl, G., & Falbe, C. M. (1990). Influence tactics and objectives in upward, downward, and lateral influence attempts. *Journal of Applied Psychology, 75,* 132–140.

Yukl, G., & Falbe, C. M. (1991). Importance of different power sources in downward and lateral relations. *Journal of Applied Psychology, 76,* 416–423.

Yukl, G., Kim, H., & Falbe, C. M. (1996). Antecedents of influence outcomes. *Journal of Applied Psychology, 81,* 309–317.

Yukl, G., & Tracey, J. B. (1992). Consequences of influence tactics used with subordinates, peers, and the boss. *Journal of Applied Psychology, 77,* 525–535.

Zenasni, F., Besançon, M., & Lubart, T. (2008). Creativity and tolerance of ambiguity: An empirical study. *Journal of Creative Behavior, 42,* 61–73.

Zenger, T. R., & Marshall, C. R. (2000). Determinants of incentive intensity in group-based rewards. *Academy of Management Journal, 43,* 149–163.

Zhong, C., Ku, G., Lount, R., Jr., & Murninghan, J. (2006). Group context, social identity, and ethical decision making: A preliminary test. *Research on Managing Groups and Teams, 8,* 149–175.

Zhou, W., & Shi, X. (2011). Culture in groups and teams: A review of three decades of research. *International Journal of Cross Cultural Management, 11,* 5–34.

Zimbardo, P. G. A simulation study of the psychology of imprisonment conducted at Stanford University. In *Stanford Prison Experiment.* Retrieved from http://www.prisonexp.org

Photo Credits

Index

About the Authors

Dr. Brian Griffith, PhD, is Assistant Clinical Professor in Human and Organizational Development at Peabody College of Vanderbilt University. A passionate and committed teacher, Dr. Griffith has earned both The Peabody College Award for Excellence in Classroom Teaching and the Madison Sarratt Prize for Excellence in Undergraduate Teaching at Vanderbilt. Students often note that his engaging presentation style and relevant content are catalysts for personal growth and development.

Dr. Griffith's research explores team dynamics, leadership, and organizational behavior. His first book, *Effective Groups: Concepts and Skills to Meet Leadership Challenges* is used as a graduate-level text in educational administration courses. His current book, *Working in Teams: Moving From High Potential to High Performance,* prepares college students to understand and lead teams within organizations. Griffith is also the creator of the *G360* online surveys used by colleges, universities, and corporations to facilitate individual and team development.

Ethan B. Dunham EdM, MBA, is a consulting executive who applies dual expertise in business and education to help people, groups, and companies solve problems and overcome challenges. Dunham specializes in organizational development and design, innovation, strategic planning and execution, conflict resolution, systems-level problem-solving, team and program leadership, and curriculum design. Previously, Dunham was Chief People & Performance Officer at Cogent Healthcare, a leading provider of hospital and critical care medicine in the United States. Dunham is also the co-author of *Burn Your Resume: How to Ignite Your Exceptional Career.*

⑨SAGE researchmethods

The essential online tool for researchers from the world's leading methods publisher

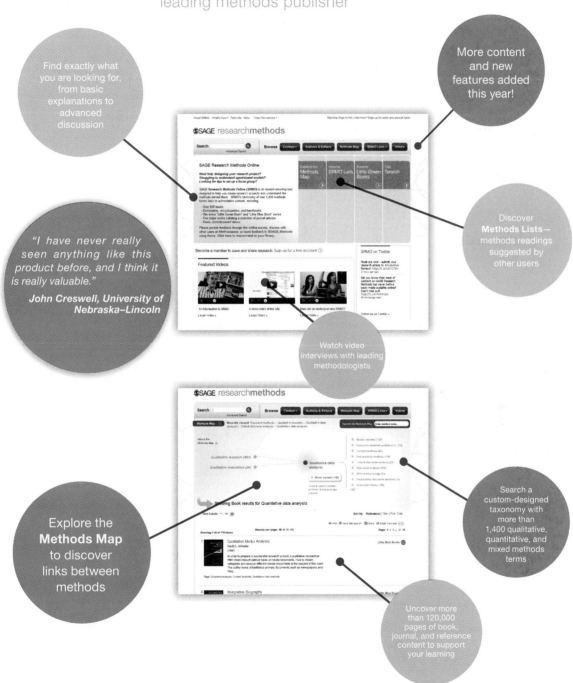

Find exactly what you are looking for, from basic explanations to advanced discussion

More content and new features added this year!

"I have never really seen anything like this product before, and I think it is really valuable."

John Creswell, University of Nebraska–Lincoln

Discover **Methods Lists**— methods readings suggested by other users

Watch video interviews with leading methodologists

Explore the **Methods Map** to discover links between methods

Search a custom-designed taxonomy with more than 1,400 qualitative, quantitative, and mixed methods terms

Uncover more than 120,000 pages of book, journal, and reference content to support your learning

Find out more at
www.sageresearchmethods.com